D0962291

ANTEDILUVIAN

BOOKS by WIL McCARTHY

The Queendom of Sol Series
The Collapsium
The Wellstone
Lost in Transmission
To Crush the Moon

The Waister Series
Aggressor Six
The Fall of Sirius

Flies from the Amber
Murder in the Solid State
Bloom
Once Upon a Galaxy

ANTEDILUVIAN

WIL McCARTHY

ANTEDILUVIAN

This is a work of fiction. All the characters and events portrayed in this book are fictional, and any resemblance to real people or incidents is purely coincidental.

A Baen Books Original

Baen Publishing Enterprises
P.O. Box 1403
Riverdale, NY 10471
www.baen.com

ISBN: 978-1-4814-8431-2

Cover art by Dave Seeley

First printing, October 2019

Distributed by Simon & Schuster
1230 Avenue of the Americas
New York, NY 10020

Library of Congress Cataloging-in-Publication Data

Names: McCarthy, Wil, author.
Title: Antediluvian / Wil McCarthy.
Description: Riverdale, NY : Baen, [2019]
Identifiers: LCCN 2019020653 | ISBN 9781481484312 (hardback)
Subjects: | BISAC: FICTION / Science Fiction / High Tech. | FICTION / Science
    Fiction / General. | GSAFD: Science fiction.
Classification: LCC PS3563.C337338 A85 2019 | DDC 813/.54—dc23 LC record
available at https://lccn.loc.gov/2019020653

10   9   8   7   6   5   4   3   2   1

Pages by Joy Freeman (www.pagesbyjoy.com)
Printed in the United States of America

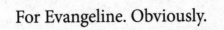

For Evangeline. Obviously.

Acknowledgments

I'm sure there are a lot of errors in this book, and I know there are some willful deviations from expert advice, for which the experts should not be held in any way accountable. Cool? That said, I'd like to thank: Dr. Jill Shapiro of Columbia University for tips on human evolution; Graham Hancock for information about ancient civilizations; Evangeline Jennifer Hoyer McCarthy for information about being a female human being; Linda Nagata and Sean Stewart for pointing out errors of logic and narration; The History Channel and The Discovery Channel for inspiring a lot of this through years of excellent documentaries; America's robust publishing industry, for filling my bookshelves with reams of obscure knowledge; and the Internet, for putting every other knowable thing just a few keystrokes away. This story was first conceived in 2004, so I'd also like to thank my 2004 self for writing such a detailed outline, and Toni Weisskopf for purchasing it almost thirteen years later, largely on faith. In a real sense, it took a whole planet full of people to write this book, so thanks to the whole planet, too. You guys rock.

Antediluvian (adj.) / ˌan tē də ˈlü vē ən

1. Ancient.

2. Out of date, antiquated, outmoded, or primitive.

3. (lit.) Pre-deluge.

4. Of or pertaining to the time before the biblical Flood.

5. Of or pertaining to the extracted Y-chromosomal memories of Harv Leonel.

ANTEDILUVIAN

Boulder Creek Apartments
Boulder Colorado
Present Day

"Are you positive you want to do this?" Tara Mukherjee asked, as the two of them rose from bed to begin their momentous day.

"Positive?" Harv Leonel asked. "What a question. What have we been doing all summer?"

They brushed their teeth and showered and dressed, and still the question hung unspoken in the air: *are you sure today's the day you want to climb into the time machine?*

And the answer, equally unspoken, hung just as loudly: *there is no doubt, Tara my dear.*

"Do you want eggs?" Tara asked him. He was usually the one to make breakfast, but today felt different—*very* different—and she wanted to mark the occasion somehow.

"Mmm," he said, thoughtfully. "And toast. We're going to need the carbs."

They ate in near silence, speaking only of the weather (sunny) and the morning headlines (gloomy). There was a sense that none of that mattered, but what else was there to talk about? He was right: Tara had spent the whole summer helping him build his damned machine. Who was she to tell him (to ask him? to *beg* him?) not to use it?

As they piled the dishes in the sink, he grabbed her and kissed her hard, and she kissed him back even harder, because she was pretty sure she loved him. How else could she explain all this? She'd been postdocing in the Paleogenetics department of CU Boulder—a prestigious posting to be sure—and he'd come in on the last day of classes to ask her a question about the

1

Y chromosome. Although he was clean-shaven, his black hair looked overdue for a visit to the barber, and like a lot of white Coloradoans, he had a tanned, vaguely weather-beaten look about him. But his crooked smile was catchy, and later that same evening she was kissing him deeply in a bar on The Hill, even though he reeked of bourbon and thic-nic vape, and the day after that she was riding shotgun in his Jeep through the mountains at a hundred KPH, with her hand on his thigh the whole time, and that night she'd fallen into his bed and done things good Hindu girls were not known for doing.

And then somehow she was spending all her spare time in his lab, in the basement of the Engineering Center. How could she not? He wasn't unusually handsome or charming, but he was *scary smart*, and a little dangerous, and he was interested in the quantum computing and quantum storage aspects of the human genome. The "quantome," he called it.

"The potential number of memory states in a single chromosome is three-to-the-two-billionth times the number of genes," he'd told her offhandedly, the first time she saw what he was building. "That's ten to the thirtieth times more than the number of atoms in the known universe. A big number! But if the chromosome has four arms, the equations don't balance and the coherent states collapse."

Tara's paleogenetics colleagues had expressed skepticism, to say the least. What did some EE professor know about genes? But Tara's specialty was tracking the Y-chromosome haplogroups—the way they diverged from the original A00 group of Y-Chromosome Adam, and split and spread and died out and conquered the world. She knew that misshapen little chromosome down to the atomic level, and the more she listened and thought and looked up and confirmed with data, the more convinced she became that Harv Leonel was *really fucking onto something*. It *did* look like a trinary quantum compiler—or "ternary," as Harv called it—in nontrivial and seemingly non-coincidental ways. Had evolution crammed such critical genetic functions into such a small, strange space because that structure, you know, *did something*?

The thought still sent shivers down her spine, and it had crossed her mind more than once, that she might conceivably share a Nobel Prize with Harv if she helped him prove his point. But that wasn't why she'd helped him. No, that wasn't why at all.

"You trust me?" he asked her as he gathered up his backpack and keys.

"Nope," she said honestly. "But I want to."

He was twenty-two years her senior, old enough that he could legally drink anywhere in the world on the day she was born. He probably *had*. He'd probably smoked pot all through her Indian school years, and fucked his way through more young women than she cared to think about. She knew that he was divorced, and that it had been ugly, and that he'd both vowed to never get married again and then, at some point, retracted that vow. She hadn't asked him why or when, or what it might mean for the two of them.

"Ready?" he asked her at the door.

No, she wanted to say. Not at all. Not at *all*. But instead she forced a smile and a nod, because this was everything he'd ever dreamed of, and she didn't want to be the thing that stood in his way. She particularly didn't want to find out that the work was more important than she was, that he would press the activation trigger whether she was in the room or not.

He drove them to work, as always, and although the traffic prevented him from really opening up the throttle, she could feel him burning beside her with impatience and reckless energy. The experiment had been funded and approved by the National Science Foundation and the Defense Advanced Research Projects Agency and the Electrical Engineering department's own slush fund, mainly because Harv hadn't quiiite disclosed that he was planning on using a transcranial magnetic stimulator to couple the output feed directly to the hippocampus of his own brain.

"It's a sort of a time machine," he'd told her on their third date. "Bringing information from the distant past and imprinting it in a living memory. Who knows? There could be a whole library in there."

And somehow it hadn't sounded crazy at the time.

Oh, Harv. God damn it.

The lab—*their* lab—was a bomb crater of wires and video displays and liquid nitrogen dewars. Over the course of the summer, the chaos had gradually faded into the background of Tara's perception—just part of the normal mess of real-world science—but today she saw it with fresh eyes, as if for the first time. Electrical and fibe-op cables ran loose on the floor, not anchored with runners or even duct tape, but just hastily thrown from one gray box to the next, streaming precious power and data and femtosecond timing pulses to where they were needed. All around were comics and cartoons, taped to the walls and to the equipment: The Far Side, XKCD, Cyanide and Happiness, Calvin and Hobbes. Anything to do with time travel. Anything to do with quantum computing or brain stimulation. The lights were already on, and Gurdeep Patel was already here, carefully stepping from one spot to another and checking things off on a clipboard.

"Hey, boss," Patel said, nodding.

"You're here early," Harv observed.

"You too."

Patel was Harv Leonel's *actual* assistant—a grad student slaving for his PhD and earning even less than Paleogenetics was paying Tara. He was a bright young man, but kind of blissfully acquiescent to whatever was happening around him. As far as Tara knew, he had no idea that what was about to happen had not been peer-reviewed or even peer-discussed. Harv had thrown some verbiage in the proposal that hinted in this direction—just enough that he could claim good-faith disclosure later on, but not enough to provoke any inquiry by the review committee.

The possibility should be explored, that the quantome interacts directly with the human brain, or that it can be made to.

Had Patel understood the deception? Would he be here if he did?

"Hey, Mukherjee," Patel said to her.

"Hi, Patel." Do you know your thesis advisor is about to fry his brain?

With surprising restraint, Harv picked his way over to the Nuclear Magnetic Resonance station—the heart of the time machine—sat down on the little wheeled office stool, and started powering up the systems one by one: Controller, check. Chiller, check. Gyrotron. Sweep generator and transmission line. Probe. Detector. Amplifier. Processor. Check, check, check.

Then he ran the primary diagnostics, and the full diagnostics, and the expanded diagnostics, and finally began reading signals from a dummy target—an *actual* trinary quantum compiler, roughly ten times the diameter and several thousand times the mass of the Y-chromosome target underneath it.

"Are you okay with this?" Tara asked Patel quietly.

Patel shrugged. "Sure. Why?"

"I have my doubts."

"Mmm. A little late for that."

She nodded. "Yeah. That's correct."

"Do you want me to hold your hand?"

That was a joke: Patel knew perfectly well that she and Harv were an item. Why else was she here? Last week Harv had finally managed to wrangle a small, retroactive stipend for her time in the lab, but it was little more than minimum wage, and she'd never specifically asked for it. No, she was here for Harv, *with* Harv, because she couldn't have stayed away if she'd tried. And she hadn't fucking tried.

"I just might let you," she told Patel.

That was a bit much, and she regretted it immediately. The fact that Patel was attracted to her was nothing unusual—a lot of men were, and in her worst moments Tara thought perhaps *all* of them were. She wasn't fond of her wide nose or wide hips, her acne scars and her too-deep voice, but she had all the right parts in all the right places, and that seemed to be more than enough to turn heads. But Patel—shy, polite, Indian to the core—was good at keeping his attractions under wraps.

True to form, Patel ignored the remark, and went back to checking items off on his checklist.

The NMR read the spin states of the Y chromosome's atomic nuclei as though they were simply four billion quantum bits. Not quite a world record for quantum computing, but certainly one of the most powerful machines ever built. That was, if "built" were the right word for something whose key features had evolved naturally. Arguably, the Y chromosome itself *was* the computer, and the NMR was just a way of accessing its computations, or alternatively, of probing the information stored within it. Of course, reading these massively entangled states would massively scramble them, which is why the chromosome sat in the center of a special microchip bathed in liquid nitrogen; this staved off "decoherence" for just barely long enough to allow the NMR to probe all two billion qubits.

The machine had performed flawlessly in last week's trials, basically proving that the Y chromosome (unlike any of the other twenty-two chromosomes in the human genome) could be made to operate as a quantum computer. That didn't mean it *was* one, but if not, then it surely was an amazing coincidence. Since that time Harv—when he wasn't drinking or vaping or being swept off to bed by Tara—had focused his attention on the Ultra High Resolution Transcranial Magnetic Stimulator and Electroencephalogram rig, known here in the lab as the TMS/EEG, or simply "the bathing cap."

"The hippocampus of a human brain actually speaks a very simple language," he'd told her, "The flow of information is basically unidirectional, with recurrent waves of inhibition and excitation tapping out the Morse code of our memories. In some minor ways it's also a quantum-mechanical process, but it's not the same language as the trinary compiler, so the signals need to be translated from what we call the frequency domain to what we call the time domain."

Time domain. The phrase was sexy, and had resonated in her mind like a kind of poetry.

But she didn't understand most of the math behind it, and she'd somehow imagined the translation code would be the work of months, or even years. In fact, it had taken just five business days, with Saturday and Sunday off for couples' stuff. Even Harv seemed surprised how easily it had come together. And here they were: no way to test it except on a live human brain.

"All systems nominal," Patel told Harv. "Test lights green. The rats have not chewed through any cables during the night."

Another joke: there were no rats in this bottom-corner sub-basement of the mazelike Engineering Center. There were no humans, either. As always, they had the place to themselves.

"Diagnostics are all green so far," Harv said. "Just waiting on the final transforms."

It took a high-end desktop computer nearly five whole minutes to convert the signals into something a human brain could read.

"You doing okay?" he asked, looking in Tara's direction and sounding genuinely interested in the answer.

"Fine," she told him, unconvincingly.

"Still think we should try it on pigs first?"

And here was yet another joke: pigs had most of the same neural and genetic wiring as humans, but they lacked the deep frontal lobe interconnections that made it possible not only to remember things, but to think about thinking about the remembered things. Without that, the hippocampus could not recognize the TMS signals at all. It was the equivalent of asking whether pigs could code the NMR's processing firmware, or write up the paper when they were through.

She answered, "I *do* think we should talk about having a physician standing by."

Harv seemed to think about that for a moment, but Tara could imagine the calculations in his mind: a doctor would insist on knowing what was going on, and would then insist on halting the experiment until some lengthy and unspecified safety criteria could be satisfied. But who was qualified to develop the safety criteria for a thing like this? Harv Leonel, that's who.

"I'll be fine," he told her. "Hell, the Wright brothers risked their brains a lot more than I'm about to." Then: "Fourier transform complete. The lights are green. TMS is accepting the input."

"Congratulations," Patel said.

"And to you," Harv acknowledged vaguely as he stood up from the stool and picked his way over cables to where Patel and Tara stood: beside the surplus orthodontist chair that Harv had fitted with a surplus polygraph, so his vital signs could be coarsely monitored during the experiment. Fitted also with the rubber TMS/EEG cap itself, and the explosion of wires trailing out of it.

Without fanfare, he smeared electrolyte gel on all the appropriate contacts, sat down in the chair, put on the chest strap and the finger bands and the wrist cuff, and finally the TMS/EEG cap itself, which he secured with a silly-looking rubber chin strap.

Tara checked all the sensor feeds and stimulator outputs—a process which by itself took almost twenty minutes. Working from a manual bank of switches, she would activate one of the seventy electromagnets in the skull cap, feeding a low-amplitude square wave into a tiny portion of Harv's brain. She would then verify that the pattern was picked up by all six electroencephalograph sensors around it, and then turn the switch off and verify that all six sensors returned to measuring normal brainwave activity. Of course, she was an expert in Y-chromosome haplogroups, not brainwave activity; the TMS/EEG connected to a computer running off-the-shelf software that handled all of the details. One by one, more lights went green, and more boxes were checked off on Patel's clipboard.

Really, it was a blessing that Harv had invested the time and budget on all these status LEDs. He'd agreed to abort the test if even one of the lights came up yellow, but none of them did, and soon the final diagnostic was complete. This chaotic mess of equipment—some new, some surplus, some scavenged from other departments—was somehow working exactly as intended, and Tara had to appreciate that it really *wasn't* disordered at the functional level. Harv and Patel—and later Tara herself—had started with an elegant design, and had simply been forced to fit it all together based on the available space and furniture and electrical sockets. Based on time and budget and the fact that nobody was checking up on them for OSHA and fire code violations. And of course, classes would be starting soon, making everything on campus at least ten times harder, and so they'd worked as quickly as they could, without ever really pausing to reflect.

Now, waking from that sex-fueled dream, she had to face the fact that she was complicit in whatever was about to happen. She might get a Nobel Prize, yes, and a cover story in Nature—the grandmommy of all the legitimate science journals. But she might also be the target of a criminal negligence probe. Walking away now would not change any of that, so she simply pressed forward, doing her best to make sure the plan was executed as flawlessly as possible.

"I'm leaning the chair back," Harv said. Another concession: he'd be in a full orthodontic reclining position when the TMS signals were activated.

"Okay," Patel said, unnecessarily. He was sitting across the room, by the emergency stop button, leaning forward slightly to get a better view of Harv as the ortho chair rolled slowly backward and then came to a halt against its rubber stops.

Harv's right hand was on the TMS activation trigger: a white handheld button assembly like they used in hospitals for requesting painkiller from an IV feed. Or lethal barbiturates for voluntary euthanasia patients. Tara touched Harv's other hand, and could not stop herself from saying, "It's still not too late to stop this."

"I know," he said.

And pressed the fucking trigger.

University of Colorado Engineering Center
Boulder, Colorado
Present Day

Harv didn't feel anything when he pressed the button, and his first thought was that the machine wasn't working. Why would it, on their first real try? His second thought was that he was glad he hadn't made any promises around this phase of the experiment. If he had, this could have been a black mark on his professorial record, which could negatively affect Patel, and maybe even Tara, if it weren't handled adroitly. See? There was nothing wrong with a little secrecy.

"Anything happening?" Patel called out from across the room.

"Not so far," Harv told him. "Not that..."

And

his

third

thought

was

that Jack was going to burn his wrist again if he didn't step back a few inches from the firehole.

"Watch your hands, laddie!" Harv barked.

Jack was flinging coal into the furnace with a square-headed shovel while Harv watched the fancy new brass-and-glass pressure gauge he'd installed on the boiler, and with every throw the bandages on Jack's left hand brushed within a sixteenth of an inch of the firehole's riveted iron lip, which stood just a whisker shy of cherry-red hot.

Except that Harv's name was Clellan Malcom Leonel, and even with no shirts on beneath their overalls it was hot as blazes

9

and dark as night in this brick goddamn shithouse, and why in Christ's name hadn't he constructed this clarty half-lever engine outside, and damn the Clyde weather anyways? Cunard had better like the design, that much was sure,

and

his

fourth

thought

was

what the fuck was that?

He sat there doing nothing, saying nothing, for several seconds.

"Harv?" Tara asked.

"I'm okay," he said, without thinking.

What the fuck was that?

"Is there a sensation?" Patel asked, holding his pen above the clipboard, ready to jot down any impressions.

Still, Harv said nothing. What could he say?

"Harv?" That was Tara again, sounding concerned.

"Yes, there's a sensation," he told them both. "If you could call it that. I may have misunderstood the nature of the quantome's stored information."

Tara looked a bit angry at that. "Jesus, Harv. Would you care to elaborate? Are you all right?"

And it was a fair question, because they were, after all, pumping strong magnetic fields into the center of his brain. He felt a faint buzzing sensation, like a subsonic hum just below the auditory threshold, and a taste like pennies dipped in apple cider vinegar.

Chuckling nervously, he said, "This is why pioneers experiment on themselves. Tara, I think I just experienced an episodic memory. *Not* an implicit informational recall. I mean, I was *there*. For a moment. In Scotland, maybe?"

To this, Tara said, "Seriously? *Seriously?*" She paused, then added, "You'd better not be shitting us. Patel, let's turn this thing off before we hurt him."

But for the moment, Patel was more curious than concerned. "That's interesting, Harv. I always thought episodic memory was a possibility. I mean, the hippocampus is basically just a switchboard. It doesn't really differentiate between different connection types. What exactly did you see?"

"Two people," Harv said. "working on some kind of steam

engine. Indoors. It was very hot. I was…I was only there for a second or two, but I felt everything. Sweat rolling down my back. This is amazing."

"Turn the machine off," Tara said again.

"I'm okay," Harv assured her. "Thank you for being worried, but the sensation's not unpleasant. Let's keep going."

And so they waited for several seconds, and then several seconds more.

"Anything?" Patel asked.

"No, I don't think so. What's the field strength?"

"Three point five Tesla, same as it was five minutes ago."

To Tara, Harv said, "My great-grandfather came from Dumbarton, Scotland, on the river Clyde. Have you heard of something called Cunard?"

"It's a British cruise line."

"Hmm. I wonder…when that was? My family lived in Scotland for quite a while."

"They weren't from there originally," she said. "Your Y chromosome is from a haplogroup called D-M174, which is very rare. Not Scottish at all. Statistically speaking, it got there by way of Tibet or Hokkaido, or the Indian Ocean. Harv, I don't like this. You're assuming you've…"

"Mmm?"

She pointed at his head. "We don't know what's happening in there. You've experienced a vivid… You're…"

"It's fine," he told her.

But that sounded dismissive, and he regretted it immediately. He and Tara had fallen in together fast and hard and dizzily, and her concern for his welfare was quite a bit more than professional. He didn't realize, until this moment, how much he'd been missing that. The divorce was almost six years ago, and while it was not particularly hard to find someone to sleep with in Boulder, he had singularly failed to locate anyone who actually wanted to hold his hand. Tinder had failed him, and OKCupid had failed him, and GeneMatch had failed him, and the women his own age who sometimes flirted at faculty parties had ultimately come up short as well. But somehow the Paleogenetics department at the University of Colorado had not. He didn't really know where he and Tara stood, or what was going to happen, or whether what they were doing was even good for her. But he cared what she thought.

More gently, he said, "I think we're really onto something, Tara. I do. I'm fully lucid, not in any pain. I feel a slight electrical sensation in my face and head, which I'm pretty sure is normal. And I swear to you, something happened. I experienced a detailed memory. That's more than we could have hoped for."

"Mmm," she said, noncommittally.

"Look, if it hurts, I promise I'll stop. Okay? But we need to do this. It could be a major breakthrough. Could be the big time, for all of us."

"Mmm," she said again. Then, "Okay, you're right. This is why we're here."

"It is, yes. And thank you for caring about me. Patel, will you please increase the field strength to four point oh?"

Patel scratched his scalp with the pen. "Um, okay. You sure?"

It was as high as the magnets could go. It was, in fact, the highest field strength commercially available for transcranial magnetic stimulation. Any higher and they'd've had to build the TMS themselves—something even Harv was reluctant to do. And yes, the machine and its accompanying instructions came plastered with all kinds of FDA warnings. But the software did allow for that setting, as long as the focal point was deeper than six centimeters past the skull. Based on the 3D brain scan data that guided the machine, Harv's hippocampus was roughly 7.5 cm from the magnets, so yes, the program would allow it.

And they were so close. So close to something. There *was* information in the Y-quantome, and they *had* written it into his memory. They had. Years of thought and study brought him to this point—physics, chemistry, electrical engineering, and neuroscience, all focused in narrowly on this one highly specialized endeavor. Was he even suited for anything else at this point? As a scientist and as a human being, Harv could no more turn away than he could choose to stop blinking his eyes.

"Yeah," he said. "I'm sure."

"*Absolutely* sure?"

"Yes, Patel, I'm absolutely sure. You may proceed."

"Okay. You got it."

Patel put down his clipboard and leaned out over the keyboard, pecking in commands.

"Unlocking. Changing the setting. Enabling. You ready?"

"Yep. Hit me."

Patel pressed enter
and
the
world
went
dark

PART ONE
The Deluge

1.1

Harv's senses crashed and blurred; they faded in and out with flickering images and feelings and smells. A forest, a desert, a campfire—no, a million campfires stretching back to the dawn of time! He felt his hands, coarse and calloused, on the steering oar of a reed boat, pushing and pulling desperately in an effort to avoid... buildings? A flooded city? No, a wave crashing through a city. His heart hammering in his throat, more afraid than he'd ever been in... his life? In someone else's life? Suddenly the flickering quieted, and he snapped into place.

"I always find you here on clear days."

Manuah Hasis turned away from the sea, toward the man speaking behind him. A man with walnut skin, black hair, and a black moustache, dressed in blue robes and bleached-white cap of finest linen, exactly the colors of the sky and the lazy summer clouds drifting across it.

Manuah bowed. "I could say the same, Your Theity."

The man laughed, because while the title was accurate, he was Manuah's half-brother, Adrah Hasis, and might just as reasonably have been addressed as "Pook" or "smallest" or "fart noise," if they were both twenty years younger.

"I come here because I work here, Harbormaster. You come to admire the view, and they only let you in because your hereditary titles make them nervous."

"I also donate money," Manuah countered, laughing along with his brother. The two of them tapped hands in a less formal greeting.

17

They were standing atop the highest tower in The City—five floors tall, and built upon the Hill of Stars, from which Adrah and his fellow Cleric Astrologers tracked the movement of planets across the night sky. They were a *hundred feet* above the valley floor—practically celestial bodies themselves! The Cleric Portenters also sacrificed animals here in the tower, presumably on the notion that it was physically closer to the gods, but fortunately today was Groundsday—hardly the most auspicious day of the week. In fact it was the day of laborers and merchants, and thus perhaps the most distant from the gods' attention.

Adrah's tone became more serious. "You look troubled, brother. I see you staring out at the waters—*your* waters—and it never brings you satisfaction. Is it not an excellent harbor?"

Indeed, it *was* an excellent harbor, mostly natural, though with a pair of cut-stone sea walls at the east, like the jaws of a dragon nearly closed, forming a barrier against storm surge and a tricky navigation for foreign sailors entering without permission. It measured nearly a full *kos*—the range of a cow's loudest moo—so that a herd on one bank could be heard by a man on the opposite one, but only barely, and only on a quiet day. Its pale blue waters were deep enough for boats and shallow enough for good fishing, except on the far west edge, where they were so shallow that at low tide a woman could walk out into the mud with a shovel and pail, and in less than half an *hurta* dig up as many clams and crabs and frogs as she could carry. The people of The City dined better than anyone else in Kingdom, by far. Well, the ones who liked fried clams, anyway.

But that was the problem, yeah? The clam beds got smaller every year. This very month, Manuah had sent his boatmen out to move the buoys again, widening the range that boats could safely travel without fear of running aground or fouling their nets.

"The water keeps getting deeper," he told his brother. Then added, "Your Theity," just in case the gods were listening, and in case they cared.

The cool shadow of a cloud passed over them, chasing out across low stone buildings and white-painted roofs, then into the harbor, darkening it for a few *kesthe* and then passing on.

Beside him, he felt Adrah shrug. "Isn't that a good thing, Harbormaster? Your domain ever expanding? Your boats safer and safer from the horrors of getting stuck on a sandbar?"

"It would be nice to think so," Manuah said.

"But?"

"But The City is built on flat ground, Adrah, between the Great River and the Grand Sea. There's no higher ground to retreat to. If the water rose another twenty feet, this whole place would disappear."

Adrah barked out a laugh. "Twenty feet! Yes, and the sky might fall on us and crack the tower. Brother, surely there are better things to worry about." But when Manuah didn't answer, Adrah became serious again. "You're a sailor, and a merchant. You know the tides. You're worried about storm surges."

"Among other things."

In fact, Manuah was worried about all sorts of possibilities, only some of which he could clearly articulate. His mother, Adrah's aunt, had often chided him as someone who worried too damn much, about too many things. And perhaps she was right about that, but while she had trained him to keep quiet about most of it, that had really only made the problem worse. The less he shared of the things that bothered him, the more power they seemed to hold over him. And yet, the more wealth and power he accumulated, the more men he had working for him, the more servants his wife commanded, the more ridiculous it seemed for him to be afraid of anything at all.

After a moment of silence he asked Adrah, "Can you people really speak to the gods? Do the gods speak back to you?"

"Not in The Language, no. You know that. But they make their patterns known. Brother, what's on your mind?"

Sighing, Manuah took his gold-leaf-covered walking stick— worth more than most men earned in a year—and pointed west to the Great River, past the edges of the city and the harbor, to where the river's waters fanned out and spilled broadly into the ocean. "That water is rising, too. Every year, the river gets a little wider, eating up a few more feet of the farms that line it. Every year, the spring floods get worse. Not just deeper, but *worse*, with faster water and more mud and debris. This water comes from somewhere, yes? Past all the towns, into the wild lands and the desert beyond that, there are hills, and the water comes from *behind those*. From the mountains.

"The mountains are white. The wildmen call it 'snow,' but they say it's what happens to water when it gets cold. And when it gets warm, it turns back to water again. What if the mountains are getting too warm? What if the land between the harbor and the delta just washes away? And Brother, the edges of another big river delta begin just thirty *kos* farther that direction. You haven't left The City in many years; you don't really understand the shape of the land, but the fan of the Other River is *close*. And *that* water is rising. Kingdom is great because the land is fertile, because we live in the flat space around these two river deltas. But what if the water keeps rising?"

"I'm sure the gods would never allow that," Adrah said, with a confidence that Manuah envied.

"Would you ask them for me?" he pressed. "I've seen some big storm surges, and I *am* afraid. If the gods became angry, it wouldn't take much to drown us all."

"Well, then we'll see to it they don't get angry. My brother, you look so tense. It helps nothing if you walk around like that. Will you try some poses with me?"

Throughout this conversation, Harv Leonel's consciousness hung just beneath the surface. He was Manuah, or felt that he was, and could not remember anything else. But here, for a moment, his own thoughts floated to the surface, and he noted (with something like astonishment) the grace of their speech. The word for Harbor-master was something like Vaivas Vakta or "Keeper of the Waters," and Adrah's title was Vaivas Jyotis or "Keeper of the Stars." The Great River was Sarudas Vakti or "stream so big it has waves," and the Other River was Chera Vakti, which meant something like "Brother of Waves." And The City was Chera Sippar, and the Kingdom was Chera Desa, and the word for brother was simply Chera. And so in their words and in their minds, everything was brother to everything else, and the result was a kind of holistic poetry Harv could barely follow, like a joke whose punchline he didn't quite get. But this was their everyday speech; they weren't composing or trying to outdo one another. It seemed this wordplay came as naturally to them as speech itself.

And Harv also took a moment to, it seemed, turn Manuah's head and survey the landscape around them. He could not, for the life of him, figure out where they were. The City had thou-sands of stone buildings and tens of thousands of wooden ones. Probably at least a hundred thousand inhabitants, which was a large settlement for almost any era. And the Great River had to be almost ten kilometers wide—wider than the Nile!—and he had the distinct impression that it flowed from north to south, and that the Grand Sea was to the south, and that this brother river to the west was parallel, and nearly as large. And although he had aced every geography and geology and world history course he'd ever taken, he couldn't think of a single spot on Earth that met this description. Adrah looked vaguely Middle Eastern, or perhaps Indian, and his clothes bore some resemblance to those of a Tibetan monk, although the colors were all wrong, and the cloth, while soft-looking, seemed to have been woven from particularly large thread. And although it was summer, the temperature here did not seem overly hot. Did any of that mean anything at all?

Anyway, was there really such a thing as a saltwater frog? Was Harv simply hallucinating? Given the strength and complexity of the magnetic fields pulsing through his brain, he supposed it was a possibility. He surely wasn't supposed to be here, *and no one had ever done anything like this before, and every second that went by might be causing irreversible brain damage. And yet, there seemed to be very little he could do about it. He couldn't feel the chair in which he was reclining. Couldn't feel himself at all. He was Manuah.*

These thoughts flitted through his mind, taking all of two seconds, or a third of a kesthe, *before his consciousness submerged again.*

Manuah grumbled for a few moments, before allowing Adrah to lead him through a series of stretches—first the fingers, then the wrists, then the elbows and shoulders, and similarly with the feet and legs and finally his back, which really did ache. He might be a lord and a shipping magnate, but when the dock crew was short a man he was not above loading and unloading cargo with his own two hands, or supervising a repair crew by getting in there and showing them how they were supposed to apply the tar. Or steering. No matter how respectable he got, he would never lose his love for standing at the stern of a boat and sculling, or pulling on the steering oar for all he was worth, to make those tricky turns without any of his sailors having to dip a paddle in the water. He never felt more free than that.

"You carry your worries on your back," Adrah told him. "I can see it from here. Perhaps that wife of yours can rub it for you, but here, stand with me. Like a tree. Like a post. Like a marsh reed in the wind. Now extend your knee, and now the other one..."

This was not Manuah's first time being led through the poses—not even his first being led by his baby brother—but it was perhaps the first time he felt that spiritual thing one was supposed to feel while doing it. Not the presence of the gods, exactly, but a kind of openness to the world beyond the boundaries of his flesh. Something pulsed in him that was neither fire nor water nor light, nor strength or weakness, but resembled all of them in some way, and when it was done—after almost half an *hurta* of jumping and posturing—he felt a better kind of tired than he had in months.

"Clarity," his brother told him. "The poses align the body in accordance with natural principles, and this in turn aligns the mind. Helpful thoughts join together, and unhelpful ones slide off you like water off a heron's wing."

"Why?" Manuah wanted to know. Why should it work that way? If the body and soul were separate things, then how could the one affect the other?

"Because the gods decree it," Adrah answered happily.

And again, Manuah envied him, because his own mind went to darker places. Indeed, if the gods had that kind of power, to reach inside human beings and affect their bodies and their souls, then what couldn't they do? If angered by the actions of human beings, what *wouldn't* they do?

"Keep them happy," he beseeched his brother, and mounted the first ladder to begin the long climb down to solid earth. In the meantime, he had an appointment to keep, here in the physical realm.

"May the next month be kind!" Adrah called after him.

1.2

The palace of King Sraddah was, without any doubt, the finest building Manuah had ever seen, which made it most likely the finest in the history of the world. It might be only half as tall as the Tower of Stars, and surrounded closely by lesser buildings that blocked the view of it, but it was covered in ornate carvings shod in gold and coppergreen leaf, and painted with red ochre and white lime. It was a battlefield of color; not only images, but also words, for those few who could interpret them. Across almost two hundred years, each generation of the royal family had added more to the display, until hardly a spot remained smooth and colorless. It was a lot to take in, and a few quick glances would hardly even convey the shape of the building, much less the carvings on it! But if one cared to spend a day studying the outer walls (which Manuah had, in his youth), they told the story of Sraddah's ancestor Kagresh, who had united all the towns along the banks of the great river, and merged several of them to form The City. A lot of blood had been shed in the process, and many grudges were formed whose echoes lingered even today. And yet, the survivors had outnumbered the dead, and had eventually come to agree that their lives were better, and that swearing allegiance to a king and being part of his Kingdom was not such a bad thing after all.

The entrance was a door in two parts, made of great wooden planks held together with copper bands, and guarded by three soldiers dressed in leather and wooden armor, almost as if they were giant toys. But these were hard men who had fought their share of battles, and had accepted this quieter job as a reward for service.

Their spears were tipped and shod with copper, and they carried nasty-looking obsidian knives. They were not to be trifled with.

One of them held a big gray dog on a leash, and the dog eyed Manuah suspiciously, as if deciding where to bite him if things went ugly. Also not to be trifled with.

Fortunately, Manuah had made an appointment, and was expected, and his golden walking stick and crimson robe and broad-brimmed sailor's hat left little doubt as to his identity. "Harbormaster" was a secular hereditary title, and "Counter of Tides" was nominally a religious one, although the priestly trappings had fallen away from it long ago. "Lord Cousin" was one he held but never used, because it sounded pompous down on the docks, but in any case, Manuah carried enough royal blood that *he* was not to be trifled with either.

"Good morning," he said to the guards, speaking familiarly, as though they were his own workmen.

"Harbormaster," one of them acknowledged.

"I'm here to speak with my cousin," he told them, and this *was* a little pompous, because he was such a distant cousin that he was not entirely sure of the lineage path himself. But still, the guards nodded and bowed and got out of his way.

"Beautiful weather," one of them said to him as he passed, and if they *had* been his workmen (or especially his sailors) this would have been the start of a conversation about winds and tides and the movement of high clouds. But these were soldiers, and "weather" to them was only a question of rain or sunshine on their backs, so he simply Mm-hmm'ed his agreement and moved on into the palace.

The interior courtyards were no less beautiful than the outer walls, though in a different way. Here, ferns and cedar trees grew, and elaborate carpets were draped along the inner walls, and so many linen-robed servants were scurrying around that Manuah wondered (not for the first time) what tasks could possibly keep them all busy all day. But the question was partially answered when three of them approached him: one woman with a clay mug of water, one with a small plate bearing an even smaller piece of oiled and salted bread, and one young man with a writing board and charcoal pencil.

"Good morning to you, Lord Cousin Harbormaster," this one said. "May I offer you refreshment?"

"No, thank you," he answered. "I broke my fast at home."

"Yes, of course," the scribe said quickly. "I meant no offense."

"None taken," Manuah assured him.

The two of them tapped hands. Then, even more delicately, the scribe asked, "May I offer to wash your feet and armpits before your audience with His Majesty?"

Manuah laughed. "No, thank you. My wife has made quite sure I'm presentable, and I haven't stepped in anything on the way over here."

"Of course, Lord Cousin Harbormaster. I'm ashamed to ask the question at all."

"We all have our jobs to do."

"As you say."

The two women melted away on some other business, while the scribe led Manuah into the sanctum, down a series of dim corridors, and into the court chamber where King Sraddah stood, holding a slip of thin papyrus up to the unshuttered window, trying to hold it steady against the light breeze.

In a corner, the young Prince Raddiah sat, playing with little tin soldiers. Nearly a hand taller than the last time Manuah had seen him, he was dressed in a finely embroidered, red-and-yellow byssa-cloth robe that was clearly too small for him, but just as clearly too expensive to discard. He looked up for a moment, saw it was only his boring Uncle Manuah, and looked disappointed.

"Hello, Uncle," he said, and turned back to what he was doing. Then, more softly: "Die, Surapp dogs! See what comes of defying *me*."

"Your Majesty," the scribe said to the king, "may I announce your Lord Cousin Manuah Hasis, Harbormaster of The City and Counter of Tides."

"You may," the king said, without looking up. He wore a thin band of gold around his head, and smelled of perfume and incense and sweat. "Damn it. One of my generals has drawn a picture of the entire Kingdom here, but I can't seem to make sense of it. There's a trick to it, like reading I suppose."

He showed it to Manuah, who said, "Yes, the sailors sometimes draw pictures like that as well. Though not on papyrus, of course." Essentially, boats were *made* of papyrus—tough reeds of it flattened and woven and bundled, and then flattened again, and curled up at the edges and ends, and decked with cedar planks. And then, in the case of Manuah's own boats, caulked at the bottom with tree rosin and oil sands. But if a sailor were ever holding a *sheet* of papyrus, it was generally saturated with tallow, and he was about to weave it into the hull to repair a minor leak. (Major ones required drydocking and, in Manuah's very strong opinion, a high-grade asphalt pour.)

"Hmm," the King said, not finding the comment amusing. "Well, I have an invasion to plan, somewhere on this little picture. Can you see Surapp Great Town on here? Damnation and rot, I wonder if my eyes are bad. But how could they be? I never have trouble seeing things far away. Wouldn't be much of a general if I did.

"In any case, the Surapp plague me. Building a city of their own! The stone there is of poor quality, but for two generations they've been quarrying granite in the Back Hills, and carrying the blocks down the Other River on boats. Two generations without a break! Which shows a lot of initiative, I think, but we can hardly allow it. Not unless Kingdom absorbs the Surapp." He smiled at the idea. "Then we'll have *two* cities: one on the east of the Great River, and one on the west of the Other River. That seems acceptable, yes? There's a symmetry to it, and it might encourage landless sons to colonize the coastlands in between. And then the industrious Surapp will *serve* me instead of blistering my bottom."

That idea seemed to please him. He spent several seconds just standing there, contemplating it. Then troubling thoughts seemed to leak in; the ease left his face. "We'd have to do something about their language, don't you think? I never could understand those bastards."

"It's not so hard," Manuah said, perhaps a bit too hurriedly. Indeed, the speech of Kingdom was more similar to the Surapp language than the faces of Manuah's sons were to one another. Two weeks' sail to the west, where the Grand Sea narrowed and finally ended, there was a collection of towns along a river of their own, and their speech was even farther removed—more a cousin than a brother to The Language. And another quite different cousin dwelt two weeks' sail to the southeast, on a river of *their* own, and although Manuah had never been farther east than that, he'd heard tales of even more distant lands, with even stranger speech. If Sraddah had to learn one of *those*, he might have something to complain about. For that matter, if one traveled fifteen days up the Great River, past Shifpar and Erituak, there were orchard keepers and wildmen who spoke a completely different language that seemed to bear no relation whatsoever. By comparison, the Surapp tongue was nothing at all. "It's mostly a matter of inflection."

"But why should *I* learn *their* language? Does it benefit me? Are they delivering it to me as tribute? No, if they're to join our Kingdom then we must all speak the same. The conqueror decides, but everyone reaps the benefit. You see? That's how to think big! One day, won't my great-great-grandchildren rule the entire Earth?"

"I wouldn't know about that, Sire." Manuah said. He tried to stay out of politics as much as possible, but he had been to Surapp Great Town many times—it was less than two days' travel!—and there were men and women there he counted as friends. If Sraddah sent his soldiers to take the place, he hoped the Surapp would surrender without too much of a fight. If they resisted, Sraddah would simply kill them all and smash their buildings, which did not seem to be in anyone's best interest. Still, it seemed better than the wars of extermination and retreat that the wildmen were perpetually fighting. Nobody ever really won that sort of war, and half the people didn't even survive it, whereas when Sraddah was your enemy, you could win best by capitulating utterly.

"No," the king said absently, "I don't suppose you would. That's probably why my ancestors stomped the crap out of yours, ah?"

"I wouldn't know that either," Manuah said, now with some irritation. *Neither would you, Sire.* Sraddah's ancestors had been larger and stronger, but Manuah's were cleverer, and he imagined they simply hadn't seen any point in battling that way. Fine, let them rule us. We'll just keep getting wealthy.

"Well," Sraddah said, putting the slip of paper down on his conference table and weighing it down with a copper knife. "What brings you here today, Manuah? Your aide said it was important."

"Indeed, yes, it is. I've mentioned this to you before, but I'm increasingly concerned: the water level is rising in the harbor, and the ocean, and the rivers. Since the time of our grandfathers, the level has risen the height of a house. If it should rise that much again during our lifetimes, it would begin to enter The

City proper. Since we live on a flat plain, Sire, with water on three sides, this is not a good situation."

"Good for boats, I should think." Sraddah looked thoughtful for just a moment, before snapping to a different topic: "Speaking of which, how many boats do you have? You, personally."

"Six. We're building the seventh one now."

"Wow. That's impressive, Harbormaster. Has any man ever owned more?"

"Not to my knowledge."

"And how many soldiers could each of them carry?"

"And still have room for crew? I don't know, maybe as many as twelve. If the crew *were* soldiers, and there was no cargo, then perhaps two twelves at the very most. But Your Majesty—"

"So seven twelves would be...what?"

"A little over sixty, Sire," the scribe piped up, making marks on his plank with the charcoal pencil. "And seven two-twelves would be almost three sixties."

And here Harv Leonel felt a stab of smugness, because he'd become more and more concerned about just who these people were. They seemed to know nothing of any organized civilizations before them, which (if true) would make them, what, older than the Sumerians? Which had to be nonsense, because Kingdom, despite being smaller than Sumer, seemed quite sophisticated. But here, finally, were some things they did badly: mathematics, writing, and cartography. He'd seen their writing on the outer walls, and he saw it on the plank now, and through Manuah Hasis' eyes and mind he could understand some of what was written there. It wasn't much; just numbers and a few dozen pictographic nouns, and the numbers greater than twelve were all unwieldy multiples of sixty. These people didn't really seem to know what they were doing in this area, and indeed, although Harv was no expert, this mishmash didn't look like any other written language he'd ever seen. It looked like something a team of six-year-olds might devise.

But what did that mean? When he put his mind to the other things that were missing here, he realized he hadn't seen any bronze, any metals at all other than copper and gold and tin. And in ancient times these were native materials on the surface of the Earth; they didn't require any knowledge of mining or metallurgy— just heat and stone hammers. And now that he thought of it, he

also hadn't seen horses or donkeys or carts, or wheels of any sort.
But that would mean... that would mean this was a Neolithic
site—a stone age *site—at least eight thousand years in the past.*
And yet these were hardly cave men!

He felt a moment of panic, as he remembered this wasn't
supposed to be happening. He was only writing patterns into his
hippocampus, like graffiti on a wall. Right? But then he was gone
again, before he could think of an answer.

"Right," the king said, "Well, I've said it before: boats are of
no military value. If the greatest boatman in all of Kingdom can
only carry three sixties of troops, then how am I to transport
half a sixty of sixties and invade the Surapp? How many boats
would I need?"

He looked pointedly at the scribe, who gulped and said, "Uh,
at least twelve and sixty of them, I think."

Sraddah nodded at that. "Ridiculous, yes, more than the
entire Kingdom possesses. You see? Boats are for fishing, and
transporting valuable goods."

"Sire," Manuah interrupted, "I'm here to talk about the rising
waters. It might be good for boats, yes, but bad for farms and
buildings. And people."

"Oh, I see," the king said, either thoughtfully or dismissively.
"You're talking about a possible flood. And you're certain of this
rising water, yes? Not just wasting my time?" He thought for
another moment and then said, "What would you have me do
about the forces of nature? Increase sacrifices? You should talk
to your brother about that, I think."

Manuah pointed in the direction of the harbor, and sculpted
imaginary structures there with his hands. "I had in mind something a bit more tangible, Sire. We can make the seawalls higher,
and build new ones between the barrier islands out beyond the
harbor. Outside the shipping lanes, of course."

"And why would we do *that*? Do you know how much a block
of stone costs? As much as a goat, and you'd need a lot of them
for a project like that."

"Yes. More blocks than are already there. I've counted over
sixty sixties of blocks."

"Well. That would be a lot, my cousin. And water has a way
of sneaking around, doesn't it?"

"It does. But waves can be broken, and storm surges deflected. I've seen some terrible storms, and if one were to hit us directly... Think of the water as an invading army, and better walls as a way of keeping The City safe from it."

"Hmm," the king said, thinking that over.

"Perhaps if you conquer the Surapp, you could demand stone blocks from them as tribute."

"Blocks? Are you serious?"

"Yes, and in the meantime, we'll cut our own. We can use cheap stone; it doesn't have to look pretty."

To prod him further, and because the king was an avid fowler, Manuah said, "When a duck swims on the water, it can't escape easily. You can kill it with a stone before it takes flight. Sire, we are like swimming ducks here, with our asses in the air."

"Hmm," Sraddah said, even more thoughtfully. But then the spell was broken and he said, "You've given me much to think about, but I have a *real* invasion to plan. Come to me another time."

Manuah felt a stab of frustration. "Seriously? What other time? Cousin, when are you not busy with military affairs?"

Sraddah clucked, as to a child. "Military affairs are what builds this country. My ancestors didn't worry about the harbor, they gave that job to *your* ancestors. So perhaps you should be grateful to be granted an audience at all."

Manuah could feel his blood rising. The king was not a bad man, nor even (on most issues as far as Manuah could tell) a bad king. Taxes had not risen during his reign, and despite his focus on military affairs, the Kingdom was mostly a peaceful place. But Gods, it was like he was deaf sometimes.

Sighing, Sraddah looked Manuah over and said, "Cousin, if there's one thing this crown has taught me, it's that our resources are finite. How many goats do you think The City can spare to feed the stonemasons? How many do you think we can steal away from the river towns, or the herdsmen up in the hills? Right now, our citizens are feeding the masons, one block at a time, to build their houses and garden walls, and that's a good thing. Everyone is kept busy and happy."

"Right up until they drown."

Sraddah laughed at that. "Drowning, is it? I have great respect for you, Harbormaster, and I promise that in two years' time you may remind me of this conversation, and we'll revisit the issue. The Surapp will be pacified, the Kingdom will be greater, and I will have more time and more resources. Until then, please do what you can with the resources *you* have, and in two years' time you may remind me. Fair enough?"

And Manuah could see that from Sraddah's point of view, that must seem like a very reasonable solution indeed. While neither acknowledging nor denying the existence of the problem, he had at least acknowledged the existence of Manuah, and delegated some vague authorizations to him. He probably thought he'd never hear about it again.

"May the next month be kind," Manuah said, resignedly. He looked again at the little prince, playing with his tin soldiers, forming quiet screams every now and then as one of them met some grisly imagined end, and it occurred to Manuah that this was a good sign, that the kid had an imagination of any sort. When Manuah had been brought here to the palace as a child, on occasions when his father had business here, Sraddah had liked to play as well, but with him it was always wooden knives, or willow spears and wicker shields, or bows and blunted darts. Or simply fistfights; Manuah had left more than once with a black eye and sore balls, or cuts and bruises across his knuckles and knees, inflicted by a triumphant prince two years his junior. In any case Sraddah had never seemed interested in using his mind. The fact that he was such a capable general owed, Manuah supposed, to the fact that his enemies' minds were even lazier, and that their hearts quailed at the ferocity of the king's attacks, and the unwavering loyalty (and thus, ferocity) of his troops. So much easier to surrender and accept a just peace! But still, it wouldn't hurt to have a thinker on the kingschair someday.

"Keep after it, Raddiah," he told the prince. "You've got them nearly trapped now."

And with that, he accepted his dismissal, bowed to the king, and allowed himself to be escorted off the palace grounds.

1.3

Manuah's home was also on a hill, of sorts, although it really only lifted his view enough to see over the whitewashed rooftops of his neighbors. Still, he liked looking out at them. A few industrious people kept potted plants on their roofs—melons and squashes and even the occasional date palm. Some kept dogs up there, who would bark and bark into the night. A few had roof chairs for enjoying the view and the night sky, and some even kept beds and chamber pots. Even the more boring houses, with nothing but whitewash on top, had a certain worldly charm to them that could not be found anywhere else.

Greater than any town or village, The City had laws requiring the ground floor of all buildings to be constructed of stone and sealed in at least a token coating of plaster. The roof planks must be a full hand wide and half a hand thick, and sealed with either plaster or earthen daub. The idea was that a second story could be built upon the first without the whole thing collapsing—a problem that had plagued The City in its early days, and still plagued the mud-brick towns of Larasha and Shifpar up north along the river.

But an unexpected side effect was to make buildings so expensive that few citizens could afford a second story anyway. Often it was the work of two of three generations to put up a proper house in the first place! Ah, but then even in the damp sea air that structure might easily last another *ten* generations, or twenty, or until the end of time; nobody really knew. Manuah had always liked the idea that The City might stand here forever, but lately he was having a harder time believing that, and his audience with Sraddah had done nothing to lift his spirits.

The best view in the house was from the kitchen, and there he found his wife, Emzananti, engaged in her favorite pastime: cooking. At the moment, she was chopping onions into a cold clay pan full of tallow, fishmeat, and shucked, breaded clams.

Here, finally, Harv Leonel saw something here that actually looked stone-age; the knife Emzananti used was a triangle of flaked obsidian, fitted into a wooden handle and wrapped tightly with rawhide. Probably glued in place as well, with some tree resin or animal-collagen adhesive. Her feet, too, were clad in extremely simple sandals: just a flat oval of leather with a bifurcated strap between the toes and tied back behind the ankle, like flip-flops designed by a child. The men also wore sandals, but theirs were sturdier and more complex, perhaps because they needed to run and climb and fight in them. Harv supposed some of the other women he'd seen on the streets were shod like Emzananti, but he hadn't really been paying attention. Quite a few of them had been barefoot, and that had drawn his eye much more strongly. The women's clothing, including Emzananti's, was also weirdly plain. It seemed the men in this society were the peacocks, or perhaps there were (again) functional aspects to their more ornate clothing that were not apparent.

"Oh, yum," Manuah said, kissing her cheek. Fried clams were his very favorite, and nobody cooked them like Emzananti. Still, he chided her:

"My most darling darling, there's enough there to feed a household for days. You're cooking for the servants!"

She turned and smiled at him, just for a moment, with reddened, tear-filled eyes, and then went back to her oniony work. "The servants can clean the bowls, and wash all the juice off your robe."

"I'm not a messy eater," he protested.

"With fried clams? Really?" She snorted in a most un-ladylike manner. Then: "How was your meeting?"

"Mmm."

"Not good?"

"Mmm. Let's talk about something else."

She continued chopping, but now somehow reproachfully. "You keep saying The City is in danger. Not talking about it will not make it go away."

"Fine," he said, gathering his thoughts. "The king refuses to provide funds for rebuilding the sea walls. He has given *permission* for me to rebuild them on my own, which of course would beggar our family." He spread his arms. "Shall I dismantle this house?"

"And why would you do that?"

"I need *blocks*, woman. Stone blocks. Even the best mud bricks wouldn't last a week in the ocean."

"Do the blocks need to be whole?" she asked, still not looking up from her onions. "Cutting stone is messy work, and not very forgiving."

"Huh," Manuah said. She was right about that; depending on the quality of the stone, a mason might finish as few as half the blocks he began. Half of those might be suitable as street cobbles, but the rest were sledded away as rubble, to be hammered by rope-ganged criminals into various grades of gravel, with which the mud-brick towns paved their own streets. Manuah had sailed upriver with more loads of gravel than he could count! But it was an interesting thought, because while blocks had value, and gravel had value, the masons actually *paid* to have their rubble piles sledded away. Not very much, of course, but if Manu were to haul it for free . . .

He laughed. "Well, that just might just work. Rubble wouldn't be as sturdy—it would break the waves, but only slow the currents. But perhaps that's enough. Especially if there's a buildup of silt."

"So I'm a genius, then?"

"Perhaps."

"And I've saved The City and all the people who dwell in it?"

He chuckled. "Perhaps."

"And tonight you will reward me for it?"

To this he couldn't resist saying "Perhaps" again, but he hugged her around the waist, and kissed her neck. Engaged as children, they'd been married at the seemly age of fifteen, and had loved each other well enough. Three live sons and two dead daughters later, they still loved each other well enough, and while Emzananti's body did not seem inclined to produce any more children, she still enjoyed the occasional attempt. Which was more luck than many couples had, and for this Manuah was grateful.

Changing the subject, he told her, "I need to travel tomorrow. The weavers in Surapp Great Town should have a load of byssa cloth for me by now, and I'm going to need that to pay for the caulking on the new boat."

"Hmm!" Emzananti exclaimed. "Will you save me a bit?"

Byssa cloth was by far the most precious cargo Manuah ever hauled, and he trusted it to no one but himself. A woven textile, it was thinner and lighter and softer and slipperier than anything else in all the world. It didn't take color very readily, so mostly it was brown or orange or yellow, and many fine gentlemen wore linen and cotton robes dyed to these same hues, to make themselves look finer still. But byssa was made from the feet-webs of pinnid sea snails, and between the harvesting of the pinnids, the drying and wrapping of the fibers, the setting of the looms and the actual weaving itself, a cubit of the fabric could cost as much as an entire bale of linen, and a bale of it (the largest amount Manuah had ever seen) was worth an entire *boatload* of linen. Sewing and embroidering it required special skill as well, so a byssa robe could cost as much as the boat that had hauled it east from Surapp.

"All right," Manuah told her, making a show of reluctance. "And a golden fleece as well."

"Oh, my. The heart flutters!"

Far north of the land where the Great Sea ended, there were magic streams where the women would lay down ram's fleeces for a month or two, and the fleeces would turn to gold. Manuah had doubted the rumors until he saw the fleeces for himself; they took on a yellow hue that glittered with countless tiny flecks and sparkles. It warmed him to know that this kind of magic could really exist in the world. Of course, golden fleeces were not as valuable as byssa cloth (and they, too, could be roughly imitated with yellow dye and mica sands), but they were more than valuable enough to be worth the trip. In this case, he didn't even have to go all the way to the world's end; he'd received word that some foreign stranger had made that journey, and all Manuah had to do was get there before the new moon, and offer a better price than anyone in Surapp Great Town, and he could claim virtually the entire shipment.

Emzananti was not a greedy woman, nor one who drew attention to herself with garish, mannish clothing. He wasn't sure what she wanted with these items, other than perhaps to make a wedding coat for their middle son, Hamurma. But that was her business, and in any case, it wasn't lost on her that Manuah stood to make a great profit from this rather short voyage, or that he planned to invest the entire profit into tree rosins, asphalt, birch tar and oil sands with which to caulk his newest boat. Four layers of caulk! He'd been talking about it for weeks, ever since the hull had started taking shape, and the wooden decking was laid down. This would be the largest boat in his fleet—perhaps the largest boat in the world—and sealing it against the corrosive ocean was *not* going to be cheap. But the alternative was to let the thing slowly rot out from under him, like a common fisherman. This he would not do.

"I'm going to bring Hamurma with me this time," he told her. "He's overdue for his first voyage."

"As you wish," Emzananti said, equably enough. Indeed, the boy was nearly fifteen, and though he was already captaining Manuah's smallest boat for measurement trips, back and forth across the harbor with a weighted sounding rope, he needed a better profession than that if he was to marry well. Manuah could let him man the steering oar on the way out and the sail on the way back, and thus acquaint him with the real ocean. If they hit bad weather, he'd move the boy to a paddling bench. He was a fine paddler, strong and with good form, and what he lacked in endurance he more than made up for in determination. When the wind was too weak or too strong, it took six paddlers to drive one of Manuah's boats, or eight if you really wanted to get anywhere, and they needed to be tough men.

Or women; Manuah actually had three of them in his crews—spinsters almost Emzananti's age—and while they weren't quite as large or as strong as the men, they tended to be very good about staying synchronized, or setting the pace if they were in front. They were tough as well, in a female sort of way—sun-shriveled and leathery and sharp-tongued when crossed. They didn't eat as much as the men, or weigh as much, but they also didn't generate as much force against ocean waves, and there was the unseemly issue of performing bodily functions in front of the men, so he tended to keep them in the harbor or on very short trips upriver.

Truth be told, Hamurma wasn't much stronger than the women at this time, but that would come with practice.

"Does he have a good raincoat? Just in case?"

"Good enough for now, yes. It's Sharama's old one, and

he'll wear it to rags before he outgrows it. Jyaphethti will need a brand new one when he's old enough to sail, but I think we can afford it."

"Hmm." Manuah knew she was right, but a jacket of stiff, waxed wool did not come cheap, and thrift was a family tradition. Where money did get spent, it was generally in the service of making more money! On the other foot, it was bad business to let his sons be seen in rags, or to let them catch their death of cold, or to disregard the advice of Emzananti, whom his parents had engaged him to largely on account of her cleverness.

He considered telling her that King Sraddah was planning to *attack* her childhood home in Surapp Great Town, but thought better of it for several reasons. First, because they would be in and out long before Sraddah's army got anywhere close. Second, because Sraddah might regard that fact as a military secret, and might take an extremely dim view of Manuah blabbing about it, even to his own wife. Third, because it would cause her to worry more than she already did. Oh, she hid it well, but what mother could be complacent about watching her sons depart for the open ocean, much less for war?

Changing the subject again, he said: "Where *is* Sharama? I'll need him to take charge of the seawalls while I'm gone."

"I believe he's crabbing. He was carrying traps when he left this morning."

"Again? Damn it, he won't rest until all my boats reek of fish. I'll have to sell my cloth to cooks and clammers!" He was partly joking, but also genuinely annoyed. This was a conversation he'd had with his eldest son more than once. He hadn't strictly *forbidden* fishing and crabbing from his boats when they were idle, but he'd pointed out logically all the problems associated with it, and trusted Sharama to draw the right conclusions. But Sharama was nineteen, and had a wife to impress, and harbor crabs brought in good money.

Here, Harv Leonel felt some confusion, because money was a thing very much on the mind of Manuah Hasis, but Harv had yet to see any coinage, or any formal system for recording transactions or savings. Kingdom clearly had a barter system, where goods had fixed values in relation to one another—ten chickens to a goat, ten goats to a cow, et cetera—but there also seemed to be some nebulous concept of credit that Harv couldn't quite pin down. These people must have good memories and a high level of trust, so that Manuah could worry about "money" without having any way to store it. Without even translating the concept into specific numbers or goods.

And again Harv felt a touch of smugness, because this system, too, was primitive and silly—hardly the stuff of civilization. And on the heels of that, he felt a wave of protective worry, because the assholes on Wall Street could bankrupt Kingdom in a month by figuring out which animals had the best calorie-to-value ratio or flavor-to-growth-speed ratio, and then executing a series of increasingly rigged trades. No one here had figured this out yet, but that didn't mean no one could. And the fact was, Harv was an amateur historian of sorts, and Kingdom was simply not a part of any historical record he'd ever come across. Something had laid these people low, and erased them from history, and their society seemed increasingly brittle to his modern sensibilities. What did they do about fires? Plagues? Floods? They were, in some ways, like babies not yet toddling—unaware of pain or the possibility of harm.

But they were clever. With no real history of their own to fall back on, without horses or wheels or bronze tools, they'd nevertheless figured out how to build a great stone city, with paved roads and gutters, with towers and sea walls and firmly established trade centers. This place was the size of a major international airport, or twenty big shopping malls. Stone age, indeed.

"It might be a ploy," Emzananti pointed out. "Sharama's been wanting his own boat for quite a while now; this may be his way of telling you. You had one at his age, if I recall."

"Yes, well, stinking up my boats isn't getting him any closer to my heart. Or my money."

"Well, then perhaps he's saving up to buy his own. How many crabs would he have to sell?"

"A lot. *Confound* it. If we can't stop him crabbing, let's at least have him put the catch in pots rather than baskets. Will he be home for dinner?"

"I would think so," she said. "You can lecture him then. Or have a real conversation; it's your choice."

With a bow drill, a plank and some wood shavings, she deftly started a little kindling fire and gently set it into the stove—a slab of slate over a square fire pit, with a square hole though the outer wall of the house serving as a sort of chimney. Her motions were as quick and as natural as chopping vegetables; something she barely needed to think about. She then carefully piled sticks into the pit, and set the clay pan on top of the slab.

Being the daughter of an aristocratic family, she also possessed a burning crystal—a type of rock that was as clear as water, and shaped by magicians so that it was capable of transmuting the light of the sun back into the fire that had spawned it. It was one of her most prized possessions, inherited from her mother and easily worth as much as a new boat. Manuah felt it was impractical and a waste of good magic, but Emzananti had been known to light a little torch with it and carry the torch indoors to the kitchen, just to prove a point. She also owned a thing called a fire tube which involved a hollowed out cylinder of wood and a thin, greased wooden plug and a little dab of wood dust, that somehow created fire without friction. It was an amazing device, and possibly also magical, but it required a lot of patience to operate correctly, and was really more of a hobby than an actual utensil. She had experimented with sulfur and sandstone as well, on the rumor that these could *also* produce fire, but she'd never gotten it to work. Emzananti loved her fire starters, but eleven times out of twelve she settled for the bow drill like any laborer's wife.

"You know," Manuah said, "you could just bang two flints together like a wildman."

"Oh, hush."

"You could cook like one, too. They drop their pots into an open fire, and lift them out with gloves and rods. Everything is roasted or boiled, or sometimes steamed. They don't fry *anything*, and since they never have salt, they load everything up with fennel and garlic."

"Nauseating," she said, wrinkling her nose.

"It's not the only nauseating thing they do."

She held up a hand. "Enough, husband. You seem bored. If this is what a day off the water does to you, then it's good you're voyaging tomorrow. The sun doesn't set for another three *hurta*; why don't you go find a stone mason and get your son some rubble for his new project?"

1.4

"Lean into it," Manuah told his middle son. "Don't steer with your arms; steer with the weight of your body. These are real waves; they'll tire you out in an *hurta* if you go at it like that."

"Yes, Father," said Hamurma. "Thank you." Unlike his older brother, he was generally eager to please, and eager to be taught rather than to learn everything himself, the hard way.

"That's it. Keep your back straight."

The waves weren't bad at all by ocean standards, but Manuah felt there wasn't much time to waste here. They'd gotten a late start, thanks to Belurin the olive merchant being a total idiot, and the sun was already low in the sky.

"We're turning toward the shore," Manuah warned. "Now you have to pull. Lean away from the oar, use your weight in the other direction. We're not in the harbor; these waves will spin you if you let them."

"Yes, Father."

The shore was a *kos* away—far enough that they needn't have any great fear of reefs or sandbars. A bit of bad steering didn't present much danger, unless it got them sideways to a rolling wave. But it cost time, and it was sloppy. As it was, they'd be hugging the coast all day and night on their westward journey. Between The City and Surapp Great Town, the currents pulled generally eastward, although they were slower near the shore and faster a few *kos* farther out. The winds blew generally westward, and they were faster close to land, where the river valleys (for some reason) seemed to suck them in much of the time. And so one traveled *to* Surapp by hugging the coast, and back home *from* Surapp by keeping the shoreline halfway between the boats and the horizon.

At this point Manuah called out, "Is this really your twentieth voyage, Letoni? Tighten that sail! Are you trying to rip it?"

"No, Captain," said one of the two men manning the sail. "Sorry, Captain."

The sail was a square made from two layers of untreated linen, which people were always advising Manuah against. *It tears too easily*, they would say. *It soaks up water and gets heavy.* Yes, well if you coated it with beeswax it was heavier still, and much more expensive, and it still had a tendency to tear without warning. And if you coated it with tallow, the seagulls would never leave you alone. No, the smart thing was to use the cheapest sails you could, and replace them often, and always carry a spare on every voyage, or two if you were going to be gone all month. And tie them down tightly so they didn't luff and flutter in the face of the wind!

Letoni was partnered with Kop—a short, heavyset man only a few years older than Hamurma—and together the two of them untied and re-tied the sail so that it was tighter. Still luffing, though, because the wind was nearly against them, and it was hard to keep the linen filled while Hamurma steered like a drunkard. But these were good sailors, and they knew that Manuah knew the blame wasn't theirs.

He'd brought a crew of ten on this short voyage, and with Letoni and Kop at the sail, and Manuah and Hamurma at the stern, that left six other men without much to do. Being also experienced sailors, they were presently sprawled on the wooden deck in between clay jugs of wine and pickled olives, with their faces covered, attempting to get some sleep while they could. One never knew when the sea's mood might change and they might need to man a paddle for several days. Too, most traders anchored for the night, often hugging the shore just outside the surf zone, or sometimes even beaching at their own preferred, quasi-secret spots along the way, and having a delightful little campout on the beach. But that was hard on the boats, and wasteful of time; Manuah's fleet sailed day and night, and the men who were sleeping now would be wide awake from midnight to dawn.

Then things went quiet for a while, with only the creak of reeds in the hull, the gentle splashing of water, and the straining and fluttering of the sailcloth against the yard arm. If the wind cut any closer against their path, Manuah would have ordered the sail lowered, and if it increased in force he might even order the men to strike the mast. But for now they were enjoying smooth—if slow—sailing. Fine weather for training a new stern.

After perhaps half an *hurta* of silence, Hamurma called out. At first Manuah though he'd lost his balance and was going overboard, and he turned toward his son, ready to grab him or dive in after him. But no, Hamurma was merely pointing.

"Father, look! A spout!"

And indeed, where Hamurma was pointing there was fountain of water and air in the distance, perhaps half a *kos* away.

Manuah felt a tingle of fear. The only animals that spouted were dolphins and greatfish, and this spout was too large to be from a dolphin. Many sailors regarded greatfish as good luck, or at least not bad luck, but Manuah's family had traveled too far and heard too much. He knew that greatfish came in a variety of sizes and shapes, and some of them had eyes the size of your head and teeth the size of your fist, and some of them would come up under your boat and capsize it for no apparent reason. He'd never heard of one eating a human being, or even accidentally drowning one, but they were certainly large enough to do either, and anyway they were unpredictable. He regarded them much the same way he might an untethered bull; not *necessarily* dangerous, but certainly not to be trusted. Of course, people were always telling Manuah that he worried too much.

"Was it a greatfish?" Hamurma asked, while Letoni and Kop clapped their hands and called out in delight.

"It was," Manuah confirmed, trying to keep the tension out of his voice.

"Will it spout again?"

"In a few *vimadi*, yes. They always come back to the surface. I think it's how they breathe."

Kop laughed at that. "A fish that breathes air!"

To which Letoni said, "Have you been sneaking wine while our backs were turned?" Then, more seriously, "We'll find it again, Hamurma. I'll look this way. Kop, you look over there."

They waited for what seemed like a long time, but presently the spout came again, much closer—barely three sixties of feet away from the boat, and loud as a fat man snoring.

"Found it!" Kop joked.

The other men were looking up now, some alert and some rubbing the sleep out of their eyes.

"Greatfish!" someone shouted, quite unnecessarily.

The thing lifted its giant tail and submerged again, only to resurface in the same position a few *vimadi* later.

"It's following us," Letoni said.

"I think it likes you," said someone else.

And from there it devolved into comments Manuah would rather his fourteen-year-old son not hear. But of course Hamurma had spent his life around sailors, and already cursed like one when he thought his parents weren't listening.

But indeed, it did appear that the greatfish *was* following the boat, just tootling along behind them—sometimes closer and sometimes farther, but always nearby. Was it looking for scraps, like a gull? That seemed unlikely for such a large animal—easily twice the length of the boat itself. Perhaps it was just curious.

In the west, the sun slipped down below the waves, and the sky grew yellow and then red and then blue and then black, and still the greatfish followed them. Despite the delight of the sailors, Manuah found his sense of foreboding growing only stronger. There was something not quite natural about this, something perhaps magical or divine, and that was a worse kind of unpredictability, because the gods seemed to get bored very easily, and you never knew what they might try next to entertain themselves.

And then Hamurma was pointing again, this time at the sky. "Father, look! There's something in the stars!"

Manuah looked where his son was pointing, and saw... something. A smudge, a glow, a little spray of stars, just above the horizon. It wasn't a cloud; it was *behind* the clouds, and also a different color. It was the color of stars, or of the thin sliver of moon that was following the sun down into the ocean.

"What is it?" one of the sailors demanded.

"I don't know," answered another.

Letoni came forward. "Captain, do you know what this is?"

It was a captain's job to know the stars, to navigate by them on the rare occasions when land was not in sight. But Manuah had never seen anything like this, and he felt a clawing superstitious dread, because he had kept a secret from his wife, and he was planning on keeping it from the inhabitants of Surapp Great

Town as well. People he counted as friends. Normally he wouldn't think himself important enough that his own actions might anger the gods, and yet... the spray of stars was immediately behind the greatfish, and it seemed to him that the thing had spouted its mist all the way up into the sky. If that was not a sign from heaven, then he didn't know what possibly could be.

But he dared not share these thoughts with his men—not in the middle of a voyage—so instead he said, "Hamurma, mind your steering!"

And then, to Letoni and Kop, "Keep to your sail, my friends. I have some thoughts about this thing, but I'll speak with my brother before I share them. Meanwhile, if it doesn't help us steer, or sail, and it doesn't help us carry olives to Surapp Great Town, then it's a distraction we can't afford."

"Yes, Captain," said several voices from around the boat. But all heads remained turned toward the sky, and several of the sailors raised their hoods up over their hats, untied the straps from behind their necks, and tied them under their chins as if to ward off cold.

Manuah's time in Surapp Great Town was marked by a great weight in his stomach. He steered the boat into their triangular harbor, noting that the mouth of it seemed wider than he'd ever seen it, even at the highest of tides. Surapp's harbor was entirely natural, with no sea walls, no dredging of the bottom, no excavation or upbuilding of the low sandstone hills around it. But here, too, the water was rising. It was rising everywhere. He supposed the ocean must seek its own level, just like the water in a bucket, but where could all this extra water be coming from? The idea staggered his mind: if the ocean rose a foot—even a hand, even a *finger*—then the volume of added water was that finger, plus the finger next to it, and so on across all the area of the ocean itself. Could a mountain be that large? Could a whole range of mountains? If all the snow melted off of all the mountains in the world, how much water would that be?

This *must* be a matter for gods, because it was all out of scale with the world of human beings. And now the sky was changing, too, and he didn't know what to do about it. Repent? Sacrifice? Reveal the secrets of his king?

He didn't trust this changing harbor. Even though it was

deeper, even though it was wider and should be safer, he felt exposed and vulnerable. Once they were past the mouth he ordered the sail lowered, and they completed the final *kos* of the journey with paddles. At the docks, by the time his men had dropped the wooden side bumpers and tied the bow and stern to the mooring pylons, word of his arrival had already spread, and before he reached dry land he was met by the merchants who were buying his cargo. Absently, he exchanged pleasantries with them while their laborers carried off the jars of olives and wine. Five minutes later he couldn't have told you what was said; his mind was racing on other matters, not least the impending invasion during which these men might lose their lives or their homes or their sons, or the virtue of their wives and daughters, and would certainly lose their autonomy. Unless they somehow managed to defeat Sraddah's army, which seemed unlikely.

Why *wouldn't* the gods of Surapp Great Town be angry about something like that? Perhaps even the gods of Kingdom would be displeased, to see so much effort being spent somewhere else.

The men asked for shore leave, but he refused them. He wanted to get out of here as quickly as he could. He wanted to get home and consult with Adrah; if anyone knew what was going on—if anyone *could* know—then surely it was the Cleric Astrologers.

Manuah had to go hunting for the byssa cloth merchants, and when he found them they didn't have a whole bale of the cloth after all.

"Our president purchased several yards of it," they apologized. "We could have refused her, could have explained that you had priority, but we desire her favor. Surely you understand."

"It's fine," he told them.

"Is it? Really?"

"It is, really," he answered, because the whole matter suddenly seemed quite trivial. Of course, he *did* need to caulk his new boat. In a world of rising waters and angry gods, a boat was perhaps a better investment than a house or an army! But he couldn't quite bring himself to care about the economics of it. He now owed a debt to the cloth merchants, but the wine and olive merchants owed a debt to him, and the whole thing had been calculated to balance out so that they would owe a debt to one another, and Manuah would be out of it entirely. But now there was an *im*balance that he was probably going to have to eat, or at least split with the cloth merchants, unless he wanted to be back here every week for a month sorting the whole thing out. And he worried—he *feared*—that that would not be the best use of his time.

He wanted to say, "My cousin will invade this place before the next new moon. Soon, if you're smart, you'll be paying tribute to a king you've never met, and it'll be more expensive than this. And if you're not smart, then this will be the last time we ever speak."

He wanted to say, "We were followed by a greatfish, that spouted pure light into the sky."

He wanted to say, "The water keeps rising, and I don't know when it will stop, or *if* it will stop, and I sometimes wonder if the whole world is going to drown."

And most of all, he wanted to say, "If all of this is happening at the same time, can it really be a coincidence? Is it even *possible* to make the gods less angry?"

But what he did say was, "I need to get out of here by midday or the tides will be murder. Have your man load the bale, and we'll sort this out some other time. And may the next month be kind."

1.5

Kingdom was ruled over by three gods, represented by stone figurines at the Temple of the Hill of Stars. Manuah, who tried to stay out of religion in the same way he tried to stay out of politics, thought of them privately as The One With The Arms, the One With The Hair, and The One With The Big Dick. Such sacrilege had never bothered him before, but now he wondered if it were part of why the gods were so crapped off. Not because of him personally, but because religion did not play as big a part in the affairs of Kingdom—and particularly the affairs of The City—as it had in times past, and the gods were widely scorned.

But which god would be angry? The One With The Big Dick seemed least likely. What would a fertility god want with a drowning world? It must be one of the other two, or perhaps some god Manuah had never thought of. Some powerful, vengeful god? The people of Surapp worshipped a god like that; a single god who would allow no others, and who was somehow his own mother and his own daughter, and was also the sun itself. That was some god! And it made a kind of crazy sense, because if the sun were conscious, it could certainly melt snow if it wanted to.

Such thoughts plagued him all through the afternoon. He let Hamurma man the sail along with Kop, and he let Letoni steer the boat, while he simply stood around and brooded, gnawing occasionally on a chunk of hard sailor's bread, wearing away at it bit by bit. To his disquiet, the greatfish reappeared as they rounded the Cape of Thorns, and stayed with them for the rest of the afternoon. Or perhaps it was some other solitary greatfish who liked to follow boats around?

47

When evening finally came, and sun slipped down into the ocean again, he allowed himself a small breath of relief. At least *that* god wasn't watching them now. But it wasn't long after that, when the celestial spray of the greatfish rose. In the constellation of the hand, at the very opposite end of the sky from the supposed sun god. And what could *that* mean? That two gods were at play here? That two gods were warring, and human beings were simply caught between them? That starry smudge seemed bigger, too. He knew one thing: he needed to consult with his brother as soon as possible. Adrah knew more about these matters than Manuah could ever hope to. For a priest he was not especially godly; he still sometimes talked like the sailor boy he once had been. But he knew his figures, yes indeed.

Manuah slept fitfully that night, and passed a groggy, surly morning watching rainclouds gather. Not *storm* clouds per se, but enough to cause them trouble if they were caught out. And the wind was against them again. Finally, Manuah took the steering oar, if only to keep himself busy.

When they finally returned to The City, his son Sharama was at the mouth of the harbor, standing atop one of the sea walls and calling out instructions to the nearby boat under his command. The tidy rectangular block wall had been broadened and heightened into a ridgeline of rubble, but right away Manuah could see what a big job this was going to be. In three days of (presumably) diligent work, the heir to the Harbormaster title had added perhaps two feet of height and ten feet of width to a twenty-foot section of one of the harbor's four sea walls. At that rate, even if Sharama worked every day at the task, it would take a year or more to complete. Assuming The City's masons even produced enough rubble! Well, at least the boy was starting in the right place.

"Ho, Sharama!" Hamurma called out. "How goes it?"

"Ho!" Sharama called back. "Just a moment, here. Basri, haul that rope! You're drifting!" Then, to Manuah, as they made their closest approach: "Hello, Father. We ran out of rocks, so we're dredging buckets of sand up against the wall."

"Ah," said Manuah. "Well, let's see if it holds." If it did, it could keep the rubble wall from leaking too much, and improve its ability to break the backs of approaching waves. Not a bad idea. Manuah steered past the lip of the wall, and around into the gap that would lead them into the harbor proper.

As the distance between them started increasing again, Sharama called out, "Will I see you at dinner? I have two matters to discuss."

"Maybe!" Manuah said over the rising wind. "But I have to meet with Adrah first!"

That turned out to be easier said than done. First he had to guide the boat into dock against an unruly tide *and* an unruly wind and then, once they'd tied off securely, he had to unwrap the bale of byssa cloth and take a cubit of material from it, then command one of the men to wrap it all up again. Then he did the same for the bale of golden fleeces, and gave both the cloth and the fleece to Hamurma, telling him to deliver them back home to his mother. Then he had to track down both the cloth merchant and the fleece merchant who'd agreed to receive these shipments, while the men stayed with the boat and guarded against thievery.

Then, once the merchants had been brought and the bales carried away, the men quite reasonably wanted to be paid for the journey, and so they all had to trek over to the bazaar, where he vouched for each man with the Master of Markets. It was an annoying process, and he wished (not for the first time) that he could simply write a note on a plank of wood and send that instead. But that would have been an insult, even assuming the Master of Markets could read, which Manuah was fairly certain he couldn't.

And then he needed to go back home anyway, to take a healthy shit in private, and by then it was nearly dinnertime. Today dinner had been prepared not by Emzananti, but by Chatrupati, who was Manuah's aunt and stepmother and the mother of Adrah. And because Chatrupati's hands and mind were not as deft as they once had been, the dinner consisted mainly of oranges and biscuits, with a single dried sardine for each person seated around the dining rug: Manuah and Emzananti, their three sons Sharama, Hamurma, and Jyaphethti, plus Sharama's wife Telebabti, and Chatrupati herself. This was Manuah's entire family; his mother and father were long in the ground, his two daughters had died before the age of five, and Telebabti had yet to bear Sharama any children. Seven people did not make for a very large family, but it did make it easier for them all to fit under one roof, which was something. They even had room for two servants: now a married couple named . . . Floopy and Poopy Gubgub or something. He was always forgetting.

"Eat and pray," Chatrupati instructed slowly. "You spend your days busy and your nights asleep, but the body and soul require nourishment."

"Father's sea walls require nourishment as well," Hamurma noted, clearly thinking the comment was funny. No one else seemed to think so, but Hamurma didn't seem to mind.

Sharama said, "I'd like to buy one of your boats, Father. The one I've been using, if that's all right. It's your oldest, and one of the smallest."

"Hmm," said Manuah. "And how do you propose to pay for it?"

"The crab vendors owe me a considerable debt—twenty baskets. I'll transfer this to you. In addition, I will share half my profits with you for two years' time."

Manuah couldn't help laughing, because twenty baskets of crabs were in no way worth as much as an operational sailboat with two paddling benches, and also because he was already getting *all* of the profits from *all* of his boats, less the small wages he paid to his sons for crewing them. And yet, Emzananti was right: Manuah *had* owned a boat at the age of nineteen. It was old when he got it, and it had rotted away within just five years, but when he closed his eyes he could still see it, could almost feel the gnarled surface of it where its edges curled up. He'd inherited his second boat when his father died, and had earned all the ones that came after that. But yes, that first one had been given to him by King Sraddah's father, King Nunuktah, as a wedding gift. Sharama had received no such gift, because he was quite a jerk growing up, and was being particularly jerky the month he and Telebabti had tied the knot. Their gifts had mostly consisted of the forgiveness of small debts.

"It's not a fair offer," Manuah said. "The boat's worth more than that."

But Sharama *was* being polite now, and he *was* the heir to the Harbormaster title, and anyway Manuah wasn't convinced the whole world wasn't about to wash away. So he said, "I'll simply give it to you, on condition that you continue to repair the seawalls. Half your time for the next two years. Does that sound fair?"

"It does, Father. Thank you, Father." Sharama was uncharacteristically quiet after that, red-faced and sweating with what Manuah supposed must be gratitude.

"What was the other thing?"

"Huh?"

"You said you had two things to talk to me about. What was the second?"

"Oh, uh, Telebabti and I would like to paint the walls of our room."

"Blue-white," Telebabti said, "Like the sky at midday. It's a lucky color, and a soothsayer told me it would bring us children."

"Huh. What do you think, Emzananti?"

"I think it's an excellent idea, as long as you pay for it yourselves. Blue-white *is* a lucky color."

And then, with dinnertime business settled, the family broke out into song.

At the Temple of the Hill of Stars, Manuah brushed past the gate attendants with a few mumbled comments, and soon thereafter found Adrah in a contemplation room, sitting cross-legged on the floor in the light of an oyster shell lamp, with a plank of wood in his lap and a charcoal pencil in his hand. He didn't look up.

"Brother?" Manuah said.

"A moment, please."

A minute later: "Adrah."

"Just a . . . just . . ." Finally, Adrah sighed and looked up. "Ah, Harbormaster. Back from Surapp already?"

"Yes, I hurried. What are you doing?"

"Attempting to predict the movements of the Evening Planet. Without much enlightenment, I'm sad to say. The venerable Goxgatar is our champion predictor, and I don't think I'm ever going to replace him. I'm not sure anyone is. Anyway, how is your darling family this evening?"

"They're well," Manuah said impatiently. "I just gave Sharama his first boat."

"I'm so glad to hear it. And Emzananti?"

"Wonderful. You really should get a wife of your own."

This was by no means the first time Manuah had made this recommendation. The priesthood didn't forbid it, but the life of a priest and the life of a family man were not particularly compatible, so the parents of potential wives were unlikely to make the match. Some women married priests anyway, either for love or

for some supposed spiritual benefit, and Adrah could probably
do pretty well for himself if he put in the effort. But he'd always
seemed weirdly uninterested.

"And how did Hamurma do on his first voyage? Did those twig
arms get the job done? I imagine *he's* about ready for marriage."

When Manuah grunted instead of answering, Andrah finally
set aside the plank and pencil and said, "All right, all right, you
look like you're going to burst. What can I do for you? Is the
water still rising?"

Manuah nodded. "Pook, I saw a greatfish spout all the way
up into the stars. It left a mark in the sky. And yes, the water's
still rising. The tide in Surapp was a full hand deeper than I've
ever seen it."

"Slow down," Adrah said. "One thing at a time. You saw a
greatfish? You know there's one in our harbor right now. I saw
it from the tower an hour ago, spouting and diving."

"Oh, gods, it followed me."

"It did?"

"It followed me all the way to Surapp and back, but if it's in
the *harbor*, if it's *diving* in the harbor, then the water must be
deeper than ever. Don't you see?"

"And this fish spouted a mark onto the sky?"

"It did. I saw it myself."

"In the constellation of the hand?"

Manuah paused. "Yes."

Adrah smiled comfortingly. "All right, yes, we've seen that
as well. It's called a comet, and it's nothing to worry about. Or
rather, we *assume* it's nothing to worry about. Manuah, the sky
isn't a solid object like a curtain; it's just empty air, all the way
up. And the stars are very far away. It's literally not possible for
a whale to spout that high."

Manuah was surprised to hear this, first of all because he'd
seen it with his own eyes, and second because it irked him to
think he might be *more superstitious than a priest*. "You sound
awfully certain," he said.

Adrah smiled again, more genuinely and a bit condescend-
ingly, and Manuah could see how much it pleased him to know
something his big brother didn't. "It's easier to show you than to
explain. Come with me to the tower, and we'll do some stargazing."

Grumbling, Manuah stood with Adrah and followed him

out into the corridor, where young acolytes were igniting tallow lamps to combat the growing darkness.

"There's a pattern to the sky, and a rhythm," Adrah said over his shoulder as Manuah trailed behind him. "It all clearly means something, but right now we don't know what. Are the planets our gods? Are they little spherical lamps set into eddying currents of air?"

They came to the interior of the tower's base, and Adrah mounted the first ladder. "The moon and the sun are the same size in the sky, but they're not the same distance away. Did you know that? The gods have set it up very carefully, so that it's possible for the moon to cover the sun exactly. And yet it rarely does, and that has to mean something as well."

"Which god?" Manuah asked, trying not to look up his brother's robe as they climbed. "The one with the arms?"

"Well, that would make sense, wouldn't it?" Adrah said, as though the thought had never occurred to him before. "Lots of arms to hang lots of ornaments. Perhaps to dance and spin and move them around. But it still doesn't answer *why*, and without that—without understanding the gods' intentions—it's quite difficult to be sure what they really want from us. Or if they even notice us at all."

Manuah was pretty sure priests weren't supposed to talk that way, but the Cleric Astrologers were a small group, and held themselves somewhat aloof from the priesthood proper.

"On the other hand," Adrah continued, "Certain things are very well understood. The solstices, the equinoxes, these predict the coming of the seasons. The lunar calendar is crap, and we should by all means expel it into the nearest chamber pot. Months wander with time; they don't predict the seasons. They don't *synchronize*, as we like to say."

"We use that word too," Manuah reminded him with some annoyance. Synchrony was what kept sailors paddling together, for maximum thrust and minimum drag. Adrah had known that long before he'd known any of this celestial nonsense.

"Of course, of course," Adrah said, unembarrassed. "And perhaps it's the same kind of thing; the events that synchronize have power over the Earth. The ones that don't..."

They arrived at the top of the tower, under a nearly cloudless sky of deepest purple, where stars faded into view one by one, with almost visible speed. Each moment both darker and brighter than the moment before it, the purple sky dividing itself into black and white.

Adrah finished: "The ones that don't, aren't helping. They might even be hurting."

"You sound like a wise old man," Manuah said, not entirely without respect.

"Not wise enough. Predicting the motions is *difficult*. The dance of Kalishiva." He laughed. "The one with the arms. All right, well, Kalishiva is both creator and destroyer, both male and female. The name means Darkness and also Destroyer of Darkness, which is as good a description of the sky as I've ever heard. So why should her dance be simple?"

Still impatient, Manuah said, "You wanted to show me something?"

"Indeed. Look over here at your comet."

With a sky-blue sleeve now as black as the sky itself, he pointed toward the constellation of the hand, where the "comet" hung. The smudge was a little bit larger and brighter than it had been last night, and its position and orientation had changed slightly as well.

"It moved!"

"Yes. They do that. They come from very far away, and approach, and then dance away again. Usually over a period of weeks."

"You've seen one before?"

"I've seen two, although neither one could be made out this clearly without a pair of burning crystals."

He produced two clear discs from a pocket in his robe, and held them up in a line between his face and the sky.

"This is secret magic, Manuah. I'm trusting you with it. It brings the sky closer to me, so I can observe it better. Still *very* far away, but closer."

"I don't see anything changing."

"No, you have to be behind the crystals, looking through. It's strange, I know."

"I don't like this," Manuah said, and was unhappy with the way his voice sounded—like a frightened boy. But when exactly had his brother become a wizard?

"Relax. It's not harmful." Adrah moved the crystals back and forth a bit, grunting and harrumphing, and finally said, "All right, there. I see it clearly. It has a bright head and a fuzzy tail. The tail of a comet always points away from the sun, presumably so the head can look at it."

"It's alive?" Manuah asked, his voice still quavering with superstitious dread.

"Possibly. Or some kind of spirit—a visiting god, from some other celestial realm. Personally, I think it's something like a boat, moving fast enough to leave a wake behind it in the empty air. Manuah, *relax*. What's the farthest you've ever sailed?"

"Twenty-five days out, thirty days back."

"All right, so about four sixties of *yojana*. That's a good, long distance. But this comet is probably sixty of sixty of thirty *yojana* away. Maybe more. It's not going to reach out and grab you."

"How do you know all this?"

Adrah sighed. "Can you keep a lid on more secret magic?" When Manuah didn't answer, he went on anyway: "Sound and light are physical substances, like wind, except that wind can travel at any speed, slow or fast or anything in between. Sound and light can't do this. They're a different sort of substance, and they travel at fixed speeds."

"What?"

"It's true. Clap your hands."

Reluctantly, Manuah did so, half afraid this would trigger some new, even more disturbing revelation. But no, just a clapping sound.

Adrah said, "Did that sound occur in a single instant of no duration?"

"Um, no?"

"No, of course not. You couldn't hear it if it did. Now clap twice, as quickly as you can."

Manuah did as he was asked. *Clapclap!*

"That sound, that pair of sounds, from the silence at one end to the silence at the other, lasted about a *nimisha*."

"All right," Manuah allowed. These were words he'd heard, words people used sometimes to describe very long distances and very short times.

"Well, now here's where it gets interesting, because from the method of drums and mirrors, we know that sound—the physical substance of sound—traverses half a *yojana* in two sixties of *nimisha.* Measurements like 'kos' and 'foot' and 'moment' and 'khyama' are *subjective.* They never mean the same thing twice. A month is at least a real measurement of time, but it doesn't synchronize, so it doesn't help. But the *yojana* and *nimisha* are precise, and repeatable. They mean what they mean, because they relate to the cosmos itself."

"Um, all right," Manuah said, his head spinning. "What's that got to do with a comet?"

"Comets don't make sound, but they do make light, and by the method of eclipses we know that in the span of one *nimisha,* light travels a distance of sixty of sixty *yojanas,* or exactly one *spakta,* which is a new unit created by the venerable Goxgatar for this purpose. And Goxgatar has assured me that the moon is twelve *spakta* above the ground—quite a distance!—while the sun is *much* higher, at sixty of sixty *spakta.* And the stars are higher still—so high that even Goxgatar can't figure the distance. If it will ease your mind, I'll ask him if he can learn the range to this comet. It might not be possible; he might need months of observations, by which time the comet will likely be gone anyway. But I'll ask, all right?"

Manuah sat silent for a long while. He'd had no idea the world was this complex. Why would it need to be? It didn't make any sense. He'd also had no idea just how *smart* his half-brother was, or how much he knew that Manuah himself did not. Manuah had noticed, more than once, that from a boat on the water, he could sometimes see men waving and shouting on the shore, and that their waving and shouting didn't... *synchronize.* It seemed at times that the sound lagged behind. He'd never known what to make of that, and he hadn't really thought about it all that much. He certainly hadn't seen it as a doorway into to these vast numbers and distances, these bewildering movements and visitations.

Here, Harv Leonel's consciousness broke through for a moment, and he had time to marvel at this sort of gobbledygook science— wrong in so many particulars, and yet right (or rightish) in so many others. These cave men knew the speed of light! Whoever this Goxgatar was, he had managed to uncover secrets that had eluded even the Greeks. And without any sort of sensible mathematics! Math savants often reported "seeing" numbers and figures without having to calculate them directly, and he supposed Goxgatar must be one of these, or else he really was in contact with some sort of divinity. Was there even a difference?

And telescopes? Galileo had insisted the idea was not original to him, that he was merely reinventing something well known to "the ancients." But what had he meant by that? Where had he gotten that information? Harv had to wonder just how many times secrets like these had been discovered, or at least hypothesized and approximated, only to be forgotten later on? And that thought filled him with apprehension, because if these people's knowledge had been lost, surely that didn't say anything good about the fate of the people themselves. Manuah was right to worry!

And suddenly it hit him: this was the Ice Age. This was the end of the last great glaciation, when millions of gigatons of ice had melted off in rapid bursts—sometimes only a few hundred years each. And this thought filled him with superstitious dread, because if these visions were real at all, then Kingdom and The City had existed more than twelve thousand years ago. As remote from the ancient Sumerians as Sumer was from modern America. The Romans maintained continuity longer than any other civilization— eleven centuries long—and yet they could have risen and fallen ten times over since Manuah walked upon the Earth.

Was Harv just dreaming after all? Could civilization possibly be that old?

Finally, Manuah told Adrah, "I want to ask what all this means, but you've already said you don't know. You say these things aren't harmful, but that's just wishful thinking, isn't it? The truth is, you don't know." And when Adrah didn't answer right away, he pressed on: "The water is rising here, and in Surapp, and all up and down the Great River. Can you honestly tell me *that's* not harmful?"

With obvious reluctance, Adrah answered: "No."

"I've seen storm surges raise the water ten feet, for a day or more. If high tide were to strike in the middle of something like that, what do you think would happen?"

Again, reluctantly, "I suppose the water would come all the way up into the streets of The City. But then it would retreat again, yes?"

"Perhaps," Manuah said. "And perhaps building the seawalls

a little higher will help, although it's going to take time. And money, whether or not His Majesty cares to admit it. But if the water keeps on rising, all on its own, then how are we to stop it?"

The two of them were silent for a time, and then Manuah added, "Plus, there's this greatfish, appearing at the same time as the comet, and following around the very person who's warning you about rising water. Perhaps, as you say, the fish didn't create the star, but even if that's true, they still happened at the same time. Are you seriously going to tell me that isn't an omen of some sort?"

"I don't believe in omens," Adrah said, clearly trying to sound reassuring.

"Here's hoping the Cleric Portenters never hear you say that."

"Hmm. Yes, well, doesn't it sound a bit arrogant, to think these grand events have been staged, somehow, for your own benefit? To help you make your point?"

Manuah answered the question with another question: "Have you ever known the gods to lean down from the sky and speak directly to human beings? In a voice we can all understand? If they exist at all, and care about human beings at all, then how *would* they get our attention? What would that look like?"

Adrah didn't have an answer to that.

After another long pause, Manuah asked, "Is there anything you can do to help me?"

"I don't know, brother. I really don't. I can talk with the other clerics, but the problem is, *nobody* knows what these things mean, including you. It won't be easy to persuade people."

"Hmm. Assuming you even believe me."

"You have raised some interesting points." Another pause, and then: "There is some indication that the moon synchronizes with the tides in some way. Some complicated way. Perhaps the Cleric Astrologers could take that on as a task. That would be less controversial, I think, and it would help you know when the greatest flood risks would occur. Is that helpful?"

One of Manuah's hereditary titles was "Counter of Tides," but other than a very loose sense that high tide and low tide each came approximately twice per day, he'd never really lived up to that name. The problem was, sometimes the tides came early or late. Sometimes they were higher than expected, or lower, and he had been to some places where the tides came in and out only once each day. It didn't make sense, and so he had never wasted much thought on it. Instead he just stood on the decks of his boats, feeling the water surging under him, telling him whether it was headed in or out.

"I don't know. I suppose it's a start."

In another moment of lucidity, Harv Leonel—more as an act of whimsy than anything else—thought very hard at Manuah: THE DANGER IS REAL. In response to which, to Harv's great surprise and distress, Manuah screamed.

"Aah! Aah! Did you hear that?"

In the darkness, Adrah looked more concerned than he had all evening. "Hear what?"

"A voice," Manuah insisted. Then, even more certainly, "A *voice*. Telling me the danger is real."

Adrah laughed sourly. "Well, that's a bit convenient. The gods speak after all? Brother, you've given me a lot to think about. Don't spoil it."

And Manuah realized that Adrah merely thought he was kidding. Which was bad enough. But if he pressed the point any further, Adrah would think he was *crazy*, and that would be much worse.

Rattled to his core, Manuah told his brother, "Look, you can ask my men about the fish. And yes, if you could predict the tides it *would* help a little."

He couldn't think of anything else to say. He couldn't think of anything else to *do*. But he knew that strange, otherworldly voice was right: the danger *was* real, and Manuah was the only one who seemed to know it.

Over the next several weeks, Sraddah completed his invasion of Surapp. To Manuah's relief, the Surappi offered minimal resistance, losing only about two sixties of men before throwing down their spears and capitulating unconditionally. Their "president," a woman named Penelebab, relinquished her office, agreed to marry her daughter to Prince Raddiah when he came of age in seven years' time, and meanwhile promised to seek employment among the byssa cloth weavers—that being one of Surapp's most lucrative industries, and therefore perhaps the one that would allow her the greatest continued influence in a conquered nation.

Surprisingly, Sraddah also demanded a tribute of stone blocks, which Manuah was free to go pick up—not entirely at his own expense, but with a slight reimbursement from Kingdom's own debt logs. It would take him a year to transport all that stone, and even so it wasn't enough—Manuah wasn't sure any amount of stone could ever be enough!—but it was a concession. Clearly, Manuah wasn't the only one concerned about the coincidence of the greatfish which continued to dwell in City Harbor, and the comet which continued to grow larger and larger in the sky. First it was the size of the full moon (though not nearly as bright), and then the size of a whole constellation, and then large enough to stretch from one horizon to the other.

"You said it would approach and go away," Manuah told Adrah. "It isn't going away."

"It's a big one," Adrah agreed, trying to brush off his brother's concerns. "But it can't stay indefinitely. That's not in its nature. Also, we've determined that it's not affecting the tides. So you can rest easy on that score as well."

That *was* a relief of sorts, but even Adrah was starting to look a bit concerned. Nothing like this had ever happened before, and of course nobody knew what it meant. Was it good luck? Was it bad luck? Was it any sort of luck at all? The greatfish was something that had never happened either, but it was less of a concern to most people, except in the purely practical sense that it was eating up all the fish in the harbor, and fouling nets and buoys as it churned restlessly from one bank to the other. Was it lost? Unable to find its way back out? Or was it indeed trying to communicate, or was the greatfish itself a communication from one of the gods? In any case, its antics were forcing timid fishermen out into the much rougher water beyond the sea walls. Manuah dared to hope this would get more people talking about how *high* the water was getting, but alas he was developing a reputation in The City as a bit of a cracked pot.

"Here comes the Lecturemaster," people would say. "Quick, cover your ears!"

And so he learned that the more he talked about the danger, and the more urgently he talked about it, the *less* people believed him. He wasn't sure what to do about this, because not talking about it also didn't result in people believing him. At times, it seemed the best he could do was wrap it into a trio of concerns, in order of their perceived importance: the comet, the greatfish, and the rising water. That, at least, kept the concept alive without actively turning people away. But how could that be enough?

While Sharama stayed behind to work on the sea walls, Manuah and Hamurma took another voyage to Surapp, along with all five of his other boats, to retrieve stone blocks. To his relief, things were not all that different in Surapp Great Town, at least along the docks and warehouses. People still did business in the same way, and while they didn't seem particularly happy about suddenly being subjects of Kingdom, they didn't seem to be directing any of this ire toward Manuah and his crews.

Of course, they didn't want to hear about the rising water, either. For them, the three big concerns were: the invasion and its attendant tributes and taxes, the war casualties and their attendant funerals, and the comet presiding above it all like an enemy banner. Here, there was no doubt that the message in the sky was an unlucky one, although perhaps not *that* unlucky, since they were all mostly still alive, and their businesses still mostly unaffected.

"You're a cousin of our new king," said one laborer as he loaded stone blocks onto the deck of a boat.

"Not a first cousin, but yes."

"Are you here to inspect us? Make sure we're up to standard?"

"What? No. I'm here to receive a shipment, same as always."

"Hmm." The laborer wasn't sure about that one.

The voyage back was slow, and the boats rode so low in the water that Manuah told all the crews to keep them close to shore, and beach them at the first sign of a rough sea. But luckily they had smooth water and adequate wind.

Once back in The City, he tasked all his crews and boats with sea wall work, gently lowering and stacking the new blocks, making sure they fit together as durably and seamlessly as possible. For nearly a week they labored, and when all the new blocks were gone, they used rubble, and when it seemed all the rubble in Kingdom was exhausted, they used Sraddah's meager stipends to buy several boatloads of gravel. This meant, of course, that Manuah's hardworking sailors were going without pay. Which meant that about half of them didn't show up for work the next day, which was their prerogative, of course. But the other half did show up, and Manuah was grateful for it. They, at least, believed in this cause, in the seriousness of it. They had been at

sea with him, during storms, during rip currents when they had
to paddle for their lives to avoid smashing onto a reef, and when
they were menaced by giant squid beneath the water, and that
one time when eagles swooped down from the sky and attacked
them for no apparent reason. At all times, their own safety was
Manuah's primary concern, and they knew it.

"You know how to read the sea," Kop told him. "You always
have, as long as I've known you. If you say it's rising, then it's rising."

"Any fool can see it's rising," Letoni added. "If you say it's
dangerous, then I believe you."

But even the gravel, bought at the cost of some sailors' loyalty,
lasted only a few days, and after that the crews were reduced to
dredging the sandy bottom up against the existing walls, making them
broader even if, at the moment, they couldn't make them any taller.

Manuah thought about going back to Surapp for another load
of blocks, but he did still have to make a living, and his sailors
certainly did, so finally he decided to take on six loads of salt and
kelp and dried fish (actually seven, for Sharama opted to sail with
them), and travel upriver to Shifpar, the northernmost of the mud-
brick towns. Never mind the stink of fish; goods from the ocean
brought a hefty price there, and Manuah's boats could return laden
with apples and plums and leather and unspun wool.

This mission brought back about half of his missing crewmen,
who quietly resumed their positions on his boats. The other half,
including all three of the women, had perhaps decided to seek their
employment elsewhere, either with Dolshavak (Manuah's main
competitor, who focused mainly on the river trade and owned only
three boats), or with fishermen, or else on land somewhere. Well,
perhaps they'd be safer there.

In any case, Manuah's crews were shorthanded on the tricky
sail upriver, and every man had to work extra hard and pay extra
attention. Shifpar was about sixty and twelve kos upriver (or perhaps,
as Adrah would describe it, twelve and three *yojana*), and although
the winds along the river blew northeast or northwest or even true
north much of the time, the river's current moved *swiftly* in the
opposite direction. When the paddles were stowed, they progressed
perhaps one *yojana* inland per day. With paddles engaged for as
long and as often as the men could stand it, they could double their
progress, but Manuah was wary of this on account of morale. The
days were hard enough, tacking back and forth into sidewinds and

against the current, oftentimes feeling like they were sweating their balls off just to stand still, and yet also running the constant risk of crashing the boats together. At least the river was wide enough to tack against, or most days it wouldn't be possible to sail inland at all. Too, the winds at night were unreliable, and as the quarter moon faded to a crescent, they had to beach every night at dusk, when it became too dark to navigate safely, even by the light of the comet, which every night grew larger and brighter in the sky.

It was already long enough to stretch from one horizon to the other; how much larger could it get? The answer was, the head of it could set in the west, and the tail could fill the sky for another hour after that. And then two hours, and then four. The tail broadened as well, going from the width of the moon to the width of two moons to the width of a spread-out hand, held at arm's length. What were the Cleric Astrologers making of *that*?

"No one knows what this means," Manuah assured his men, night after night. "My brother and his people are counting and measuring and practicing secret magic, and yet all they can tell us is that the moon is farther away than any of us have ever voyaged, and the comet is higher than that, and does not affect the tides. And if that's as much as the wisest men can learn, then really you know as much as they do."

And the men's voices would come back with, "Maybe it's a giant cock, come to fuck us."

Or: "Maybe it's Min, the fertility god."

Or: "I still think it's a greatfish. They say the sky is the mirror of the Earth, and we have a greatfish down here. Why shouldn't there be one up there as well? It has more room to grow, for one thing."

Or: "Maybe it's a *rip* in the sky."

To this one, at least, Manuah could say, "The sky can't rip. It isn't a material object, like a curtain. It's just empty air."

"Forever? Just up and up and up?"

"I suppose so, yes. The stars are higher up than the Cleric Astrologers can measure."

"Well then, how do they know it isn't a curtain?"

Manuah sighed. "I'm not sure. But even if the sky were a curtain, it's much farther away than this comet."

He didn't know how such a remark could be in any way comforting, but it did seem to mollify the men.

On the third day, they passed the little town of Erituak, and on the fifth, they passed the larger town of Larasha. Both were made of mud and straw and gravel. To be fair, a sun-dried, mud-straw brick was nearly as hard as a fired clay pot, and nearly as light as a wooden beam, so as building materials went, it wasn't entirely awful. But unless you could afford paint (which few of the townies could), it literally looked like shit. Neither town had proper rain gutters down the sides of the streets, either, so both of them *smelled* like shit, even from the safety of the river. Both had been added to the Kingdom by Sraddah's ancestor Kagresh, at the cost of considerable bloodshed which the townies here had never fully forgotten. This made them a bit surlier than the other peoples Manuah had met in his travels, and so he tended to avoid these towns, leaving their trade for men like Dolshavak. They were, in Manuah's mind, the Big Shit and the Little Shit. And then, on the seventh day, they passed the Least Shit—a town whose name Manuah couldn't even remember, because he had never bothered to stop there.

For several days after that, they saw nothing but tree-lined riverbanks, uninhabited save for the occasional hut of grass or animal hides, almost like something the wildmen would build. The men took to calling out different wild animals they saw. This was difficult, because traveling by river made for a narrow journey, with usually not very much to see. Nevertheless, the men called out:

"Bear!"

"Eagle!"

"Leopard!"

"Three wolves!"

"Six deer!"

But then boredom set in, and the callouts became more fantastical:

"Giants!"

"Dragons!"

"An army of turtles waving the Surapp Presidential Banner!"

And then, inevitably, they became obscene.

"Your mother!"

"Your *grand*mother!"

"Your sister, in deepest embrace with a pair of oxen!"

Manuah put a stop to it there, before the word *daughter* could be mentioned. And morale suffered accordingly. More than once,

he heard a sailor muttering, "I see *Manuah* in congress with a
pair of oxen." He got them started on bird colors instead, and
that kept them busy for a few hours.

On the eleventh day they passed the little mud town of Tesk,
which had been conquered by Sraddah's father Sretekan, and once
that was behind them they were in the North Kingdom, which
held a special place in people's hearts because everything there had
been conquered by Sraddah himself, with almost no loss of life.

"We could have walked here by now," complained Hamurma.

"Oh, wise little worm," Letoni answered. "It might even have
been quicker, but could we have carried all this fish? Ah? Anyway, on the trip back we'll be like songbirds. Woosh! Woosh!
You'll like that."

Finally, on the fifteenth day, they arrived at Shifpar. It was the
largest of the river towns, and while it too was mostly constructed
from mud brick, there were some nice wooden buildings as well,
and three (the governor's mansion and a pair of temples) that
were actually fashioned partly from painted stone. Shifpar had
proper docks as well, fashioned from flat wooden planking and
stood up on heavy wooden piles driven deep into the riverbed,
and nestled in a little backwater cove that made getting in and
out a lot easier than it might have been. These features cemented
Shifpar in Manuah's mind as a civilized place, albeit barely.

And with his newfound sense of urgency about rising water,
Manuah now also noticed that Shifpar was built on a series of
hilltops, set well back from the river and significantly higher. If
a flood were to strike, Shifpar would weather it better than any
of Kingdom's other towns or cities. It was an interesting thought,
but he didn't know what to do with it.

Once the boats were securely tied and the cargo sold off, Manuah
granted the men a night of shore leave. Not because it was a good
idea (it certainly wasn't), but because he feared a mutiny if he didn't.
And so, while the little town of Shifpar tried to absorb the appetites
of thirty men, and tried even harder to figure out a reliable way to
charge them for it, Manuah took Hamurma to the house of Qitsturt, a man with whom he'd done frequent business, and who had
offered him hospitality in the past. This disappointed Hamurma,
who wanted to hit the town with his fellow sailors, but Manuah
figured that on the brink of his fifteenth birthday, Hamurma was
better off with disappointment than he was with sailors on leave.

1.6

"So, what does your brother make of these disturbances?" Qitsturt wanted to know. His thickly accented voice reminded Manuah of the wildmen: high and quick and clipped.

The two of them were up on Qitsturt's roof, sitting in leaned-back wooden chairs, looking up at the comet and drinking beer from clay mugs. Manuah always expected the beer in Shifpar to taste...inferior somehow, but it never did. Their wine was sour and dry and took some getting used to, but the beer was, if anything, even better than what Manuah could get in The City. Perhaps it was fresher?

Manuah snorted. "He says it's nothing to worry about."

"Hmm. And do you believe him?"

Manuah didn't need to say anything. The comet's length stretched from one horizon to the other, and its width stretched across a third of the sky's remainder, now bright enough to blot out many of the familiar constellations.

Qitsturt said, "Dolshavak is a man from your city. He told me last week you'd gone crazy, prattling about greatfish and floods. He says no one listens to you anymore, but you have never struck me as a prattler. There *is* something going on. The river grows swifter and deeper. And colder."

"Yes."

"And The City is built on flat ground. And spring floods do occur, as do storms."

"Yep."

"And the sky is, forgive me, rather foreboding."

"Uh-huh."

"Well, my friend, there is nothing crazy about all that. Perhaps it's your countrymen who prattle. Or, forgive me, *our* countrymen. My thanks to Sraddah for liberating us from our former condition."

"You shouldn't joke about that," Manuah cautioned.

"Who says I joke? Before we had an army that Sraddah could easily defeat. Now we have Sraddah's own army. This is meaningful, when the lands of the wildmen begin just a day's march away, with nothing but a few rude farming villages between us. Which also belong to Sraddah, and are also protected by his army. We gained peace by losing a war. Sraddah is a clever man."

Manuah snorted at that.

"Now who jokes? You think your cousin is not wise?"

"He doesn't seem so at times."

"No? Well, perhaps it is difficult for him. He is accustomed to winning. When the forces of sea and sky begin lining up against him, what is he to do? I tell you this, my friend: if there *is* a flood in The City, your family is welcome to seek refuge with mine."

Manuah paused before saying, "Thank you, my friend. My family is small, but not *that* small. You're a generous man, but I couldn't possibly."

Qitsturt laughed. "We'll see how reluctant you feel, if the time comes. Now drink! Drink! You leave at dawn, yes? What manner of host am I, if I send you home without a headache?"

Dutifully, Manuah drained his mug, and turned it over to show it was empty.

"There, see?"

"You don't look happy yet. I'm going to keep serving you until you look happy."

"Ah. Well, I'll try. The beer and the company are fine, and I thank you, but the view up here is shit. I've had enough of this comet."

"Yes? Well, it won't stay around forever."

"Huh. Yeah. May the next month be kind."

If the current had seemed swift on the way upriver, it seemed even more so on the way down. At first, Manuah ordered that each boat have two paddlers in the bow and a steersman in the stern, with the sails stowed away, but the Great River wasn't the sort of waterway that had rapids. Almost half a *kos* wide and well over twelve feet deep, it suffered the occasional sandbar or tree, but otherwise presented few navigational hazards. So once the men had found their rhythm, and were rolling down the river under comfortable control, he ordered the sails raised.

"Whooooosh!" the men exclaimed as the wind caught and filled the linen, making the boats leap forward so quickly that they all lost their balance for a moment. In hardly any time at all, their downriver speed had nearly doubled. The boats left wakes now, like comet trails of their own, and when the steersmen started crossing paths to make each other's boats roll sickeningly, Manuah didn't put a stop to it. He liked this as well as anyone—the wind in his hair! The thrill of being fastest!

"You see? You see?" Letoni said to a frightened-looking Hamurma. "Songbirds! Whoosh! Whoosh!"

The men in one of the other boats got out their paddles and started churning the water hard, taking a few *kesthe* to find their synchrony and then, finally, adding even more speed. Though initially they were in the middle of the pack, they began to pull out ahead, until the men in the other boats shouted their objections and unstowed their own paddles.

Now there was no need to keep people busy, to keep them from focusing on how hot and tired and out of breath they were. This was dangerous work and even more dangerous as play, but they'd done it before, and Manuah wouldn't have thought twice about it if not for the presence of Hamurma. But Hamurma was nearly old enough to get married, and had not been promised to anyone yet, and a little danger would make him more interesting to the young women of The City. Probably not to their fathers, but that was their own problem.

"Race!" he called out to the crew of his own boat. "Pull with your backs! Pull with your legs! Bury those blades, you toads! Plant and pull! Plant and pull! Now! Now! Now! Now!"

They didn't quite get out in front—no one was about to let the boss beat them in a fair contest!—but they acquitted themselves well enough.

Of course, no one could keep up a race pace for long, so eventually they all settled down into a more leisurely (though still challenging) rhythm, with one boat or another occasionally putting in the effort to take the lead for a while. It was a fine thing, on a fine day, and for a while Manuah was able to forget all the troubles of the world. They made it all the way to the delta, through the widest channel, and back to the Grand Sea a full hour before nightfall, grinning and whooping at their accomplishment. Let's see Dolshavak beat *that*.

But at the mouth of the Great River there were *lots* of sandbars, and they had to pick their way more carefully around the harbor's cape, and then through the interlocking sea walls, tacking back and forth in the sputtering wind. The sun set, and the sky turned yellow and red and purple and blue. And then the comet appeared, its head hanging low in the northern sky, its tail streaming *way* out behind it like a ghostly white flame.

"It's bigger," someone said.

"It's *closer*," someone else said.

"It's nothing to worry about," a third person said, in clear imitation of Adrah's voice.

The men burst out laughing. And then the greatfish appeared, blocking their way into the harbor, and the laughter stopped.

Yes, blocking their way! The fish spouted and thrashed its tail, raised up an eye to glare at them, then dove and breached and spouted some more. Exactly as though it were trying to get their attention.

1.7

Manuah was stricken with a fear he dared not show. Who had ever heard of such a thing? A greatfish blocking a harbor mouth, on purpose! Hadn't the gods made their point already? But no, apparently not. Whatever or whoever controlled this fish, didn't want them entering the harbor. Or perhaps the fish was wily enough to control itself. *Go back*, it seemed to say. *Go back, this is not the place for you!* Or perhaps it was only lost and confused, and maybe even frightened by the strange light in the sky, and had had enough. *Out of my way, I'm getting out of here.* Was that any better?

"That rips it," Manuah said, to no one in particular. "I'm moving to Shifpar."

He'd meant it as a joke, and to his relief it came out sounding like one. A few of the men in his boat even chuckled weakly at it. But he realized it was true. He couldn't take this stress anymore. Something *was* going to happen—something awful—and if he couldn't stop it and couldn't convince anyone else of the danger, he could at least get his own people to safety.

The thought made him sick. Was he a coward? A deserter? A traitor? His family had looked after the harbor for generations. He was an important person in the life of The City. Did that fact oblige him to die here? To let his children die here?

"Go around the fish!" he called out to his crews, as calmly as he could manage. "It can't block seven boats at once."

"Race!" Sharama called out. But that fell flat; the men were tired, and scared, and no longer in a racing mood. But the boats fanned out, working their way around the massive fish. To its

70

credit, the fish didn't seem to want to hurt anyone. It never got closer than sixty feet, and never raised enough waves to risk swamping anyone. But it surely did seem...agitated. Finally, it sank beneath the water and let them all pass unmolested.

"There's something you don't see every night," Hamurma said, clearly struggling to sound cheerful.

The wind was dead, now, so as tired and sore as they were, they paddled the rest of the way. No man complained. However, one of them did say, "The comet is moving," as they were maneuvering into the docks by its light.

"Northward," someone else said.

"*Down*ward," said a third person.

Manuah looked, and saw that it was true. In the *hurta* they'd spent mucking around in the harbor, the comet had visibly changed position in the sky. Not by much, but it was more than enough to notice. In an *hurta*! And that was something you didn't see every night, either.

"Don't unload the boats," he said to the men.

"What?" "What?" "We can't leave these unguarded." "What?"

"Don't unload the boats," Manuah repeated. "We're going back to Shifpar, any man who wants to. I believe we'll be...safer there."

There was silence at that, until one of the men said, "What about our families?"

And that stopped Manuah, because he hadn't thought about it. His own family, yes, but there were thirty sailors here. The boats could probably carry thirty more people and still have room for this cargo, but he didn't actually know that much about the personal lives of most of his men. A few were single, a few had wives, a few had wives *and* children, but here in this moment he couldn't dredge up a single detail.

"As many as we can safely carry," he finally said. "*I'll* decide."

There was silence again, until someone said in the darkness, "Captain, you *are* crazy. I'm going home."

There were murmurs of assent here and there, and several of the men started climbing out of the boats. But another voice—Letoni's—said, "I believe you, Captain. I'm staying right here." And there were murmurs to that as well.

"Get what you need, and *whom* you need, and meet me back here as quickly as you can," Manuah said to whomever was still listening. "Letoni, do you have a family?"

"Only my ma," Letoni said, "and she's half blind and half lame, and sworn never to set foot on the water. I think she'll be better off at home."

Manuah didn't agree. He didn't agree with that one tiny bit. But then again, did Letoni, really? They couldn't take the entire population of The City with them, and what good would it do anyone, to fill the boats up with the old and sick? He didn't argue the point.

"We've eaten up all the food," he said instead. "We can eat the cargo—plums will keep for another six or twelve days, and the apples for longer than that—but that's not going to be enough. And there's no time to dry or pickle anything, so we'll have to bring our meat still on the hoof. Go to the houses of the animal vendors, and buy some chickens and goats. Tell them we'll pay double. Triple if they carry it all down here, in cages, within an *hurta*. And get some hard biscuits if you can. As *many* as you can."

Letoni looked uncertain. "You'll pay for all this?"

"Yes! Yes! Now go!"

To Hamurma he said, "Go home and gather up the family. All of them. Tell them to gather up only what they can carry, and bring it here immediately. No arguments."

To Sharama he said, "Go to the Hill of Stars and bring back your uncle. Tell him his older brother commands it. If I'm wrong, I'll tithe heavily, but in the meantime he is to get his skinny blue robe down here on the dock. Is that understood?"

"Yes, Father."

Letoni and Hamurma and Sharama departed, with all the haste he could have wished for.

"You're crazy," another one of the sailors said.

"Fine," Manuah told him. "I'm crazy. Get out of here."

He busied himself counting rope and spare sails, trying to figure out how well provisioned they were *really*. Not that there was much he could do about it.

"The comet's gone," someone said.

Manuah looked up. The statement wasn't precisely true, because the tail of the comet still dominated the sky. Broader than ever, and seeming now to shimmer and flow right before his eyes. But the head of it had somehow slipped down below the northern horizon. It had moved quite a bit while they were looking away.

But now they looked, and where the tail of the comet met the skyline of The City, there was a distant flash of light. Nothing all that big—like lightning in a far-off thunderstorm—but nevertheless unambiguous. And frightening.

"What does it mean?" someone asked. It was Kop, right there by his side.

"Nothing good," Manuah said. He watched the horizon for a while longer, waiting to see if there would be more flashes. When nothing happened, he went back to his inventory.

"You don't have anyone?" he asked Kop as he counted extra paddles.

"No."

"Hmm. Too bad."

"Or not," Kop said. "Something bad is going to happen, isn't it?"

"I think so, yes." He paused, not sure what else to say. He had no idea what was going to happen, and he was *not* a crackpot, and he was not ordinarily superstitious. And yet he was somehow very certain: the danger was real. The high water made this place vulnerable even to ordinary Earthly dangers, and what was happening here was neither ordinary nor Earthly. But how could he explain all that to a man like Kop? He could barely explain it to himself.

Finally, he said, "We need to prioritize our deck space. Let's get this wool out of here. I don't think we're going to need it."

"Hmm," Kop mumbled. "Plenty of wool in Shifpar."

So Kop and two other men began grabbing the bales and setting them up on the docks. It didn't take long. A little while later, they were moving paddles around, making sure each boat had exactly two spares, and Manuah was trying to remember to station the smaller men in the boats with the shorter paddles, because everyone knew you shouldn't use one taller than the bottom of your ribcage—

The ground jerked. He watched it. While the water remained stationary, the whole landscape dropped a hand, and then raised two, and then dropped again to its original position. There was a sound like sixty sacks of gravel being dropped all at once, and then silence. All in the space of two handclaps. He might almost have thought he'd dreamed it, except that the boats were now lurching as well. Neat, round, foot-high rolling waves spread out across the harbor, rippling in the light of the comet's tail. From inland, voices began shouting in The City.

Dear gods.

To the three men still here with him, he said, "Guard the docks. Don't let anyone down here but our own people."

"What *was* that, Captain?"

"Nothing good," he repeated. "And nothing final." He still didn't know what was happening, but he knew that wasn't the end of it.

The other sailors began to trickle back. Some brought valuables with them—a copper lamp, a golden bracelet, a fine wedding robe. Others brought loved ones.

Manuah called out, over and over again: "Passengers remain on land! Thank you! Sailors with me! Leave all your crap on the dock!"

But he exposed himself for a hypocrite when Hamurma showed up with Emzananti in tow, and Sharama's wife Telebabti, and Manuah's youngest son Jyaphethti, and he let them all straight onto the largest of his boats. "Wives of my family, sit down on the deck and stay out of the way," he barked, in a way that he wouldn't dream of under ordinary circumstances. "Sons, get on the bow and stern and await orders."

"I can sail," Emzananti offered. And it was kind of true; he'd taken her on pleasure cruises around the harbor, and occasionally even out into the open ocean. But always in good conditions.

"Not tonight," he said, more firmly than he probably should have. But he just didn't know how much time they had, and Emzananti (gods bless her) didn't argue.

However, Manuah's stepmother, Chatrupati, trailed behind the rest of the family.

"What's going on?" She demanded to know.

"We're moving to Shifpar, Mother."

"All of a sudden? In the middle of the night? Don't be crooked with me, young man. I've known you too long. You're escaping."

"Something's happening, Mother. Didn't you feel it?"

"You're escaping with your family, yes? Well, I'm not going."

"Mother..."

"I'm not your mother, and I'm *not going*. Do you know what's happening? Exactly?"

"No."

"No, and how could you? These are strange days, and running away may be smart, but you listen to me, Manuah: you bring enough men and boys to crew these boats, no more. You fill them up with women and girls, and bring *them* to safety. Then you're a hero, not a runner."

Manuah started to object, on several grounds. First, because he was already planning to transport as many women and girls as he could, and didn't need a lecture about it. Second, because he'd been warning against disaster for a long time now, and didn't need a lecture about that, either. Third, because he didn't want people to see him getting yelled at by an old woman! But there was no time for any of that, either. What he said instead was, "Yes, Mother. May the next month be kind."

"And to you," she said back, and then hugged him warmly. She *wasn't* his mother, but something more like an aunt twice removed. But she'd lived in the house with him since he was five years old, and had been the *only* parent once Manuah and Adrah's father had grabbed his chest and dropped dead on a voyage one day. Manuah didn't know what kind of fate Chatrupati would face here—what he was abandoning her to—but he knew he didn't like it.

"Be *good*," she said, very sincerely. And then she released him, and then she was off, marching back toward land, merging with the growing crowd on the Street of the Warehouses.

To the sailors he—

The ground shook again, more violently this time, sliding sideways by two full feet, and then sliding back, and repeating the motion several times. The sound was a deep rumble, like thunder, and the water of the harbor began sloshing back and forth, almost like the water in a bucket. Manuah's boats were tossed around like toys, and everyone lost their balance.

And then it stopped, and the water was just lapping heavily against the dock's piles, and the boats were just rolling and rocking in their berths. And then everyone was shouting at everyone else.

As loudly as he could, Manuah called out: "Sailors to me! Lash these boats together! The big one at the center!"

"What, you mean side by side?" Kop shouted back over the hubbub.

"No, in rows!" Manuah thought for a moment, and then said, "Two, then three, then two, then one! Like the shape of a fish. Like a sandbar in a river!"

Looking around, he counted eleven sailors, including Hamurma and Jyaphethti. Was that enough? He hoped more would return. He hurried onto the dock, and thence to the cobblestone street, looking around.

Presently, Sharama appeared, with his uncle Adrah in tow, gently carrying an oyster shell lamp as though its meager light were more important than moving fast.

"It didn't spill," Adrah said, as if reading Manuah's thoughts. "The whole city shook. Walls cracked. Roofs fell, *I* fell, but this lamp stayed right in my hand."

"You're an idiot!" Manuah shouted back to him. Then, to Sharama: "I stole your boat! I'm sorry. We're lashing them all together. I think it might get rough out there!"

"All right," Sharama agreed. "Where do you want me?"

"At the center. At the sail."

He wanted to hug his eldest son, but they were both in motion, in opposite directions, and there simply wasn't time.

Including Manuah, that now made *twelve and two* sailors, for Adrah had crewed boats for several years before deciding he loved the stars more than the sea. And that still probably wasn't enough, so Manuah prayed silently for more, and almost immediately Letoni appeared, with a parade of merchant men and women behind him, dragging animal cages on sleds. The bleating of goats and the clucking of chickens and the quacking of ducks added to the general sense of disorder.

"Stack these cages up!" Letoni shouted over the crowd noise. "Onto the boats!"

And Manuah looked around in the crowd. There were over sixty people assembled here, some because they were the family members of his crewmen, some because they were warehouse workers or fishermen or crewmen on other people's merchant boats who hadn't gone home yet, and some because they were ordinary citizens curious about all the commotion down on the docks. But the whole city was full of commotion now: fires and smoke and dust and even some rubble here and there. It wasn't obvious that anyone should think Manuah's boats were the safest spot in The City. Manuah was by no means sure of this himself!

But still, if everyone here wanted rescue, he was not going to be able to take them all.

"Raise your arm if you know how to sail!" he shouted to the crowd. Several arms went up—both grown men and good-sized boys. "I'm sailing tonight for Shifpar. Keep your arm up if you want to come with me!"

Some of the arms went down, leaving him with three new sailors between the ages of ten and twelve-and-eight.

"On the boats!" he told them. Then: "Women and girls who want to come! Show of arms!"

That netted him a total of twelve-and-ten passengers.

"Get out on the docks!" he told them. "Wait for further instructions!"

"Not without my son!" a woman shouted indignantly. Several others joined her, and once all that had been sorted out, the passenger count rose to almost half a sixty.

Manuah wasn't sure he could take any more, so he asked everyone else to wait, except the people who didn't want to come with him. Those he asked, as politely as he could, to disperse and go back to their homes. Some did; others didn't.

From there, it took a surprisingly long time to get everything settled. The seven boats, all lashed together, formed one giant boat—surely the largest the world had ever seen—and while it was capable of flexing rather than flipping as the harbor's waves rolled under it, it was still an unwieldy contraption, far too large for the docks. And so only the rear two boats were moored, to the outermost dock, while the rest of the thing flopped and wagged like a skirt in the wind. And there was always one more passenger or apple basket to be moved from here to there, to balance the loads. One more line to be tied or untied or adjusted or moved. It was well over an *hurta* before they were ready to undock, and when they did, it was barely a noticeable event at all. The handful of remaining mooring lines were released, and the leather-wrapped wooden bumpers were hauled in, and still more weights were shifted around, and Manuah took up a position at the steering oar of the rearmost boat. He had actually intended for the boats to be lashed the other way around, so that this single boat would have been at the *bow* of the giant boat, rather than its stern. But he supposed it might be easier to steer this way.

And so, before he even realized what was happening, they

had drifted five feet away from the outermost dock, and their journey had begun.

There were immediate shouts of protest from the crowd, which had gotten bigger again, and which surged out onto the dock as if to grab them. But Manuah looked around, and feared his contraption already held more people than could possibly be safe. He didn't know anything about how this giant boat would handle—how they would tack it upriver with seven independent little sails, how it would pitch with a good-sized bow wave or—gods help them—a broadside wave.

But among the milling throng he saw a girl, about fourteen years old, standing almost close enough to touch.

"You have my brother," she said, matter-of-factly, in the guttural accent of Larasha, the Big Shit.

"Where are your parents?" he asked her.

"Don't have any. Just him."

"Let her onboard!" said an urgent sailor's voice from one of the other boatlets.

"What's your name, girl?" The distance between them had now grown to six feet.

She rattled off something guttural and complicated: "Na'elta-a-ma'uk."

"Let her on!" The sailor shouted again.

And because it was the right thing to do, and because she seemed like a nice, smart girl, (and, truthfully, because she was very beautiful and his middle son Hamurma needed a wife), he reached out his steering oar to her and said, "Grab hold and jump."

And she did, and he caught her with his right arm, and set her down on the deck in front of him.

"You're strong," she said, without any particular emphasis. "Thank you."

But then there were more protests from the dock, at least twelve-and-ten people screaming at him. "Hey! Hey! Get back here, Harbormaster! Where do you think you're going?"

With a calm that wasn't entirely feigned, he said, "I'll be back in a few days. Anyone who still wants to come, can come with me then." It wasn't entirely a lie, because it might be true. He didn't know. And so he started calling out commands, and together he and his men learned how to paddle this giant raft of boats.

✧   ✧   ✧

Harv noted that he'd heard two different words for boat: tari *and* karsa. *The word for raft was* tarika, *and he wasn't sure how he knew that, because he hadn't heard anyone say it. But in Manuah's mind the concept of a "raft of boats" was rendered as* tavitarka, *and Harv grasped it instantly, marveling again at the beauty of this language. Some sort of proto-proto Indo-European?*

And then, when they were perhaps half a *kos* from shore, the sky started raining fire. Well, not fire exactly. They were streaks of light: first one or two here and there in the sky, and then a dozen, and then sixty dozens.

"Shooting stars!" Adrah called out, loud enough for everyone to hear. "Don't worry; they're usually harmless."

"What do you mean, usually?" Manuah asked, annoyed, because everyone knew what a shooting star was, and everyone knew they were just lights in the sky. How exactly could they *not* be harmless?

"Um, they're little rocks," Adrah admitted. "Sometimes we can see them reach the ground, or the ocean. They can even bounce."

And that was not good news, because the *whole sky* was turning to shooting stars. "It's the tail of the comet," Manuah said. "It's made of little rocks!"

And indeed, the tail had widened to encompass the entire night sky, and instead of a featureless blur it was now intricately braided, and visibly moving, like white fire. And yes, the shooting stars seemed to be coming from it. And yes, one of them landed sizzling into the harbor, less than a *kos* away from them! One out of many sixties, but still terrifying!

"Where do we go?" he asked Adrah. "How can we hide?"

"We can't. It's going to be same all over."

And so, with slowly growing skill they wallowed out into the center of the harbor, and turned, and began making their way toward the sea walls. It occurred to Manuah to wonder if they would even fit through, but of course he knew the dimensions and spacing of the sea walls very well indeed, and so by looking across the width of the *tavitarka*, he could see that it would be possible, through tricky.

"This wind is shit," he said to no one.

"I think the sails are blocking each other," Kop said. "That makes it worse,"

But the paddles weren't much good either, except for turning them in circles. At times Manuah felt he was propelling the entire contraption by sculling the aftmost steering oar, and at other times he felt they simply weren't moving at all.

And still the little rocks rained down, sometimes disappearing behind the horizon, sometimes splashing and sizzling into the harbor, sometimes very clearly landing within the confines of The City. What would they do there? Were they tossed pebbles, or sling bullets hurled downward with all the might of heaven? And since they trailed fire behind them, would they set wooden roofs ablaze? He did see the red glow of fire here and there, although its sources were hidden from view. The shore was too far away now for Manuah to hear the shouting there, except as a low, indistinct roar, barely audible above the din of goats and chickens and passengers and sailors. He couldn't tell what was happening back there, and he had a lot to pay attention to right here.

"All quiet!" he called out more than once, and also "Heads in the boat!"

People obeyed these commands (more or less), and when they quieted, so (more or less) did the animals, except for one stubborn goat that would not stop bleating. But it was never long before people started talking again, because they were scared and confused and therefore agitated. What was happening? *Why* was it happening? Where were the gods in all this? Was there a war in heaven, so fierce that its effects were spilling down to Earth?

It was almost midnight before they got anywhere close to the sea walls, at which point—

The water dropped a foot, and then raised again, making a tremendous thumping sound, like several sixties of gigantic drums. All around them, it turned to foam, and the boats swamped in it, and the foam poured over their edges. Once again, Manuah's sailors tumbled to the decks, now several hands deep in foam. Once again, large waves began to rock the harbor.

"Bail!" Manuah called out, for the foam was popping and sloshing and turning to water. Lots of water. Without bothering to get to their feet, the sailors dropped whatever they were doing and grabbed the nearest bailers: wooden buckets and fired clay pitchers and small wicker baskets sealed with pitch. Each was for a different type of bailing (the wicker was for getting the last little bits out), but every man grabbed whatever was handy and started moving water as furiously as he could. There were shouts of alarm, because one of the boats in the second row was fully swamped, and sinking, and would have gone down if it weren't lashed tightly to its neighbors.

People clung to its edges as apples and empty baskets poured over its sides and into the water of the harbor. The boat might *still* go down. It might bring all of the rest of them with it! Papyrus reeds were lighter than water, and would float by themselves, but pitch was heavier, and so were the cargo and passengers.

"Bail!" Manuah shouted again, and then followed his own advice as a bucket floated towards him in the shimmering foam. The task was urgent and consuming, and left little room for thought. And yet he still had time to wonder: what the Giant-Dicked God was *that*? Had the top two feet of the entire ocean turned to foam in less than a *nimisha*? What colossal magic could create so much chaos over such a large area, so quickly? And *why*? The gods must be very angry indeed, but what could human beings have done to make them so upset? Could a human being cause pain to a god?

They bailed until the water was down to their ankles, and then kept bailing as though their lives depended on it, which of course they did. How many more cosmic events like that could they take? And then finally Manuah commanded them back to their paddles and sails and steering oars, and they began working their way back to the sea walls again. They needed to get out into the open ocean, and thence to the channels of the river delta. He wasn't sure what they would do then, but that was too many problems from now.

Crawling, inching, they wormed their way between the walls, and finally, *finally*, out into the ocean. It had taken all night; dawn was already showing on the eastern horizon, like a streak of blood across the lip of the sky.

And right away, Manuah could see that lashing the boats together had been a good idea. The ocean was rough, in a sort of *confused* way, because the wind still wasn't all that strong. The waves were chopping every which direction, and some were as high as three feet, and were swamping into the boats all over again. However, the *tavitarka* remained stable.

Overhead, the shooting stars were tapering off, as the tail of the comet finally set in the western sky, slipping below the ocean.

"East!" Manuah called out, unnecessarily. "Toward the sun!"

The dawn brightened, but declined somehow to shift from red to orange.

"I don't approve of this!" a child said loudly, only to be answered by the nervous laughter of two dozen men and women who didn't approve of it either.

"Steady," Manuah said quietly. As the laughter tapered off, the whole world had gone quiet.

And then...

And the ocean began to sink. More slowly this time, but in a much more pronounced way. At first it was hard to notice in the dawn light, when they were four sixties of feet from the ocean's flat, sandy shoreline. But the beach was getting larger as the water retreated from it.

"The tide is going out," someone said.

"This is no tide," someone else said.

"Gods help us!" shouted a third voice.

And now there was no mistaking it, because the sea walls were exposed to fully half their depth, and the water of the harbor was pouring out from the gaps between them, and then they were cracking and crumbling, and the *tavitarka* was being pushed farther out to sea by the current this created.

"What's happening?" a female voice demanded.

"I'm afraid!" said one of the children.

Manuah felt a fluttering sensation in his stomach and a tickling on the sole of his feet as the *tavitarka* dropped and dropped beneath him, and then finally paused. And then began, slowly, to lift again. And at this moment he felt that something very awful was indeed about to happen; he felt aware, as never before, of the sheer *mass* of the water beneath him, surging outward toward the watery horizon and then, just as inexplicably, surging back in toward the shore again. Because yes, *that* was what was about to happen. This outward current would reverse itself, and the ocean—*the entire mass of the ocean*—would...

He screamed: "Paddlers! Sterns! Steer for your lives!"

This order seemed to confuse the men for a moment or two, but then they felt the boat lifting beneath them, and they understood what it meant. Manuah's stomach dropped out from under him, and suddenly they were like children playing in the surf. Lifted by a wave and, if they weren't careful, tumbled by it. The water rose and rose, and if Manuah didn't bring the stern around to meet it, then the whole *tavitarka* would roll up sideways, like a floor mat. The wave was that big!

"Steer!" he screamed, but already the surf was louder than he was. Already the boat was twelve feet above the break line, and the water around them was a churning of black foam unlike anything Manuah had ever seen. His passengers were tossed like rag dolls, and his sailors... well, a lifetime on the sea had taught them how to stay on their benches in rough water, but it was hard to say they were paddling, exactly. Battered by the great steering oar, Manuah lost his feet for a moment, then gained them again, then lost them. The oar couldn't get a grip in this foam, so he raised it and raised it until it was nearly above his head, and still couldn't find clean water. Regardless, he *pulled* for all he was worth.

And as the wave lifted them, it also rose up behind them—a great pushing wall of water—and they began to slide forward down its churning face, and now they were looking *down* at the beach, and now the beach was gone, and now the *tavitarka* was higher than the harbor ridge, and when Manuah looked up he could see the lights of The City.

Rushing toward them.

For a moment his mind couldn't make sense of what he was seeing, of what was happening around him, but really it was only the *scale* of it that was unfamiliar. His boats were a scruff of coconut wood being rolled ashore by a wave much, much larger than it was.

Already they were into the harbor, and it seemed the world was bisected: on one side, the low, peaceful waters he had tended and monitored all his life, with a great city hugging 'round. The human world. On the other side, behind and below him, it was the realm of gods, against which human beings, and all the things that human beings had built or ever could build, seemed very small indeed.

"Steer!" he screamed again, uselessly.

They were picking up speed, now going as fast as sails had ever carried him, and now as fast as the Great River had ever carried him, and now faster, and faster still. Had any living person ever traveled so fast, or so noisily? Was this what it felt like, in the moments before a boat rolled and flooded and sank and vanished forever? No mistakes, no errors of judgment, just vast forces beyond human reckoning? He pulled on the oar with everything he had, and it did almost nothing, almost nothing at all, and why, oh why had he ever mocked the gods? The gods, who were capable of this!

And then they were halfway across the harbor, and then two thirds of the way, and The City was still hurtling toward them. But now The City looked small. From his current height, everything was *down* except the walls of the palace, and the Tower of the Hill of Stars, and the rooftops of a few scattered buildings whose owners had dared to build three stories high. The air was full of the sound of screaming, louder even than the crashing water, and Manuah spared a glance below him, at his tiny boats lashed together and falling, falling, falling down the face of this black wave.

I love my wife, he thought frantically. *I love my children and their wives and all of my brave, hard sailors, and I'm about to get all of them killed.* He'd started too late. Believed too little. Trusted too much in the way things had always been.

And yet, he would not let death take them without a fight. He steered. He did! If the water carried them in a straight line—and why wouldn't it?—they would smash straight into the south wall of the king's palace. Not only tall but *wide*, covering more area than any thirty buildings had a right to, the palace was simply too large a target to miss, unless... Unless he turned slightly, sliding *that* way instead of *this* way down the wave. He couldn't imagine anything more dangerous, and yet it was what needed to happen.

"Left!" he screamed. "Left! Left! Steer left!"

In a better moment this kind of aspiration would be broken into a dozen separate commands: Left side hold! Right side *dig*! Left front draw! Right front pry! Everyone with a steering oar, *pull*! Don't push, *pull*! But here in the realm of gods, it was every man for himself. Did they hear him? Did they figure it out on their own? He could see a dozen sailors doing a dozen different things, but most of them were, in one way or another, struggling to rotate the *tavitarka* in the required direction. So slowly! So laughably, against the churning madness all around them! But the men—even the boys—held to their stations while chicken cages smashed and apples rolled and tumbling passengers shrieked in terror.

And it worked; they were going to pass between the Palace and the Tower of the Hill of Stars, with several sixties' feet of clearance on either side.

"Good!" He called out, again unsure if anyone could hear him at all. "All ahead!"

He wanted to get a better position on the wave; less vertical and crushy. When it finally broke, he didn't want it to be on their heads! But even as he thought this, he could feel the wave flattening behind them. Not breaking, like surf against a shoreline, but merely *slumping*. The crest of the wave was too big and too heavy to curl over, so instead it slid forward on top of itself in a boiling mass that soon raced out ahead of the *tavitarka*. And that seemed good for a moment, because who wanted a giant wave towering over their heads? But the next few moments brought a new terror, because they were lower to the ground, now, and there were all kinds of hills and rooftops and ladders and poles jutting up into the space they were about to occupy.

And then they swept over what must have been the docks and warehouses of the harbor's northern shoreline. The deep rumble of the water became a hiss, and then a rumble again, and then a cacophony of breaking and crashing and great, glooping bubbles that burst to the surface out of spaces that, Manuah thought, must surely be the insides of buildings. He tried to ignore, up ahead, the sight of people running and the sound of their screaming. So many people! But the wave was much faster than they were, and there was nothing at all he could do for any of them, and the whole situation was so much worse than anything Manuah had ever actually imagined.

"Right!" he called out to his men. "Turn right! Turn right!" And he braced his feet against the hull of the boat and pushed the steering oar as hard as he could, because the *tavitarka* was going to collide with a house if he didn't. *That* was something he *could* do: steer his own boats, save his own skin, his own family and friends, or at least make the effort so when he washed up on the starry shores of heaven, he could hold his head up without shame.

"Right!!"

Steering the *tavitarka* was like blowing on a falling feather; it seemed like it ought to work, but in practice the thing did whatever it wanted to, no matter how dizzy you made yourself. Or it was like piloting a boat in the heaviest of river rapids, or it was like being attacked and beaten by a platoon of soldiers. The best the men could do was *petition* the vessel and the surging water beneath it, and hope to live another few *kesthe*.

One of the tall houses swooshed by them, impossibly fast and almost close enough to touch, with a lone, shrieking woman clinging to its roof, and in its wake they were sucked so hard to the left that the *tavitarka* spun a full circle around before (approximately) righting itself again. Above them the sky was tuning bright red, and by its light Manuah could see that the path ahead was a forest of obstacles and a snake pit of sucking vortices, and there was no way, there was *no way* they were going to get all the way through it and out the other side without wrecking.

The river was closer. If they could make it over to the river, they'd be all right until . . . Until . . .

Only then did his heart realize what his gut already knew: this wave really was going to sweep all the way across the face of The City and keep on going. There was something heavy and endless and final about it. It wasn't really a wave at all anymore; it was the ocean itself, redefining its relationship to the land around it. Manuah hadn't known it could do that. Would it *ever* stop? Was this the *end of the world*? Already the water was full of planks and baskets and robes and loaves of bread—all the stuff of the world—and also with corpses: men and women and children and goats and dogs, and for them it was already the end. Did they see it coming? Did they know what had happened to them, or were they just standing and breathing one moment, tumbling and drowning the next?

Well, even if it were the end for Manuah as well, he'd still rather meet it in the river.

"Right!" he called out. Then, more explicitly, "The river! Head for the river! HEAD for the RIVER!"

And then he had to call out more lefts and rights, as they navigated around the higher points of what had once seemed like a very flat city. But the message and the plan were clear, and through the chaos the paddlers and sterns did what they could to nudge the boat in a generally westerly direction.

Here and there, strong swimmers carried along in the water would grab the *tavitarka* as it passed them. Most lost their grip immediately and were swept away, screaming and weeping in bewildered terror, and *how could the gods be this angry?* What in Hell's depths could human beings possibly have done to deserve this? But here a lucky soul managed to hold on long enough for two of the women to haul him aboard, naked and bloody as the day he was born. And there another did the same, except this time it was a young woman.

And then there were no more living people in the water, just corpses and pieces of corpses, and then the *tavitarka* was picking up speed again, being pulled slantways down a low embankment or waterfall of some sort, and then all seven of the boats dug their prows into the water, bounced and sank and bobbed to the surface, half of them flooded to the rims, and...

And they were in the river.

At least, Manuah assumed it was the river; it was much too wide and much too flat, with none of the islands and sandbars and reeds and willows that ought to be here in the delta. It was as wide and featureless as the harbor, and was flowing in the wrong direction, yes. But suddenly there was nothing for them to crash into.

"Bail!" he shouted, unnecessarily, as the *tavitarka* spun. Each bench had a bailing implement tied to it, and each sailor knew that water was death as well as life, and if the flooded boats were allowed to sink they would drag everything else down with them, and that would be that. The men set to it with a vigor Manuah had rarely seen. There were fewer corpses here, and less debris, and certainly less sense of immediate peril, and also the sheer *scale* of this catastrophe had a kind of numbing effect. It was hard to think about anything much beyond the next few *kesthe*.

Except that Manuah's oar station was a standing bench with no bailing bucket attached, and the raft dynamics of the *tavitarka* were such that he was raised slightly in the air, with no water at his feet. And there was nowhere to steer toward and nothing to steer away from, and so he took a moment to really look around.

The river had filled up now, and the low hills and banks separating it from the harbor had either been wiped away or drowned. The lashed-together boats were still rising, yes, and now he could see The City again, or rather, he could see the last of the houses disappearing beneath churning brown water. He could see the walls of the palace crumbling like those of a sand castle, and he could see the Tower of the Hill of Stars—now immersed to fully a third of its height—falling over. He would have thought it would fall toward the land, but as its base was swept by the moving ocean, it basically lost its footing and fell *toward* its attacker, breaking in half as it fell and then simply vanishing.

And with that, beneath a sky of fiery crimson and streaks of bright yellow, The City was gone. And the churning water was somehow quieter.

Up ahead of them, there was land visible, perhaps two or three *kos* away. Even though it seemed, yes, that the entire ocean was moving inland, Manuah didn't think the water could have swept that far ahead of them that quickly. No, there was still a rolling mound of water up ahead, perhaps half a *kos* away, and it was obscuring the ground in front of it. The *tavitarka* was still riding the giant wave, albeit on the back end, and the wave was still tall enough that the olive trees it scythed down were mostly blocked from view—just heads of broccoli snipped and rolled and drowned up there in the distance. And here was a strange thing, because this wave was *long*—impossibly long, much longer than it was tall—and it seemed to have quite a bit of run left in it. Was it the last wave the world would ever see?

As the sailors bailed furiously, he became aware of the squawking of chickens and the bleating of goats and children. And then the weeping of women, and the groaning of injured and heartbroken men.

"Secure the cargo!" he called out, when enough water had been bailed that they were no longer in immediate danger of sinking. Because that was their next biggest problem: panicked animals trying to run around on the very limited space of the *tavitarka*'s seven decks, and getting tangled up in ropes and baskets and people.

And when that was taken care of, he commanded, "Passengers, see to each other! Secure the injured!" Some of the more alert women had already started doing this, but the thirty-odd passengers were mostly shocked into passivity, and needed now to be shocked into something else.

✧　　　✧　　　✧

And here, as men and women started seeing to one another's numerous injuries, Harv was shocked to observe a kind of systematic first-aid process at work. He supposed injuries must be commonplace in a world like this—even without catastrophe—and dealing with them promptly must be a matter of mutual survival. Is this wrist broken? Can you open that eye for me? Let me see, let me feel. You! Help me lift him onto the bench. Still, three of the children were incoherent and inconsolable, and three of the adults could not be roused to action of any sort, and by a kind of triage these were ignored for the time being, while attention was focused on those who could describe their own symptoms. The whole process seemed familiar and calming, and not at all what Harv would have expected. Could the people of his own time respond so well? He doubted it.

A few minutes later, Sharama called out to Manuah: "Should we keep the boats lashed together?"

Manuah thought about this, and didn't have a clear answer. The *tavitarka* was spinning slowly and drifting aimlessly, and that rankled his sailor's sensibilities. A boat of any sort must be under control at all times, or bad things tended to happen. And yet, the water around them was increasingly . . . well, not *calm*, but less like river rapids and more like an ordinary, fast-moving river. And there was nothing for them to crash into or run aground on, and even with everyone at full attention this awkward assemblage of boats would be exhausting to control for any length of time, so perhaps they could just let it be for now. If the seven boats were separated, then paddling to keep them close to one another—but not too close!—was a headache they didn't need.

"For the moment," he answered. "Let's see how it goes."

The sky gradually got brighter, but the sun never really did come out. There was blue sky above them, but to the northeast was an ugly wall of charcoal gray clouds that spilled across the heavens like a stain. Could something like that be considered a bad omen, when so much actual badness had already occurred? No one discussed it, but everyone kept looking up, occasionally making the sign of the half-closed eye in hopes of warding off any further evil.

"What are we going to do, Captain?" Letoni wanted to know.

"Stay at your station," Manuah told him. "I don't like the look of these clouds."

That answer was both obvious and unsatisfying, so Letoni turned instead to Adrah and asked, "Hey, Your Theity. Is this the end of the world? Is there any point doing anything at all?"

To which Adrah replied, "Jump overboard if you like." And then, perhaps feeling that wasn't a priestly enough response, he added: "The fact that we're still here is significant. I don't really know what to make of it. Why should we be saved? Aside from the obvious, that we happened to be in a boat when the flood arrived."

As for *why* the flood arrived, he didn't seem inclined to venture an opinion. How could he? Who knew the minds of the gods, to whom human beings were just so many goats and chickens, or perhaps even ants.

About half an *hurta* after the flood began, Manuah finally felt it stop and, very tentatively, reverse direction. There were no reference points against which to judge this motion, but he could feel it in his belly. They were dropping slightly, as well. Was that a good thing?

"It's stopping!" Hamurma called out excitedly. It seemed a strange thing to be excited about, since it in no way guaranteed their safety, nor even implied it.

The sense of movement increased, until Manuah could actually feel a breeze on his face. This worried him, because when he dipped his hand into the water and tasted it, it was bitter with salt and dirt. There seemed to be no boundaries now between land and river and ocean, and if the water had reversed direction, it could mean they were about to be swept out to sea. Did they even have seven working sails? Or fresh water for thirty passengers and twenty crew, or any fishing gear at all, or any of the dozen other things a proper ocean voyage required? Would they be able to get their bearings? Did The City's harbor even exist anymore? Was the concept of safe harbors even relevant?

He began to see material protruding above the water's surface again. Things that might have been rooftops, things that might have been trees. Something that might have been the top of the Hill of Stars, and the base of its shattered tower, with water swirling treacherously inside the stone ring that remained.

It was all much farther away than he would have guessed,

nearly a *kos* to the south, and they were now racing back toward it with alarming speed. The river still had no banks; there wasn't anything immediately around them to run into, but the sensation nevertheless filled him with helpless dread. These forces continued to be vastly out of scale with anything he'd ever experienced, or heard of in old sailor's stories. The anthill had been kicked over and drowned.

"How long will this continue?" someone demanded of Adrah.

"Until it ceases," Adrah answered, now testy again. And why not?

"Or until *we* cease," Yaphethti said, loudly enough for everyone on the *tavitarka* to hear.

And with that, Manuah had had enough. What did ants do, when their home was destroyed? They got right back to work, without pause or complaint. Either these four-twelves-and-two people would survive, or they wouldn't. Right now he couldn't really imagine what that survival might look like, but he could at least admit the possibility. And this was *his boat*, and he was responsible for everyone's welfare, and all this talking was not going to help.

"Stow the chatter!" he snapped. "Right front, draw. Left front, pry. Everyone else: if you don't have a steering oar in your hands, sit down and shut up. We're headed back toward The City, and we may have to dodge buildings all over again."

But things were still changing; below the water, even though it was an opaque brown that admitted no light, he fancied he could somehow sense the banks of the river. The *tavitarka* was out of its channel again, and its speed was dropping. *They* were dropping. The water was draining away beneath them, and for the briefest of moments Manuah thought they might just be gently deposited on the floor of an orchard or a farm or a pasture. For a moment, yes, but then he heard the distant roar of the ocean, and saw another evil churning out there.

"Paddlers!" he screamed. "All ahead, full strength! Dig! Dig! Sterns left left left left! Pull, you motherless bastards! Get us back in the river! Now, now!"

And although being hit with a second giant wave was not all that different than being hit by the first, it seemed this time that his sailors understood what to do. The wobbly *tavitarka* was grunted and hauled to the waterfall of the river's bank, and

over and down without swamping, and thence into position, a
two-sixties' feet or so into the channel, all lined up to catch the
wave beneath its stern, and ride it upriver as far as necessary.

The men accomplished this in less than a *vimadi*, which was
good, because that was all the time they had before the second
wave scooped and lifted them into the air. Higher than before,
louder than before, *more vertical* than before, and this was amazing
to Manuah, because the wave had already traveled a *kos* inland
before reaching them. If it still had this much energy, then it
must be a *lot* larger than the first one.

We're surfing, *Harv thought for a moment, and although he
was safe and sound in his regression chair, many thousands of
years in the future, he felt a tremendous fear wash over him. Or
perhaps it was Manuah's fear. And yet... And yet, if Manuah was
in Harv Leonel's Y-chromosome lineage, he must somehow have
survived this disaster. Which meant things could not be quite as
bad as they appeared.*

Be brave, said a voice in Manuah's head. Or something like a
voice, a thought, a feeling from outside of himself. *All is not lost.*

And a part of him thought: well, all right, perhaps the gods
can be kind amidst their cruelty. Or perhaps one god is kind
amid another's cruelty, or perhaps it was more complicated than
that. But another, larger part of him was fixated on the steering
oar in his hands, and the flat water below and in front of the
tavitarka, and the battering sense of speed and falling, and the
impossible task of somehow keeping this makeshift craft from
rolling and sinking in the wave.

As the moments slithered by, the stern of the rearmost boat
lifted higher and higher, until Manuah was literally dangling
from his steering oar, with a heel hooked on his bench to keep
him from falling into oblivion. But then the stern began to lower
again, and the *tavitarka* was *bending*, each of the seven boats
rigidly straining against its lashings, finding its own awkward
path up the boiling face of the wave.

And it happened that the highest part of the wave was rolling
forward along the deepest part of the Great River's channel, and
indeed the *tavitarka* was sucked in that direction as it gradually
slipped behind the wave's crest, and this time there was nothing for

them to crash into or maneuver around. So even amid the terrible churning of the water, even though they lost control at the crest and began a slow spin, Manuah was not swallowed by his fear.

All was not lost.

Time moved slowly—the *vimadi* as ponderous as *hurta*—while the wave gradually slipped out in front of them, and they were left in calmer and calmer water.

Except for occasional (and halfhearted) steering commands from Manuah, no one spoke. What was there to say? Would there be a third wave? A fifth? An eighth? Would there be any land for them to steer toward? As the water quieted, as the wave sloshed out farther and farther ahead of them, the fact that they were all still alive began to seem more and more miraculous.

"Were there any other boats on the water when it hit?" Sharama finally asked, breaking the silence.

"I don't think so," Adrah answered. "I didn't see anyone."

"I don't see anyone now," Manuah said. And this was telling, because the water around them, while not exactly flat, stretched out for many *kos* in all directions, giving way to barely-visible hills in the distant east and west, and the blue expanse of ocean far to the south. To the north things were harder to make out in the roiling of black rapids, but nevertheless, if there were another boat out here it couldn't stay hidden from them for long.

"Keep your eyes open," he said then. "Someone might need our help."

And so, with little else to do while they bailed water and lashed down cargo and set broken bones, the people on the *tavitarka* scanned the waters around them. And found nothing. Even the corpses and debris were far behind, now.

"Keep looking," he encouraged occasionally, because it seemed to be keeping people calm.

And finally, it was Hamurma who spotted something. "Look!" he called out, pointing excitedly.

Manuah looked up from what he was doing, and saw nothing at first.

"What do you see?" he asked his son.

"A spout. It's gone now, but something spouted. About half a *kos* that way. I think it must be our greatfish."

"There's more than one greatfish in the ocean," Kop said dismissively.

"But only one in the harbor," Letoni answered. Then, to Adrah, "Your Theity, can a fish be an omen?"

"Anything can be an omen," one of the women said. It was Emzananti, Manuah's wife. She was big on omens and signs, following them closely where they presented themselves.

Then everyone paused, until the water broke once again into a fountain. Closer than Hamurma had indicated, and also farther north.

"It *is* a greatfish," Manuah said.

"It's swimming upriver," said Emzananti.

"We should follow it," said Letoni.

"We appear to have little choice," said Adrah.

And with that, several people broke out into laughter, and *that* was the moment when Manuah first really began to believe in a future that was more than five *vimadi* away.

1.8

Manuah figured it was around noon when the rains began. Just a few sprinkles at first, as if the sky were weeping for the lost Earth. But then it was sheets of storm water, and within just a few *vimadi*, a frigid torrent. Those ugly gray clouds had swept from horizon to horizon with an unnatural speed, surely faster than any wind could carry them, and they were heavy with an unnatural burden of rain.

"Bail!" he called out, again over a racket that hid his voice, and again unnecessarily, because at this point there was little else for the sailors to do except stand by as the *tavitarka* drifted upriver. There *had* been a third wave, smaller than the other two, and a fourth one after that, but they were low enough that they didn't present any real threat to the boats. Low and long, *unspeakably* long, like a gentle hand pushing and pushing and pushing them northward. The river had become a moving sea, dotted here and there with branches and dead animals and even the occasional tree, uprooted and floating freely. Once they'd encountered a pair of rainbow-gray pigeons clinging to what looked like the middle third of an olive tree, and these leapt eagerly to the *tavitarka*, finding it to be a better resting place for their tired wings. Someone stuffed them into one of the chicken cages to keep them out of the way.

But mostly there was nothing happening, and when water began pouring down on them—like a sixth endless wave, from an unexpected direction—the idea that the sailors wouldn't bail it out of the boats was absurd. Similarly, the passengers (mostly listless and weeping up until this point) sprang to life, chilly and awake and "rain-day naked" in their linen robes that clung wetly to their bodies. Under normal circumstances this might provoke shame among the women and playful laughter among the men, but not today. Almost as soon as the sky began dripping, they were up and working furiously, forming makeshift tents out of woolen blankets and unused sails, bales of linen, and even a few bolts of precious, precious byssa cloth. It was amazing how well and how quickly they saw to their own survival, when there was something specific they could do.

As for Manuah and his sons and sailors, their hose and hooded jackets were wax-rubbed woolens, warm enough for rough winter seas, and warm enough to keep them from chilling dangerously even in a rain like this. They just tied down their chin straps and made do. Adrah, however, was rain-nude in sky-blue linens that plastered at once to his body. His white cap seemed to have fallen off somewhere along the way, and his long black hair was in his face no matter how many times he flipped it back. Fortunately, without Manuah having to say anything, he abandoned his post, helped the passengers on his boat erect a crude shelter, and then crowded underneath it alongside them.

And so the day passed, with sailors on their benches periodically dumping out buckets of water, and otherwise not very much going on. Nobody went thirsty, and while a few of the sailors ducked under a tent roof every now and then (perhaps to dry off a little, perhaps to check on the passengers, and perhaps to grab a bite to eat before the stores became waterlogged and rotten), Manuah stayed grimly at his post, watching through the rain for any sign of anything helpful or dangerous or noteworthy.

Sometime in the afternoon, another wave rolled by, lifting and bending the *tavitarka* and then racing out ahead into the gloom. Manuah felt vaguely as though they had slowed down, and that this wave sped them up again, hastening their pace upriver, but without any reference points to measure against, he couldn't be sure.

His mind began to wander. So: these four-twelves-and-two people had survived a calamity that must surely have killed tens of thousands. So: Manuah was responsible for them, because he owned the boats. Except for Sharama's, but since Manuah owned Sharama it made little difference. He had gotten them into this (apparently for the better, not the worse), and it was his job to get them out. But how could he accomplish this? Should they row, in the pouring rain, toward distant hills that were no longer visible? Should they raise a sail or three, and see where the wind might carry them? Should they drop a rope-wrapped anchor stone, wait for it to snag on something beneath the water, and then wait even longer for the water to subside?

This last course of action seemed by far the riskiest, since Manuah had no way of knowing how deep the water was, how fast it was moving, or when it might choose to retreat back into the ocean. If it ever did! Here was the warning he'd brought to King Sraddah, made real and then some. The water was rising, yes, but whatever made him think it must rise at a constant rate? Especially with the gods flinging comets around? For all he knew, it might be the desire of the gods to remake the world, to wipe it away and start it fresh, like a sand table drawing gone slightly wrong. He thought probably not, or there wouldn't still be hills in the distance, but he was taking nothing for granted, and dropping an anchor sounded like an excellent way to capsize the *tavitarka* and spill these few survivors into the cold, dark water once and for all.

In fact, the safest action he could think of was simply to drift along with the current until they ran aground on something resembling actual ground. In a way, that was also the most difficult action, because it was no action at all. And yet...

"Stow the paddles!" he called out over the roar of the rain. "Raise and lash the oars! If they're lost or broken, we could be done for! Let's let it drift for a while!"

And then, when this was done, he finally consented to leave his own post and seek a drier place.

The people of the *tavitarka*, like all people everywhere with nothing to do, grew bored. They began—despite the obvious risks—clambering from one boat to the next, rearranging themselves into different groups. Beneath the tents, they were all rain-naked and huddled together for warmth in a way that transcended lust or humor or shame, but at least they would choose with whom they would and would not huddle. And so it was that Manuah's own family—his wife and three sons, and Sharama's wife Telebabti, and His Theity Adrah Hasis—all gravitated back to the rearmost boat, where Manuah was. They were joined by Letoni, and by the teenage orphan girl with the complicated name, Na'elta-a-ma'uk, and her brother, Ku'ulta-do-ma'uk—who was one of the sailors Manuah had acquired at the dock. They were both from Larasha, and didn't seem to know anyone, but Manuah was the leader here, and perhaps they knew him and his family by reputation, and so felt less alienated here than in any of the other boats. Better a known family of strangers than an unknown mob?

"Welcome," Hamurma said, more to the girl than to the boy, as they settled in.

And perhaps they weren't beyond lust or shame after all, because his eyes lingered a bit too long on her breasts and hips, taking in the torrent-soaked shape of her, until Ku'ulta-do-ma'uk said, "Eyes off my sister! We appreciate your hospitality, Family of Manuah, and the fact that we're alive. But I will find a different place for Na'elta if *this* one doesn't behave."

"I'm Hamurma," Manuah's son said, holding out his hand for tapping. "And please let me apologize. In here there are only so many directions to look!"

And that was true; here were nine people huddled under a two-ply sail of unwaxed linen, half of them bailing or looking for dry footing, and the other half trying to stabilize their makeshift roof to keep the rain out, and all of them in shock from the deaths of nearly everyone they'd ever known. Including Chatrupati, their own grandmother! Fortunately there wasn't much wind, and the rain was just so damned *heavy* that it fell straight down from the sky. There were goats and chickens out there drowning in it! Even the ducks were drowning!

"See if you can cover some of those cages," Manuah said to both Ku'ulta-do-ma'uk and Hamurma, hoping that might form the beginnings of some sort of bond between them. Making peace was generally the right thing to do, but also, also, he could not stop his own eyes from flicking toward Na'elta-a-ma'uk and assessing her as a potential mate for his son. Here in the midst of calamity! If Hamurma and the Larashan boy were friends, or at least allies, it could simplify that process later on. These were rather cold thoughts, as if the girl were no more than a bale of cloth to be traded and sewn, but this kind of thinking had become habitual for Manuah almost the moment Sharama took his first steps and—as someone who was apparently going to survive—received his name. Yes, it was a father's job to watch the crowds, to listen for rumors, to look at the daughters of his friends and business associates in order to identify the girls that were clever enough and honest enough and kind enough and pretty enough to grow into wives his sons could be proud of. With strong birthing hips, and acceptable breasts, and if this meant Manuah had to ask himself whether he, himself, would want to fuck these girls, well, so be it. Such imagined trysts lasted a few *kesthe* at most, and Emzananti didn't have to know, and would probably approve anyway.

And as these thoughts flitted through his mind, he realized that he now really did believe they were going to survive this, that there was a future long enough and real enough that marriages still needed to be planned for. And that was certainly good news, but also bad in a way, because it meant he was going to have to come up with some kind of long-term plan. But how could he, with the world in flux and the sky raining down?

If the afternoon was miserable, the night was intolerable. The air—which was already cold and damp—became wintery, and the animals bleated and squawked about it while the humans huddled together for warmth. There was no light—no way to make fire, and no stars or moon peeking through the torrents of rain—and so in the darkness of the blind they really *were* beyond shame. Manuah curled into a ball as best he could in the cramped quarters, and his hands and feet and face and buttocks were pressed against a mass of linen and wool and human hair and human flesh, and he did not know or what part of whose body it was. Amazingly, he did manage to sleep for a time, but when he woke up it was still dark, and when the light of day finally returned it did not bring any warmth.

When enough people on the *tavitarka* were awake, and announcing their awakeness by complaining of hunger rather than screaming, Manuah thought it was a surprisingly good sign. He had no appetite whatsoever, and he would have asked his sailors to pass around a breakfast of apples and plums, until he realized the people were already helping themselves. And that was fine for now. They might have to ration later on, but for now it was probably best to let everyone fill their belly that wanted to.

Sometime into the meal, it was realized that two orphan children had died during the night—one apparently suffocated under living bodies, and the other left too far out in the cold to die of exposure, because nobody was particularly paying attention to them. And so Manuah ordered that any remaining orphans be adopted on the spot, under his authority. But there were no more orphans, unless he counted Na'elta-a-ma'uk. And she was huddled with his family, but he didn't want to adopt her for obvious reasons, and so he let the matter drop, and ordered the bodies thrown overboard. They quickly drifted off and vanished in the torrential rain, and if anyone wept about it, their tears were hidden among the tears of heaven itself.

Later in the day, some idiot sailor from Dolshavak's crews took it upon himself to slaughter a goat. Word spread quickly, and when Manuah heard about it he marched over to the man—as well as one can march when stepping between moving, lashed-together reed boats drowning in rain—and demanded, "What are you doing? You gods-damned idiot, what are you *doing*? Are you going to eat this raw? Are you going to light a fire on the floor of my boat? Or are you just butchering it for when we beach the boats and camp tonight?"

When the man said nothing, Manuah continued: "Look around! You *idiot*, look around you! I'm not surprised Dolshavak let you sail with him, but I don't let idiots crew my boats. You'll do no thinking from now on. You'll do nothing, and I mean *nothing*, without specific orders from me. If you need to shit, you ask me first. Is that clear?"

Still the man said nothing, which prompted Kop to hit him across the shoulder with a large clay mug. "Captain asked you a question."

"Ow!" the sailor said, his tongue now loosened. "Ow! That really hurt!"

Not satisfied, Kop hit him again, this time in the gut. "I can do this all day, friend, and may the next month be kind. Are you going to listen to our captain, or am I going to throw you overboard? With the captain's permission, of course."

"I'm going to listen," the man said sullenly. "And furthermore, I apologize for killing a goat."

"It wasn't yours," Kop reminded him, striking a third time with the mug for good measure. "Now grab a bucket and get bailing, if that's the pleasure of our captain."

"It is," Manuah confirmed, while thinking to himself, *we haven't heard the last of this one.*

And that was the day's excitement. The rest of the time was spent huddling miserably, until Manuah could scarcely remember any other form of existence. He napped fitfully throughout the day, dreaming of rain.

They lost three more people along the way, and after that was all over, Manuah would be amazed to realize that they were only four nights and four days on the water altogether—hardly a proper voyage at all. But it felt like eternity, like sixty sixties of years, before the rain finally eased a bit, becoming something more like a natural rainstorm, a little less cold and violent. It wasn't much, but it was something.

At the same time, visibility expanded from sixty feet in all directions to a quarter *kos*, and then a few *kos*, and with this newfound visibility, Manuah could see that there were hills around the river valley. With this sighting he began to feel less like a speck floating above a drowned world, and more like a collection of boats traversing a river, albeit one much greater than the Great River had ever been in the past.

Manuah ordered the men to bring out the paddles and unlash the oars, but before this operation had really gotten going—as they dragged their stiff, freezing bodies out of whatever shelter they'd been able to find, and started trying to get their fingers to work again—the *tavitarka* began to lurch beneath them.

Manuah's mind took a surprisingly long time to figure out what this meant: the river had stopped. Beneath them it was churning and roiling, not like during the initial waves, but not gently either. Against the hills—several *kos* away on either side—they were no longer drifting forward. Instead, they spun for a while. The men fussed with leather cords and slender hemp ropes that, sodden with four days of torrential rain, refused to give up their knots.

"Should we cut them?" one of the sailors wanted to know.

Manuah thought about it for a long moment before answering, "Not right now. We might need the ropes later, and there's nothing to steer toward anyway."

Indeed, the hills looked surprisingly steep, offering no places to camp or even land properly. They looked *barren*, too, as though they had also been scrubbed clean by giant waves. Did that make sense? A particularly high tide could sometimes briefly reverse the flow of the Great River as far upstream as Erituak, twenty *kos* from the sea. How far inland were they now? Manuah could not find any recognizable landmarks, but if they had been traveling upriver for four days then even if the river moved slowly, they could easily have passed Shifpar by now.

Which was *really* bad news, because even though Shifpar was a hilly town, no part of it stood any higher above the river than the Hill of Stars had above the harbor. And if the river had flooded this badly, this far north...

Pulling Adrah aside, he said, "I don't think we're moving to Shifpar."

"Indeed, I've been thinking that for a while now. What are we going to do?"

"Find a flat spot to camp."

"Now?"

"No, not now, Your Theity. Do you row for Dolshavak or something? Look at these hills. We have to wait."

"For what?"

"Brother, I was hoping you could tell me."

1.9

The question was answered for them about a quarter of an *hurta* later, when the river started flowing south again. The sailors all noticed right away; a murmur went through the crew, and then, a *vimadi* later, through the passengers.

"Praise gods, the flood is over," said Ku'ulta-do-ma'uk.

"Doubtful," Adrah said to him. "All this rain has to go somewhere. It has to *drain* somewhere. All this means is that four days of rain have finally overwhelmed the ocean. It's retreating now, but only because it's being pushed."

"How much more water can the sky possibly hold?" the Larashan boy demanded.

"I don't know," Adrah admitted. "I fear the comet may have turned to water."

"Yeah? Why?"

"Who can say? Because the gods desired it."

"Did they desire this flood?"

"I don't know. Probably, right? The alternative is that it happened without their bidding, or in spite of it. Does that sound right to you?"

"Well, how big is the comet? How much water are we talking about?"

"I don't know that either."

"You don't know much," Ku'ulta-do-ma'uk said, though his tone was not unkind. They had shared the warmth of their bodies for four days, and were still sharing it now.

Two boats over, the troublemaker (whose name was Ruk) called out, "Are we landing?" No one answered him, or paid attention.

"I do think the water level is dropping," Manuah said. Unlike those two, he was standing up and looking around. "The rain has been slacking off for at least an *hurta*. And yet, we're picking up speed. With the river this wide and this deep and this *fast*, just think of how much water it's draining!"

"Take it all, sister ocean," Letoni muttered—an off-color joke to which everyone, even Na'elta-a-ma'uk, laughed.

And then Manuah said, "I see a village! We *are* north of Shifpar; these are the Clifflands. And I think there's a village at the top over there!"

"Where?" Adrah asked, climbing out from under the sail again. Like all Cleric Astrologers, he had abnormally good vision.

"There," Manuah said, pointing.

There was no smoke rising from it, and indeed through the rain he couldn't make out much about it at all, except that it looked more like a cluster of buildings than like anything else he could think of.

"You're right, it's a settlement of some kind. I'm not sure 'village' is the word."

Somehow, Adrah had managed to hold onto his burning crystals, and he now pulled these out and looked through them, moving them backward and forward. They were covered in water droplets, and more rain was falling onto them every *kesthe*, and yet Adrah seemed undisturbed.

"That's a wildmen camp," he said.

"Is that good?" Emzananti and Hamurma both wanted to know.

"At this point, I would say so, yes. I fear our entire Kingdom has been swept into the ocean, and Surapp with it, and perhaps every town in the whole world within ten *yojana* of the shore. So yes, I'm very happy to see any human beings at all. It means my brother has, in fact, saved us."

"Not yet, I haven't," Manuah said.

To which Adrah replied, "Nonsense. You've had the gods whispering in your ear all along, or there's no way we could have made it this far. Sending you subtle warnings, years ago. Sending you *dire* warnings, *days* ago! Sending greatfish to block your way! Telling you to lash the boats together. Do you deny it?"

Manuah wanted to. He didn't really believe in all that stuff, but could any person really be so lucky? Or skilled? Or did he simply have all the right materials lying around?

Adrah beamed. "I wanted to be closer to the gods, to know their ways. But who'd've thought *you'd* become their prophet?"

"Not a prophet," Manuah said, a bit too sharply. "Just a harbormaster with a fleet of boats."

And with that, they ran aground.

It was a loud and messy affair, with two of the boats snagging on a sandbar or the top of a hill or something, and the whole rest of the *tavitarka* pivoting around them, and then breaking loose, and then grounding again, this time less gently. Everyone who was huddled beneath a sail got landed on by everyone who was standing, and for a *vimadi*, chaos reigned.

But order slowly reasserted itself.

The floodwater was indeed draining around them; whatever hill they'd grounded on, the *tavitarka* was now *bending* around it, conforming to its shape. A pair of ropes snapped. People yelped, and some of them started trying to climb to other boats

"Steady!" Manuah called out to them. "Everyone hang on and stay where you are!"

That wasn't necessarily the best advice, but it did calm everyone down over the slow, agonizing *vimadi* while the water dropped a foot, then another foot, until finally all seven boats were on solid ground.

Solid ground! A cheer went up: "Manuah! Manuah! MAN-UAH!!"

An *hurta* later, the water had receded enough that Manuah permitted the passengers to climb off the boats for the first time in four days. They were still cold and rain-naked, but they were standing on the mucky ground, and for the moment that was good enough.

As for the sailors, Manuah called out, "Men! Unlash these boats! Cut the ropes if you have to. We're going to turn these over and make houses out of them!"

They were busy with this task until darkness fell, and although they technically had the means for making a fire, they had no dry wood, and so they huddled miserably once again, perhaps even colder this time since their bodies were pressed against wet sailcloth lying on wet mud, rather than against the reeds and wooden decking of the boats. But without the rain pummeling them, they were certainly drier!

When Manuah slept that night, he dreamed of home, with

Emzananti's voice gently scolding the children (who had become young again) and the smell of fried clams filling the air.

The next morning, the sky was still a deep, flinty gray, and a light, damp fog had descended that made the world seem small and vaguely magical around them, but the rain itself was down to a sprinkle. More importantly, the flood water had receded so much that the river looked more or less like a normal (though still very great) river. Its edges were nearly half a *kos* away from the boats, and fully sixty feet lower. The ground was littered with shattered, leafless trees.

Manuah, no longer dreaming, shrugged off a lot of pointless praise from his followers as he looked around, realizing that apart from the hatchets that were part of the standard voyaging equipment, he and his people had no means of making a new town for themselves. Had he rescued any carpenters or stone masons? Any hunters or farmers or thatchers? They were already out of food, and yes, once they got some fires going they could butcher all the birds and goats and eat for another couple of days. But then what?

The crew and passengers spent the morning truly setting up their camp, arranging meager possessions and expedition equipment, gathering stones, chopping firewood and cutting crude shovels out of the better-formed pieces. Here on land, everyone finally felt purposeful and in control. But for how long?

Manuah spent the morning walking around, asking each person what they were doing, what they planned to do next, what their skills were. He was not particularly encouraged by the answers. Adrah, for his part, walked around providing spiritual encouragement, telling everyone that they had literally been chosen by the gods to begin the world anew. He really seemed to believe it, too. Emzananti rounded up a group of women to head out and scavenge for food. This sounded improbable to Manuah—what could still be edible around here?—but also harmless enough, because what could be dangerous, either?

He had completely forgotten about the wildmen, until five of them appeared out of nowhere, striding up the hill just as Emzananti's crew was getting ready to set off. A few of the women screamed, and were quickly silenced by their peers.

Manuah had seen wildmen before, but only from a distance.

This was a group of three men and two women, dressed all in leather and fur, and yet not so roughly or rudely dressed as he would have imagined. Those boots, those hats, those jackets... although the overall effect was strange, none of the individual pieces—with their clean cuts and tight stitching—would have been particularly out of place in the river towns, or even among the poorer residents of The City itself. Of course, linen and especially wool were preferred, and Kingdomites generally chose sandals over boots, but...

The men were carrying long wooden spears, and all of them, the wildmen and wildwomen, looked tense and suspicious, even as Manuah's own people melted away from them.

"Hello!" Adrah said, moving toward the wildmen, against the tide of bodies.

No response.

"We saw your camp yesterday," Adrah tried.

Again, no response, until finally one of the wildmen blurted out a string of nervous, nonsense syllables.

And here the orphan girl Na'elta-a-ma'uk spoke up: "He's asking what's happening here, and where we came from. He says everything here was water yesterday."

To this Adrah said, "You speak their language?"

"My mother was half wild."

Adrah laughed. "All women are, I find. Very well, tell them that this"—he gestured grandly at Manuah—"is the Great Prophet Manuah Hasis, who was warned by the gods that a flood would come. He rescued all these people from The City, far to the south."

Dutifully, Na'elta-a-ma'uk spoke a series of words to the wildmen, then listened back, then spoke again. After quite a long exchange, she asked Adrah, "And the animals, too? He seems quite confused about this."

"And the animals, too," Adrah confirmed.

And here, Harv's experience of the events seemed to cut off, or rather to blur into years rather than moments. He knew that Manuah's people went to live with the wildmen, not as conquerors or refugees but as something like lifelong honored guests. The name "Adrah" sounded like "wisdom" in the wildmen language, and "Manuah" sounded all at once like "hand" and "person" and "industry," and so Manuah and Adrah Hasis became known as

the Two Wise Men. Harv couldn't remember much else about their
lives, except that they had mounted two expeditions downriver,
and never found a single trace of The Kingdom or its people, or
indeed of the coastline they'd always known. It seemed the harbor
had finally swallowed The City and merged with the ocean, and
the river towns had all washed away, leaving only some vague
suggestions of unnatural flatness here and there.

And Harv knew that he, himself, was descended from Jotholan
Hasis, a fourth son born to Manuah two years after the flood,
and he knew that this particular tribe of wildmen had grown
and prospered and divided, and eventually changed their name
to "Humanu Shya," the children of Manuah, and had refused to
build settlements close to water for generation upon generation,
a vast stack of unbroken time, until nearly everything about the
great flood had been forgotten.

University of Colorado Engineering Center
Boulder, Colorado
Present Day

When Harv finally opened his eyes, Tara gasped in relief. Thank God. Thank *all* the gods.

"Harv? Can you hear me?"

He blinked at her, and tried but failed to sit up, due (she thought) to the curve and lean of the orange orthodontist's chair.

"Harv?"

"Oh," he said. "Oh my God."

"Harv, will you speak to me, please?"

Harv was looking around, blinking. Clearly disoriented. He said, "I'm in the lab. My name is Harv Leonel, and I'm in Boulder, Colorado."

"She didn't ask you that," Patel called out from across the room.

"How are you feeling?" Tara pressed.

"What? Strange. Very strange."

Angry tears were rolling down her face now. "You just had a seizure. Patel's on the phone with 911 right now."

"Seizure?"

"Damn it, Harv. Yes, a seizure. You didn't move, but your EEG went nuts, and the software started blaring out seizure alarms. I didn't even know it could do that."

He looked squarely at her for the first time. "Tara? Tara Mukherjee? Oh, God, I'd forgotten how beautiful you were."

"You're scaring me," she told him. She'd never actually seen anyone have a seizure before, and didn't know what was or wasn't normal. Could he be having a *stroke*? "Can you feel your fingers and toes?"

"Um...yes." He nodded. "Yes."

"What happened? What do you remember?"

"Everything," he said. He finally did manage to sit up, and then he looked around again, fumbled for the controls, and raised the seat up behind him, lifted one of the armrests and swung his legs over the side. "How long has it been?"

"What?"

"How long! How long was I out?"

"I don't know. Thirty seconds? That's not the point. I think you should lie back down until someone gets here."

But he didn't lie down. Instead, he asked, "Is there a river in India called Sarudas Vakti?"

"What?"

"Is there?"

"There's a Saraswati river in Pakistan, but it's a dry valley."

That seemed to surprise him. "Oh. Wow. It was so big! And are there two sunken cities nearby, off the coast?"

"What? What? Harv, just calm down."

He looked squarely into her eyes now, and said, "I'm calm. I'm very calm. Tara, I've just experienced *years* of someone else's life." He slapped the chair underneath him. "This thing worked *so* much better than we expected."

She stared back at him, uncertain what to say.

Looking across the room, he said: "Patel, hang up the phone."

"I'm talking to 911," Patel said.

"Tell them I'm fine." He turned back to Tara. "Are there drowned cities near the mouth of this river? I need you to look it up for me."

"Harv—"

"We're in the middle of a science experiment," he reminded her gently, "and this is data. Will you Google it? Please?" And then, when she didn't move, he added a more tender, more plaintive, "Tara?"

Sighing, she pulled out her phone and started typing. But she called out over her shoulder, "Do *not* hang up, Patel. This man needs a full brain scan or something."

"I'm not hanging up," Patel assured her.

Pecking words into her phone, Tara was just humoring her boyfriend-turned-boss, trying to keep him calm. She wanted something to refute him, so he'd slow down and listen, but to her surprise the words "drowned cities off the coat of Pakistan" produced an immediate hit. *The discovery of what is believed to be a ten-thousand-year-old city off the coast of India...*

"Oh," she said. "Oh wow. Harv, I think you might be right." She then quickly added, "It doesn't mean anything. You could have heard that somewhere. I need you to calm down and breathe for a minute."

"I'm calm," he assured her once again, then contradicted himself by fist-pumping in the air. "Yes! Yes! I need you to look some other things up, my dear. There was a comet impact, and a *huge* flood. And a man named Manuah who sailed a big boat to safety."

Tara's blood went cold.

"Manu? Are you talking about Manu?"

"That wasn't his name."

"Harv, Manu is a Hindu myth from the Rig Veda."

"He wasn't a myth. He had a brother, and a wife, and three sons who were also sailors. He lived in a city at the mouth of the river. There was a tower. There was a *whale*. My God, it's all so clear. Can you bring me something to write with? Please? I need to make some notes while it's fresh."

Tara could feel her tears starting up again, because a lot of those details were straight out of the Vedas, but it didn't mean anything. Harv *wanted* this experiment to work. Harv had just done who-knows-what to the memory centers of his brain. Harv had just woken up from a seizure, and was clearly disoriented. It didn't mean anything. But she brought him a pad of engineering paper and a mechanical pencil.

"Thanks," he said, and immediately set about scribbling on the top sheet. A rough map, annotated in hurried words and symbols. Without looking up he said, "It must have been the end of the Ice Age. Sea levels were rising, and then there was a comet impact. I'm thinking it was at least ten thousand years ago, maybe more. Could you look that up, please? A comet impact?"

Again, she complied to keep him from getting too agitated. Again, she got hits right away with "Neolithic comet impact." *Ancient stone carvings confirm that a comet struck the Earth around 11,000 BC...* But it still didn't mean anything. Neither did the astronomical details she confirmed for him next.

But when he said, "There were seven boats tied together,

loaded with people and farm animals," Tara's blood ran cold again, because Manu's boat from the Rig Veda supposedly had seven decks. She'd seen a thing about it on YouTube.

"Stacked vertically?" she asked weakly. "A tall wooden ship?"

"No," he said, still not looking up from his drawing. "Reed boats, like an Egyptian painting. Seven of them tied together."

And that made sense, it *made sense*, and it wasn't anything she'd ever heard before. Where would Harv have gotten a detail like that? Her skin shriveled into goosebumps, so that the hairs on her arms stood up.

"Harv, are you saying we extracted information from a Y chromosome *inherited from Manu?*"

"No," Harv corrected. "I'm not saying that."

"*Everyone* is descended from Manu," Patel called out from across the room. Then said into his phone handset, "Yes, he's awake and lucid. He wasn't unconscious very long. I don't know, maybe thirty seconds."

"Not everyone," Tara murmured. The whole human population was very definitely not descended from one single Neolithic Pakistani male. However, the Y chromosome's F haplogroup *had* started in India, and was ancestral to more than eighty percent of non-African humans. And many Indians were proud of the fact that Indo-European languages—languages that *actually originated in the Indus Valley*—were spoken throughout Europe and across much of Asia. It meant that sometime in the distant past, people from the Indian Subcontinent had colonized broad swaths of territory, absorbing or edging out nomadic tribes. If Manu had been a real person, there at the beginning of that group-F surge...

Nobel Prize, whispered a voice inside her head. But no, wait, this wasn't at all what was supposed to be happening. Not at all. According to Harv's theories, the TMS would create new structures in his hippocampus that would be detectable in an fMRI scanner and could be traced point-for-point to patterns in the Y-chromosome quantome. These would be "memories" only in the very narrow sense that information would be retained in Harv's brain. At most, they should prompt what Harv called "scattered bits of generic recognition." Even a momentary flash of old Scotland was far beyond what they'd been hoping for.

And even if they'd succeeded in writing a memory, that *still* wouldn't prove the chromosome was a computer or a storage device. For that, they would have to hunt for similar patterns in the hippocampi of other men, and then probe *their* Y chromosomes to prove the exact same patterns existed there. Some genes in the Y chromosome, like DDX3Y, coded for subtleties of gender-specific neural development, and Harv wanted to prove a connection between these genes, the quantum information riding on top of them, and the classical neural networks of the brain itself. Tara had never been entirely sure what *that* would prove, either, but it would certainly be a momentous discovery.

Would it mean that only men had quantomes?

"Not necessarily," Harv had told her, back on that magical date that had changed the course of her summer, and perhaps her life. "They could be in the mitochondria or the cell membranes, or anywhere, really. If we can figure out where to look, the human body may be *full* of time machines."

Hmm.

She wanted to tell Harv to keep writing on his pad, to get down every detail. This could all be unspeakably important! But she held her tongue, and simply undid the chin strap on the rubber TMS/EEG cap and slipped it off his head. She ran her fingers through his hair, combing gently through the matted electrolyte gel.

"It's going to be okay," she said to no one in particular.

Was this his vindication? A discovery even more earth-shattering than the one he'd set out to make? The idea made her angry for some reason. Did he deserve to discover something like this? The way they'd crashed forward, like Brahma bulls, did he deserve to discover anything at all, except perhaps a seizure and a migraine?

"They had magnifying glasses," Harv told her absently. "They knew the speed of light. I want to thank you for all your help, Tara. We literally could not have gotten any data out of that thing without... This is amazing."

"Okay," she answered. "I'm going to get you some water." Her voice sounded warm and chilly and angry and sad, all at the same time, and she knew that was her own fault, that she had in no way prepared herself for what might happen today. Not just the experiment itself, but the fact, the *proof*, that Professor Harv Leonel had seen her as a means to this end. His young paleogeneticist girlfriend; had she been anything more than that?

God damn it, Harv.

She got the steel water bottle out of her backpack and, finding it nearly empty, went upstairs to the drinking fountain to fill it up. Then she used the restroom, because she realized she'd been dying to all morning, and took another moment to stand in the blast of an air conditioning vent, letting it cool the sweat off of her. When she finally got back to the lab, he was still in the chair, scribbling on what looked like his tenth sheet of paper.

"How are you feeling?" she asked, uncapping the gray steel bottle and handing it to him.

"Hmm? Oh, not very good." He took the bottle and drank from it, then took a deep breath and drank again.

"I'm sorry about this," he told her then. "I didn't expect anything so messy."

"None of us did," she assured him. And it was true; her vague forebodings hadn't meant anything, even to her. They hadn't *stopped* anything.

"I don't just mean the experiment," he said, a little sadly. "There's a power asymmetry between us, you and I. I don't know. Intellectually we disdain that. We try to ignore it. We pretend it isn't there or that it doesn't matter, or something. But the limbic system has its own ideas, right? Your innocence is romantic. It's *sexy*, and I haven't tried to resist. But should I? Are we fucking with *your* head?"

She sighed. "I don't know, Harv. You're worried about that now? Right now, really?"

"What's wrong with now?" he asked. "Time is full of moments. Overflowing. I watched them moving all around me." Then: "Oh, I *really* don't feel well. I really don't."

Was he delirious? Was his brain swelling or bleeding internally?

"Paramedics should be here in a few minutes," Patel said.

"Okay," Harv answered, no longer protesting. He drank again from the bottle, and then dropped it clanging onto the floor. And dropped his pad of paper into the spreading puddle. "Okay," he said again, and collapsed back into the chair.

PART TWO
The Monsters

2.1

"See? Look at this," said Argur. And then, when his wife didn't reply, didn't turn to look at him, "Dala, look."

Now she did turn, favoring him with a look of amused impatience. "What."

Their daughter, Dele, turned with her. The two of them were husking wheat for breakfast, fishing it out of a basket, dropping the husks on the hard-packed floor and the kernels of wheat into little hardmud bowls. They sat knees-together on their cut-log benches, the daughter a smaller version of the mother. She held a hardmud figurine of a bear in her lap, and the bear wore a little kerchief of brightly colored linen, and had a little hardmud ball sitting next to it. The toys of a child. And yet she was almost a woman now. Almost old enough to leave the hut and start a family of her own.

"What?" Dala repeated.

"I've made some hair," Argur said, shaking free of his thoughts and holding up the oval of bearskin. "See? With a strap to hold it on my head. Ha! I'm young again!"

He demonstrated.

Dele laughed. Dala tried not to, but did anyway. "Honey bee, it looks like a sandal."

"Sandal? A sandal? Nonsense. When I walk around the village in this, everyone's going to want one."

Dala threw a handful of grain husks in his direction. "If you go outside like that, everyone will say I'm a fool to love you. Of course, they say that already."

"Then we have nothing to lose, eh?"

✧ ✧ ✧

Harv Leonel was not actually present, was not actually seeing through the eyes of this man. Harv Leonel had not yet been born. And yet, sometime in the future, the Y chromosome inherited from this man, Argur, would release information about this time and place into Harv's hippocampus, which would then read it back as episodic memories. Vivid ones! And this really wasn't supposed to be happening, because he knew he wasn't even hooked up to the machine any longer. Why was he still traveling in time?

He caught the smell of the air, cool and fresh and piney with a hint of ice, like being in the mountains of Colorado in summertime. The woman and the girl were wearing clothes—coarse, loose-knit fabrics dyed blue and yellow and brown, dull in the morning sunlight slanting in through the hut's doorway. The cloth was dirty-gray and coarse-woven, and as rough as the crudest blanket Harv had ever personally seen with his own eyes. But colored, yes. Not just colored, but patterned, as was the curtain that partially covered the doorway. Argur himself wore a gray tunic belted across the waist.

Was this the Middle Ages?

In the hut's center, away from the bedding and the chamber pot and the gaming circle, the three of them were sitting around the fireplace on the logs Argur had chopped and flattened and smoothed for that purpose. And finally, with a great deal of ceremony, Argur's wife and daughter served him a breakfast of toasted malt grain and blueberries in a fine hardmud bowl.

"Sir," Dala said, with false respect.

"Ma'am," he said back to her, smiling, enjoying her discomfort.

"I think your sandal hair looks good," Dele offered, watching her father eat.

"And that is why you are the best daughter any man has ever had, anywhere."

He accentuated these words by balancing the bowl in his lap, pulling out his flute and tooting a few bright notes.

"Da da daaaaa!" Dele sang, in deliberately poor accompaniment. She actually had a beautiful voice—perhaps the best in all of Nog La—but as a toddler she had begun singing with far more enthusiasm than skill, and once she was old enough to realize this irritated her father she continued the habit, long after her true talents had become apparent.

"Beautiful," he assured her, puffing out a few more notes.

Dala groaned. "*This* is my family? This is my home?"

And so Argur put his flute away and grabbed her around the waist. "If this child is such a disappointment, perhaps we should send her out for the morning and get started on another one."

"Not today," Dala said, lightly pushing him away. "I'm leading a gather this morning. Berries don't grow in bowls, you know."

"They don't? Well, wouldn't that be something if they did! Perhaps a blueberry bush could be woven into a basket shape and covered in mud, and planted here indoors? It might even keep rats out. Better than a regular basket, anyway."

Mother and daughter rolled their eyes in unison, and Argur could see the reasons behind their eyes. First of all because they thought the idea wouldn't work, second because Argur was always coming up with annoying ideas like that, and third because there was no point explaining all the pertinent facts to him. He didn't have the patience to sit and listen!

Well, indeed, Argur hadn't even finished his breakfast when he stood up and told them both, "I'd like some milk. Wouldn't that be nice? I'll find a nursing orr-ox and squeeze her teat right into this bowl. Cereal and milk! I'll even try to bring some back, although it may spill along the way."

"Ha!" Dele said.

"Don't encourage him," Dala chided. Then, to Argur: "You're serious? Oh my, you are. All right, will you please be careful? Mayga's husband, in the south village, was *kicked* by an orr-ox last year, and hasn't been the same since."

"Bronon! Yes, good man. Not very careful. Not like me."

"Seriously, Argur."

"Yes, seriously."

And with that he was off, tightening his belt, gathering up his hunting bag and his spear and his skinning knife, just in case the orr-ox put up a struggle and things got ugly. He was halfway out the doorway when he stopped, turned, and said, "I forgot my breakfast! Wouldn't that be a fine move."

He scooped up the bowl and took it outside with him, and then set about rounding up a hunting party. "Orr-ox! Orr-ox! Who wants to hunt an orr-ox?"

He pretended to be recruiting from the general population, but in fact he already knew whom he wanted for the mission.

"What's that on your head?" His neighbor, Tom, wanted to know.

"What does it look like? I've grown my hair back."

"It's not even the right color," Tom protested.

"Well, then perhaps we'll kill a black bear along the way. What do you think?"

"I think you've got rocks in your head. Or your heart, or wherever it is stupidity lives. But yes, okay, I'll kill an orr-ox with you."

"We're just after the milk," Argur warned.

"Eh? Really? You want the thing alive?"

"That's the plan."

Tom screwed up his face at that, as if wondering whether Argur could be talked out of this, or whether it was just one of those things he was going to have to go along with. "You know, we can also get the milk if we kill it. That's a lot of meat."

"Well, obviously. But I have an idea, or anyway half of one." Argur puffed on his flute. "We could try to bring it back here! Tie it up with a rope or something. Then we can all have milk, all the time."

"Hmm. Wouldn't that be somewhere between stupid and crazy?"

"Maybe. Some things are. But if it doesn't work—" he made a flourish in the air "—we can always change plans."

And with that, Tom's face resigned. This was one of those things. "Huh," he said. "Well, all right, that sounds like a day. Let me get my stuff."

From behind Argur, a voice opined, "You're going to get kicked."

He turned to see Tom's wife, Birgny, shaking a finger at him. "You just see that you don't get my husband kicked as well."

"Nobody's getting kicked," he assured her. "We'll throw nets on it from three different directions, keep it from going anywhere. We'll make a *plan*."

"You bring it back here it could kick children and the elderly," she warned. "And who's going to clean up all its shit? You?"

"You'll make yourself sick drinking all that milk," said another woman's voice, from two houses over. Yula, the cousin of Dala's sister's husband.

"Perhaps!" Argur said brightly. That hadn't even occurred to him, but it was hardly the worst thing that could happen. When people drank orr-ox milk it was usually mixed with orr-ox blood, and divided among everyone who could make it to the site of the kill. A few sips here and there, ah? But if a whole udder's worth left him exploding from both ends, well, then the people of Nog La would have gained some valuable knowledge.

"And what is that thing on your head?" Yula demanded.

Not seeing a need to prolong the conversation, Argur simply handed the women his empty breakfast bowl, bowed respectfully, and went on his way. Three houses over, two houses down... his search was not random, and he needed to be quick about it if he wanted to catch the right people before they went off on other business. Although the castle contained ten sloppy hunters and ten decent ones, only some of these were also Knights of Ell, charged with protecting the valley of Nog La from monsters and human invaders. And only these few possessed both the skill and the physical courage he thought might be needed for this little venture of his. Any idiot could heave stones at an orr-ox until it fell over. Any *skilled* idiot could load a leverthrow and hurl a spear through an orr-ox's heart from a safe distance. But for something like this, they were going to have to get close. He could already imagine the smell of orr-ox breath! The buzzing of flies around her rump! Oh, today was going to be a day, all right.

"Headman," said another voice—an adolescent young man suddenly tagging along at Argur's elbow. He had no beard, and his hair was still short from the last time his mother cut it. It would be another year at least before it started to form grown-up dreadlocks. He was too small for his clothes, and his boots had burst through at the toe and been patched.

"Yes, Nortlan?"

"Have you thought about my idea?"

"Hmm. Which idea is that?"

"Putting mud on the outside of the castle wall."

"Ah! No, I haven't given it a thought."

"I tried it on my house," Nortlan said. "Fireproof. Even a torch couldn't burn it!"

"I thought your house fell down," Argur said, with some amusement. Young Nort had moved out of his parents' place and tried to build a little shelter of his own in a corner of the castle, without help from anyone wiser. Argur admired the spirit, but not really the sense. "And anyway, why do the walls need to be fireproof? Who's going to attack us with fire?"

"I don't know," Nortlan said. "Bandits? Trolls? Jabrajab men from the East Hill Country?"

All of these had been problems in the valley of Nog La at one time or another, and were the main reason for the existence of the Knights of Ell. But none had dared launch raids against the castle or its nearby villages even once in Nortlan's lifetime, and none had entered the valley of Nog La at all for the past six years. And none had ever been known to burn things down indiscriminately, or why bother raiding at all? This was hardly a situation that called for innovative measures.

"Are you imagining them stumbling across the valley with kindling and fire jars in their hands, sneaking up against the base of the wall with no one noticing, and building a fire there?"

Nortlan sniffed. "It sounds stupid when you put it like that. What if they hid in the forest, and ran at us with torches?"

"And kept them lit while they sprinted across the meadow?"

"Yes. Why not? With a fat-soaked rag wrapped around the head, it could burn hot for quite a while."

Argur laughed. "You've thought a lot about this! Ah, Nort, you remind me of me. If only you were big and strong, I'd let you marry my daughter!"

"I'm strong," Nortlan said, defensively, puffing himself up and squaring his shoulders.

"Indeed," Argur reassured him. "Indeed you are, very strong for a man of your size."

"Hmm."

Oh, great. Now Argur felt bad. And why not? Nobody liked to be called small or weak, even if it was true, and no young man liked to be told whom he wasn't allowed to marry. Sometimes Argur's words ran out way ahead of his thoughts.

"It's good to think," he conceded. "Really. Very good. Most people never do. And it's good to know *how* to make things fireproof. We can keep it in mind, right? Not every idea is useful right away, or even at all. But ideas are a kind of strength, yes? And you've got that."

Nortlan looked somewhat mollified, though not entirely.

"Now, I've got to be moving along," Argur said. Then, on impulse, he asked Nortlan: "Would you like to come on a hunt today? With your mother's permission, of course, and with your promise to stay *well* out of the way."

This might be a bad idea; Nort was no hunter at all, and certainly no fighter. But he *was* good company, and also needed to learn some common sense from somewhere.

"I'll go ask," Nort said, not bothering to find out what they'd be hunting. *Now* he was mollified, because Argur had shown him real respect. "Oh, and Argur? One more thing?"

"Yes, Nort."

"What *is* that thing on your head?"

Argur laughed again. "It's hair. You want some?"

While Argur walked, Harv Leonel looked out through his eyes, and saw... well, he wasn't sure what he saw. A collection of domed huts made of woven sticks, thatch, and yellowish animal hides—maybe fifty buildings in all, with smoke rising from some of their centers, and everywhere men and women and children moving busily about. All this was surrounded by a fortification wall of sharpened timbers that enclosed a rough rectangle perhaps two hundred meters across. Thousands of timbers! A whole forest worth! There were even two crude watchtowers at opposite corners of the fortress: each one a tilted ladder lashed to the wall, with a little seat on top, like an inward-facing diving board. Neither was occupied at the moment, which probably said something about the actual threat level around here.

The settlement looked like a cross between a medieval village, a Wild West frontier fort, and an African or Native American nomad encampment. There were no animals here, no wheeled carts or even sledges, and on close inspection all of the tools were made of wood or stone or bone, sometimes fastened together with resin and rawhide. No metal anywhere, so he was in the Stone Age, not the Middle Ages. There were long, narrow, leaf-shaped tools everywhere—as spearheads, as knives with wooden hafts, as needles and as scrapers. The workmanship seemed competent enough, but none of them seemed to be barbed or curved or fluted or grooved. They seemed primitive, compared to other Stone Age artifacts Harv had seen in museums. The huts, too, looked extremely basic; except for dyed cloth curtains, they could be from anywhere or anywhen.

And yet, these people were well organized. They had pottery and fortifications and fitted textile clothing, and... some sort of warrior caste? That didn't make sense to him, and for the second time he was left wondering where the hell and when the hell he was.

Over the next little while, Argur rounded ten of the Knights he was looking for. There was Chap, the sprinter, and Pagel the distance runner, and the three brothers Snar, Gower, and

Gouch—easily the three strongest men in the entire valley. There were Perry and Ronk and Max and Timlin and Tom. And last of all there was Jek, whom Argur half-hoped would not be able to make it.

"Your new hair looks *amazing*," Jek told Argur when he and ten Knights (and Nortlan) showed up in front of Jek's house. "So, I hear we're going on a *hunt*? For Mommy's milk? Aw. Does the headman miss his Mommy?"

This was how Jek generally spoke, and Argur only put up with it because Jek was by far the best hunter and wrestler and stone thrower he'd ever met. What little he lacked in raw strength, he more than made up for in precision and sheer aggression. He had once punched a troll! In a fair fight he could certainly beat Argur, although in order to get away with it he'd have to beat all the other Knights as well, and he'd never quite been stupid enough to try. Not quite.

"It might be tricky," Argur said to him. "I need good men."

"And *boys*, evidently," Jek mused, eyeing Nortlan up and down.

"This one's a trainee, and he's with me, and you'll leave him alone if you want to stay on my happy side."

"Oh, and I do," Jek assured him. "And although he evidently can't speak for himself, I assure you both he has nothing to fear from me."

"And I am thus assured," Argur said, in a tone that implied otherwise. And yes, this was another of Jek's talents: to get everyone else speaking and acting like him, if they weren't careful. Then he said, "Do you still have that net we used last summer? Not the fishing net, the other one."

Jek nodded. "My trapping net? Yes. I do. Would you like me to bring it?"

"Yes, and some rope, if you don't mind. I've got a bit of a plan."

"You always do," Jek agreed.

He went back inside his house, and several of the men made rude gestures behind him.

"Oh, stop it," Argur told them.

"You stop it," Gouch muttered back.

Argur chose to ignore that, instead calling into Jek's hut: "Don't forget to bring water this time. And some food, and whatever else you might need."

"Perhaps some otter fat for my lips," Jek said from inside. It wasn't clear if the comment was intended to be funny, or literal, or what. Fatting the lips was mostly something women did, and mostly in the winter. For a man in the height of summer, it was a strange thing to say. Argur sighed inwardly; this could be a long day.

To the assembled Knights he said, "I've brought my flute, of course. Has anyone got a little drum? Or a rattle?"

"Or a singing voice?" Pagel asked.

There was some laughter at that, for the awfulness of their voices was legendary throughout Nog La.

Finally, Jek emerged from his hut, with one red and one blue hawk feather jutting out of his headband, the two colors crossing together in the center of his forehead like a visor. This was foolishness, because one feather was more than enough to keep the sun out of his eyes, and so that was what most men typically wore. The second one was apparently just there for symmetry and color. But given that Argur himself was wearing a circle of bearskin on his nearly bald head, perhaps now was not the time to criticize other people's clothing choices.

Jek was also loaded down with *way* more equipment than he needed. This puzzled Argur for a moment, because Jek was a veteran of countless hunts and patrols and even battles, and knew perfectly well how much a man should carry. But when he tried to hand some of this bric-a-brac off to Nortlan, Argur understood, and shot a warning glare at Jek, who then had to go back inside for a moment to drop some of it off.

"My mistake," he muttered.

And then, finally, they were on their way.

Tom leaned close to Argur and asked, "Why you always got to bring Jek? Nothing's ever fun when he's around."

Argur murmured back, "Yeah? Well, maybe not everything needs to be fun. Maybe this is serious, dangerous business, and I'm worried what will happen if he's not there."

Tom snorted. "Now you say. Are you having second thoughts?"

"Not at all. This is worth trying! I think it's actually a pretty good idea, but who knows? Orr-oxen are feisty creatures."

Argur emphasized the point by whipping out his leverthrow, loading a spear onto it, and hurling it at the image of an orr-ox painted in yellow on the inside of the castle wall. It struck, of course, right where the heart would be.

The wall's inner surface was decorated with all sorts of images: trees and flowers, suns and moons, clouds and rivers and oversized leaves of important medicinal plants. But mostly it was animals, and mostly the men used them for target practice. And since the wall was made of sharpened logs lashed together, this had a tendency to weaken and fray it much faster than weather alone. This caused some grumbling among the carpenters, who had to splice in repairs several times a year. But since the carpenters were also hunters, and also used the wall for target practice, the grumbling was mostly good-natured. Mostly.

"Nice shot," Tom said, with no more than routine enthusiasm.

Then he fired a spear or his own through the eye of a red-painted mammoth, and Jek landed his own spear right up against Tom's, and then everyone was killing imaginary snow leopards and wooly rhinos, and Timlin even attempted a long shot at a boolis, and very nearly hit it.

There were compliments and other chatter as the men gathered up their spears, and some cursing as Gower realized he'd broken the tip off his. Some time was lost as he ran back to fetch a replacement, but soon enough they approached the castle gate, guarded by a sullen-looking boy and a resigned-looking old man, who set about opening it without being asked.

Based on these animal drawings, Harv immediately revised his estimate of how far back he'd gone this time. If there were wooly mammoths around here, then he was in the Ice Age for sure, at least as old as Kingdom and The City, and probably older. But now he was confused about the place, because these people were black. Well, medium brown, but they had a definite African-ish appearance, and there were leopards and rhinos here. But nothing about the scenery here reminded him of Africa.

The opening of the gate involved fishing a loop of rope off of a pole with a tall stick, and then lifting the gates on their creaky rope hinges and walking them out. Each half of the gate was about half as tall as the wall itself, and made from trees about half as wide as the wall's own timbers. It was a rickety setup, and even a very small battering ram could knock it to pieces with a couple of hits, but Harv supposed battering rams weren't considered an important threat. Overall, he couldn't help being impressed. The gate's timbers were just as pointy as those of the "castle" wall, and climbing over any part of the fortifications would be quite dangerous, assuming these Knights of Ell ever gave you the chance.

The word "knight" was an approximation in Harv's mind; this language was wholly unfamiliar, and it didn't contain concepts like "soldier" or "warrior" or "elite," or anything like that. The word for "fight" and "fighter" were both "bork," and the word for hunt/hunter was "heezh." The descriptor for the fighters of Ell was "makla," which also meant "stick," or perhaps "club" or "spear." "Ell" itself was some sort of proper name that conferred respect, though in a not-entirely-serious way. He supposed it was like calling themselves the Spears of Uncle Sam, or the Bludgeons of Saint Gerome.

And yes, there was some inherent respect in the way the old man and the boy opened the gate for these knights, but that wasn't why they were opening it. It was simply morning, and time for people to start coming and going. There wasn't really all that much inside the castle except tromped-down, vaguely muddy soil, which the residents had covered here and there with straw. Most of the daily business—hunting and gathering, apparently—would be elsewhere in the valley.

And here, Harv's mind seemed to blur into Argur's own, for Argur seemed to be thinking similar thoughts. It *was* time for the daily in-and-out traffic to begin, and indeed, Argur's gray-haired parents waved and nodded to him, lining up for their daily fishing trip.

"Good hunting today," said Argur's father, Urdo.

"And you," Argur said back warmly.

"Oh, I can only dream," Urdo mused. "These bones won't carry me fast enough, or flick a dart. I'm done with hunting, or it with me."

"Nonsense. Someday soon you should come with us."

Unlike Urdo's father—Argur's beloved grandfather, Kostna—Urdo himself had never been a Knight of Ell. He was capable, but never interested in the time commitments or the organization. The spirits within him were too restless for that. He *had* been a skilled and avid hunter, and a skilled and avid carpenter, but for the past four years he'd been settling for a net and a fishing spear instead.

"Fish don't run," he said. "They don't fight back, they're not heavy, and they taste just as good as any mammoth or orr-ox. I'm content, boy."

"As you wish," Argur told him.

Argur's mother, Ilga, added, "And he can bring me with him. What man doesn't want his wife at his side all day and all night, telling him how to do things?"

"Indeed!" Urdo said brightly.

Argur nodded. Yes, all right. As you wish.

Nismu, the Wizard of Sunrise Castle, was walking around with a smoldering stick and a handful of feathers, nodding at people.

"Spirits guide your journey. Spirits guide your journey. Spirits..."

Dala's gather group was also assembling nearby, with scythes and baskets and feather-woven sun visors. Off to harvest grain, it appeared, and perhaps some turnips—both staples of the Nog La diet.

Argur had suggested many times to Dala that she scatter some of the grain outside the castle, in hopes that it might grow there. What could it hurt to have some growing close by? But no, she never liked that idea. The soil wasn't right, and it wouldn't get enough water or light or whatever, and no it didn't make sense to break the soil up with a stick, because blah blah blah. The simple fact was, she liked getting out into the meadows with her "cattail females" and holding forth, away from the ears of men and children. Sometimes their laughter could be heard from a long way off.

It seemed a rather slow affair, for the men to shuffle out of the gate. They didn't stride out confidently like masters of their environment, and they certainly didn't cower or shirk, but there was a certain staged caution in the way they moved, the way they looked around, like a SWAT team exiting a building. A rather lazy and good-humored SWAT team, not expecting any trouble but still ready for it in some vague, habitual way.

Per tradition, Argur was the last man out of the gate, and took point after that. For several minutes they traveled in formation, spiraling outward around the castle, alert for tracks and droppings that didn't belong. Alert for smells and sounds, for wheeling vultures in the sky, and anything else that might indicate trouble. The full complement of Ell didn't *always* patrol the area first thing in the morning. Sometimes it was only two or three of them. Sometimes it was small groups of ordinary hunters, or even bands of well-armed women, when the Knights had their own matters to attend. Indeed, it would be inconvenient to arrange things any other way. But still, Sunrise Castle was situated within easy walking distance of the mouth of Ketlan Pass, which threaded its way uphill to the High Vales, where monsters dwelt, and it was never wise to be too lax.

Just last winter Argur and Tom had killed a snow leopard lurking right outside the castle walls, and two summers ago the Knights had stumbled on a freshly excavated den of gray hyenas. Not *right* outside the castle, but a bit too close for comfort. They'd ended up skewering and braining half of the stoop-shouldered beasts, and chasing the rest far into the mountains—hopefully instilling in them a fear and hatred of all things human. Because that was how Nog La was kept safe for the children, and for the adults.

"All clear," said Jek—nearly always the first to sound off.

"All clear," said Nortlan soon after, perhaps believing his opinion was sought.

"All clear," said Tom a little while after that. And this *meant* something, for Tom was a thorough and careful man. After that, the rest of the men gave their final suspicious glances this way or that way, and sounded off one by one. And again per tradition, Argur was the last to sound, and the loudest. "ALL CLEAR!" he shouted back toward the castle gates. And so the women spilled out in a laughing mob, a few of them mocking the voices of the men.

"All silly!"

"All self-important!"

"All headed off on some crazy errand!"

Nortlan didn't like that; here he was, among men, being treated (more or less) like he belonged there. This disrespect reflected poorly *on him*, and it showed in his face. "All shut up!" he called back to the women indignantly.

This brought chuckles to the lips of the men, though not for the right reason. "Ho! That's telling them."

"Good, work, Nort."

"You know, some of us have to go home to that."

But then, after a bit of standing around, it was time to get down to business. The air was cool and damp, the sun just about to break clear of the groves of trees that presently hid it.

"Where *exactly* are we headed, Headman?" Jek wanted to know.

To which Snar said, "There've been orr-oxen down by the lake for the past several days."

"Mating," Gower replied, adding a rude hand gesture just in case he wasn't understood.

Argur laughed politely and then said, "It's actually the *calving* ones we're concerned with."

"The ones who mated ten moons ago," Gouch explained, making the same rude gesture.

Nort made the gesture, too, for some reason.

And then, after a bit of nodding and shrugging they were all off as a group, whistling as they marched down toward the lake.

The valley of Nog La was broad and long; it would take a strong man all day to walk its full width, and three days to march its length, to where Sunset Castle protected its other end. The land was about evenly divided between meadows and woods, and Round Lake sat more or less in the middle of it all, taking up a quarter of the valley's width, and was one of the main reasons hunting was always so good here. When Snar indicated there were orr-oxen down by the lake, he meant simply that they were by the part that was close to the castle itself. There were *always* orr-oxen somewhere around its shores. And bison, and giant elk, although the bison tended to roam farther out into the grasslands, and the elk into the forests. There were also voles and hares and ponies scattered so plentifully throughout the valley that even a pair of lazy hunters could be assured of catching dinner for their families.

There were also carrots and cabbages in the summer, and turnips and parsnips enough to fill any pot year-round, even if the lazy hunters came home empty-handed. And there were grains aplenty; wheat and rye and barley that the women cut with scythes, and shook in fat sheaves onto threshing blankets. That was what Dala and her cronies were doing today, and it meant that in a few days' time there would be *ogabred*—a delicacy that had been invented right here in the valley, that visitors were always anxious to sample. A sort of hard-baked porridge, it was solid as a piece of fruit, and yet dry and fluffy inside, unlike any other food in the world.

The only real problem was rats. There were plenty of those in the valley as well, and they could gnaw their way through a basket and lay their filth all over everything they didn't eat. They seemed particularly attracted to *ogabred*, so you had to eat it quickly, or they would find it and do it for you. Or the mold would get it. But anyway, fresh from the fire it was warm and delicious and full of love.

"I'm looking forward to the smell of baking," Nortlan said, as if reading Argur's thoughts.

"Maybe some girl will even let you *eat*," Jek said. Some of the men laughed at that, for Nortlan's mother did not participate in the harvesting or grinding or baking, and smells might be all Nort could expect from the venture.

"Come to my house," Argur told him. "We'll have some extra for you."

That raised some raucous suggestions about Argur's daughter— would she feed Nort by hand? Would she stroke his hair while he ate? Would she drink *gargo* with him, and go all swoozy in his arms?

Gargo was another grain product, not invented in Nog La but arguably perfected here. Wetting and rotting it was a fickle process that often left nothing more than jars of putrid gruel, but the women of the lake villages were particularly adept at it, and often traded *gargo* to Sunrise Castle in exchange for *ogabred*. The castle women were always complaining that it was too much work, and that the men drank it all too quickly, that it led to... indiscretions.

These insinuations of course required Argur to throw some punches to defend his family honor, and to receive some punches in return, as the men he'd punched defended their own honor. Sometimes these things flared up into genuine brawls—the Knights of Ell were proud men!—but today it settled down quickly enough, and they all decided to lie down in the dewy grass and rest for a while, and watch the clouds turn into different shapes. Why not?

"I see a mammoth," Tom said, settling down with his hands behind his head.

The men laughed at this, because Tom said it literally every time he looked up at the sky, day or night. He seemed incapable of seeing anything else up there, or unwilling, or else just really running on forever with a tired joke.

"I see pine trees," said Timlin.

"I see wolves," said Max, pointing to a particular spot in the sky. Argur had to agree; the clouds looked very much like wolves, at least for a moment. And then the conversation trailed away.

"Your daughter is very beautiful," Nortlan said, after a seemly interval had passed.

"*My* daughter?" Max exclaimed, drawing fresh laughter, for his daughter was only three years old.

"No!" Nort said indignantly. "Argur's daughter."

"Ah. She *is* beautiful," Argur agreed.

"And kind."

"Indeed."

"And funny, and a good provider. She can gather and weave and sew."

"All true."

Argur waited to see whether Nort would press the point at any further. Part of him wanted to say, "Stay away from my baby girl." He'd always figured Dele would end up with a Knight, or at least a hunter, and Nortlan showed little inclination in those directions. What right did he have to come sniffing around, with nothing to show for himself? Another part wanted to test the boy, to see how strong he was in other ways. Was he a good fowler or craftsman, weatherman or peacemaker? Could he sing and dance? So far, none of the usual talents had made themselves apparent, except perhaps a slight gift for fishing.

But who could fail at that? He rarely even used a net and spear, but built traps out of vertically driven stakes, like little castles with entrances that were wide and then narrow and then wide again. Fish and craw-pincers would find their way in and get confused, unable to find their way out, and Nortlan would simply go and harvest them, like gathering turnips from a tended patch. Was that clever, or was it lazy? Nort wasn't generally a lazy boy—in fact, he could be surprisingly energetic—but he was a boy nevertheless. What could be made of him? His father, Pock, *was* lazy, and tended to tag along with hunting groups so he could claim a share of the kill, and spent the rest of his time sleeping and tossing pebbles and borrowing things. Nort's mother, Nanka, was about the same.

Well, at least Nort was popular with old people and little children. That was a start, and perhaps here among Knights and hunters, he would find a bit more of himself. Weirder things had been known to happen.

Still, a third part of him wanted to ignore the problem and get down to business, and it was this part that won out. "Enough rest. Enough clouds," he said. With a grunt, he was up on his feet again, and the Knights were up with him, brushing grass and dirt off their tunics and trousers, and break time was over just like that. Soon they were on the path again, whistling and marching and throwing pine cones at one another, and generally having a good time.

2.2

Life hadn't always been this easy in Nog La. Argur's grandfather used to tell stories, passed down from his own grandfather, of a time before Knights and castles. A time when monsters outnumbered human beings, when trolls and giant bears roamed the valley freely, when villagers were routinely dragged away by leopards and lions without warning. "This place used to belong to the trolls," Granddad would say, "and the beasts of the forest knew better than to mess with *them*, when it was so much easier pluck off humans like raspberries anytime they liked."

This, of course, made Argur wonder why humans have ever bothered to settle here, if it was so dangerous. He knew, in a vague sort of way, that at the beginning of time they had lived in a much warmer, much safer place, with no requirement for Knights. But they'd been forced to vacate because of snakes or fruit or something, and had wandered for ten generations. He supposed the whole world must have been very dangerous indeed, for his ancestors to have thought this a haven! And it made him wonder, too, how many generations of brave, hard work it had taken to push the trolls and monsters out of here. Or mostly push, for Argur knew of at least one troll who was sometimes spotted at the edge of the valley, hunting small game and turnips when the light was dim. Sunrises and sunsets and rainy days, mostly.

As the men walked, a hare bounded right through their midst, barking in dismay. A silver fox was soon spotted running in the same direction, and at first it seemed the fox was chasing the hare, until it overtook it and kept on running in its sly, foxy way, flowing like water between the trees.

"Alert," said Tom quietly.

The Knights of Ell tensed, readying weapons and turning to look in the direction the two animals had vacated.

For a moment, nothing happened, and then...

And then the saplings along the forest floor were bursting apart as a black and white spotted animal charged out from the treeline. At first Argur thought it was a boar, but he saw it was too large, and then he saw it was *much* too large. It skidded to a halt when it saw its way blocked by ten armed humans, but it snarled and raised its front legs and then brought them back down, stamping the earth flat beneath gigantic feet.

"Boolis!" someone cried out.

"Shiiiit!" cried someone else.

"Plant spears!" Argur commanded, for bracing one's spear against the ground was the only plausible way to survive a fight with a boolis. But the men were only armed with shortspears and leverthrows today, because they were hunting orr-ox, and not with lethal intent. All they needed to do was goad a mare into the nets, and maybe, if things went really wrong, launch a spear or two through her heart with the leverthrows. A shortspear was, by definition, only chin-high, and offered scant protection against a creature such as this. With a single gigantic horn on its head—tall and blunt as a stone hammer, and waved around just above the level of human heads—the boolis was almost two men tall at the shoulder, and weighed as much as a whole herd of orr-oxen. It vaguely resembled both a mammoth and a wooly rhinoceros—and yes, a very large boar—but it outmuscled all of these by a long throw, and its white-and-black coloration were enough to strike fear into even the bravest hearts. Though a solitary herbivore, it was faster than a cave bear, meaner than a wolverine, and easily the most dangerous animal these woods had ever known.

Still, the men did as he commanded, and Argur was surprised to see Nortlan copying them, with a brave, proud look struggling against the terror on his face. Fighting monsters with the Knights of Ell! But he might not feel so brave if he really understood what they were up against.

The boolis growled, stamped its feet, brushed a gigantic hoof against its gigantic mouth, and screamed.

The men screamed back, for boolises could sometimes be spooked that way.

The young of the species were pure white and frail, with a long sharp horn. They resembled deer or horses, if horses were armed and dangerous, but they were also lonely creatures, and they occasionally fell prey to packs of lions or wolves. Even human hunters had been known to take one down if the opportunity arose, although the meat was tough and flavorless. As a boolis grew, its horn widened without growing longer, and its body thickened with bitter muscle as tough as rawhide, and ribs the size of saplings. Killing an adult boolis involved getting *underneath* it with a well-planted spear, driving the point into its heart, and then somehow getting out from under before it fell on you or trampled you to death. Argur had heard of people surviving the experience, but it was definitely not a position you ever wanted to be in.

But perhaps boolises never forgot that early vulnerability, even as they grew into monsters. They tended to be suspicious of humans and carnivores, and to shrink away from fire and movement and loud noises. Waving a rag at them was recommended, if you had a free hand. Spitting water at them was another trick that supposedly sometimes worked, if you happened to have some water in your mouth.

Unfortunately, this particular boolis wasn't spooked by the men's shouting, and it wasn't intimidated by their spears. Instead, it took a step forward, and then two more, and then it charged right through their midst, knocking Knights aside like leaves in a wind. It screamed again, and then thundered off into the trees, trampling everything in its path.

As it slipped from view, Argur noticed that its rump was bleeding from a number of circular wounds. Huh. Weird. Were they not the first men to fight it today? But who would spear it in the rump, and for love's sake, *why*? If a boolis is leaving, you let it leave!

"Sound off," Argur said.

"Intact," Tom answered at once. Several other men responded similarly.

But then Gouch said, "Hurt. The spear broke. I think I sprained my wrist."

And Timlin said, "Face wound. Bleeding. I'm not sure where."

There was a pause.

"Anyone else?" Argur inquired, and when no one answered, he said, "Bravely done, people. That was no joke."

Then he swiveled toward Timlin, took the man by the chin, and clucked. "Oh, ouch. You've split your lip! Or bitten through it, I don't know. There's a lot of blood. Put some pressure, yeah, put some pressure on that. I know it hurts."

"Is it bad?" Tim wanted to know.

"Well, it's not good. You've got an opening the size of my fingernail. If you press on it it should seal up before the end of the day, but that lip's going to swell. Are you dizzy?"

"No."

"Teeth hurt?"

"Yes. Front teeth are loose, but intact."

"Hmm. Well, you're going to be eating soft food for ten days, I'm afraid. Get back to Sunrise Castle and have someone wash that out. By morning your lip's going to be the size of a pine cone. But keep the pressure on, or you're going to leave a blood trail all the way home."

It wouldn't be Timlin's first split lip, and he certainly knew what to expect, but Argur generally found it a good idea to tell people what they already knew, especially when they were hurt.

"Should I go with him?" Gouch wanted to know.

"Yes. Definitely. And since neither of you can fight, bring Snar with you as well, for protection. You three are out for the day." And then he repeated: "That muddy mud mud shit was no joke. Thing could have killed somebody. We didn't have the weapons or the armor for a fight like that. It could have killed *everybody*."

"I'm fine," Nortlan added, a little late. "It ran right past me. I felt its breath! And did you notice those spear wounds on its hind end?"

Several of the men nodded and grunted at that. Yeah, yeah, spear wounds.

Yeah.

"That's not right," Tom said. "Something's not right."

"That thing was *goaded*," Jek said. "Someone *drove* it here to cause a *problem*."

"Why?" Pagel asked.

And then the answer seemed to dawn on everyone at once: as a decoy.

"But who would do that?" Chap wanted to know. "Who would dare?"

And that answer was not so clear, but the question hung

heavy in the air. Who would dare attack the valley of Nog La, risking the wrath of its Knights and hunters? Even the women of Nog La were notoriously skilled with knife and cudgel. Or perhaps skill was less the issue; the people of Nog La were *well equipped.* There were always knives and spears and clubs and leverthrows ready at hand. There were shields and helmets and armor and piles of big, round rocks! And baskets and hardmud bowls full of food, too, which meant the people here were big; at least half a head taller than any of their neighbors. And Argur liked to think they were smarter as well. And they had two fine castles to retreat to and attack from! It didn't make any sense.

And even more worrying: who would dare attack a boolis? Who would dare goad it from whatever mountain forests it was haunting, and drive it down into the valley? What kind of courage or desperation did that take? The thing had come from the direction of Ketlan Pass, which wasn't good.

"I think we'd *all* better get back to the castle," Argur said. Then, after a moment's thought: "Except you, Chap. I want you to run to the lake villages and warn them about the boolis, and what it means. And you, Pagel. I'd like you to run all the way to Sunset Castle. I'm sending you both alone, and lightly armed. Pagel will be *spending the night* alone. You can certainly both refuse if you're not comfortable with it. But you two are *fast,* and I fear we may need that right now."

"I'll do it," Pagel said at once.

"Yeah," Chap agreed.

With that agreed, the men spent a few minutes checking and trading their gear. Chap and Pagel needed to travel light, but not stupid. One knife, one spear, one leverthrow, a good belt to hold it all, and a strong pair of sandals. A warm cloak for Pagel, plus a small hammock, fortunately carried along by Jek for some reason. Everything else the two runners could offload. Water and food were luxuries they could obtain along the way.

"Ready?" Pagel asked.

Chap nodded. "Yep. Let's go."

And then, with no additional fuss, they were off. Running in the same direction for now, but before long they'd have to split up, violating one of the most basic rules of Nog La: never go anywhere alone.

"Wow, this day went bad quickly," Nortlan said.

"That's how it happens," Max told him.

"Nobody expects to have a bad day," Tom agreed. "You wake up planning for a good one. And it's good right up until it's bad, and you have to *notice* when that's starting to happen."

"I definitely noticed," Nort agreed, his voice shaking a little.

"Let's get going," Argur said.

And so the ten of them—ten able-bodied and two slightly wounded, plus a boy who had stood his ground. As bad days went, this could be a lot worse. But then again, it could get still get a lot worse. In fact, they didn't really know what was happening. It could already be worse, and they just hadn't learned the details yet.

"Stay sharp," he said. "Move fast."

Harv surfaced here for a befuddled moment, wondering first of all why Argur—a seemingly intelligent fellow—kept referring in his thoughts to ten of this and ten of that, when the actual numbers were clearly different. It seemed the man didn't actually know how to count, or that "ten" was not just a word for the maximum number of fingers a person could hold up, but perhaps also a synonym for "many" or "who cares how many," or something like that. As an analytical person, Harv was offended to think one of his ancestors—even one as remote as Argur—could think such imprecise thoughts.

But Harv was also thrown off by what had just happened. The "boolis" was nothing he'd ever seen before, even in artists' conceptions. It appeared to be some oversized relative of the rhinoceros, although its single horn was farther back, near the center of its head. But in coloration it was more like a modern dairy cow, and in temperament like a rodeo bull, and he wondered, for just a moment, whether he was dreaming or hallucinating. Could such a cockamamie animal really have existed? But it was all too vivid, too specific for him to remain suspicious for long. No part of his brain was capable of imagining all this. It must be something long extinct.

But that led him to ask again: when the hell was this? A few mammoths were actually probably still alive in Manuah's day, and the orr-ox drawing was perhaps not so different from the sort of cattle some people still kept in Africa in Harv's own time, so that didn't tell him much. But this wasn't Africa; from the maple and oak trees and hawthorn shrubs and rolling hills all around him, he thought he must be somewhere in Europe. And although it was the height of summer here in Nog La, Harv could feel a whisper of cold in the air, and a sense in Argur's mind that a brutally cold season would be coming soon, and staying for a long time, and could be deadly if they weren't prepared.

Europe in the middle of the Ice Age, then? That wasn't much help, either; wasn't the Ice Age millions of years long? Homo sapiens hadn't been in Europe that long, though. While his mind was active, he tried to dredge up anything he might ever have learned about when they'd arrived.

But okay, why were the people black? Or nearly black; while not quite the color of stout beer, Argur and Dala and all of the Knights of Ell ranged in color from red ale to, perhaps, a nice dark lager, and all of them sported deep brown eyes and wiry black hair that formed into natural dreadlocks and was trimmed to just above shoulder length. Their beards were short and close to the skin—apparently naturally so. Tall and strong, they looked like no native Europeans of Harv's own epoch. Really, they didn't look like anyone of Harv's epoch, except perhaps Samoans or Tongans or something. One of those islands that produced a lot of football players.

But these people weren't cave men either, any more than Manuah and Adrah. Their clothing was too advanced; Harv had never seen a cave man wear dyed, woven cloth, or dyed hawk feathers, or dyed rope necklaces and bracelets. There was color everywhere on these people (dull and muted color, but still), and not a stitch of animal fur anywhere to be seen. Oh, they wore sandals and boots made of pale but otherwise cured-looking leather, and their leather carrying bags—worn by both the men and women, and strikingly similar to the purses and messenger bags that were popular in Harv's time—were something he could picture on a cave person. But the knights also wore hooded leather half-cloaks that would have been at home in almost any era, and also wore what Harv could only describe to himself as tool belts. Held up by a pair of large, rectangular wooden buckles, they looked like something a cartoon policeman or construction worker would wear. Or some stone-age Batman.

The implements carried on the belts and in the bags provided a bit more information, because the men did not have bows and arrows.

These short spears and "leverthrows" seemed to fill a similar purpose, but with a more limited range and a lot less ammo. The spears themselves were as straight and smooth as signposts, and tipped with sharp, symmetrical stone points shaped like bamboo leaves. These also appeared well made, and well secured to their hafts with slots and resin and rawhide lashings. A nasty weapon in any era! But they lacked any sort of barbs or lashing grooves in the stone itself. Compared to Native American artifacts, they looked a bit rough.

The knives were interesting, too; basically half-sized spear points mounted to eighth-size spears, and sheathed in that same pale leather. They reminded Harv of the knives Manuah's wife, Emzananti, had used back in her kitchen in The City. He supposed it was simply a good design, hard to beat and relatively easy to make. The "hardmud" bowls and jars and pots the people used here were clay that had been fired but not truly vitrified. This material was too weak to be made into anything with handles, and so it was fashioned into a few standardized shapes that reminded Harv of wine carafes and plant pots, and those oversized cups you sometimes saw in coffee shops. He also somehow knew that they imparted a faint flavor of dirt into anything boiled in them.

These implements seemed stone-age enough, but Dele's toys—the bear and the ball—were made of the same stuff, and struck Harv as anachronistic. The men also carried bean-shaped water skins of the sort that could still be purchased in Harv's time, and also various cleverly made bits of rope and string and wood and wicker whose purpose he could not immediately divine. The Knights of Ell looked, more or less, like African tribesmen attempting to dress up for a Renaissance festival.

Putting the clues together, Harv figured this must be somewhere between twenty thousand and thirty thousand years ago. Still a broad range—longer than all of recorded history!—but it gave him enough sense of orientation that he was able to lose his train of thought and . . .

"What do you think is happening?" Nortlan asked Argur.

"I don't know," Argur answered. "Nothing like this has ever happened before, that I've ever heard of. Goading a boolis is fool's work, deadly and not lightly undertaken. So the question is, who are the fools? And what do they want? It must be something very important to them."

"Any ideas?" Tom asked.

"Only that someone wants to take the valley away from us. But that doesn't make any sense. They'd need to have ten ten ten *ten* people to do it, and even then most of them wouldn't survive. I feel like I'm missing something."

"I'm missing something, too," Jek said. "Why do you have a furry sandal on your head?"

There was uneasy laughter at that, and then someone threw a pine cone at Argur's hairpiece, and then there was genuine laughter, because *that* was *funny*. A pine cone! In the head! And for a while the conversation turned bright again, if only because they didn't know enough—and frankly couldn't imagine enough—to dwell on anything dark. These were hard men, but their experience was limited, and although their job involved occasional losses and tragedies, they'd never encountered anything fundamentally beyond their strength and wit. Argur even blew a few notes on his flute to emphasize the point: theirs was a hard world, but they were the bosses of it, and could not stay worried for long!

That was, until Argur's wife, Dala, came running up to them, with Tom's wife, Birgny, trailing behind. They were within sight of the castle now, but both women were gasping for breath, as though they'd run a distance much longer than that. They carried nothing: no bags, no scythes, no feather visors, no water. More importantly, Dala had blood trickling down her forehead, turning against one eyebrow and running from there down her cheek and neck, to stain her dress a forbidden color. Women's clothing was white or yellow or blue or green, or brown if it was old and worn out, or sometimes even *orange* if the right gourds were in season—but never the color of blood! Blood meant danger, or perhaps carelessness at the wrong phase of the moon, in defiance of spirit law. In any case a major problem!

Birgny did not appear to be bleeding, but she had a long, ugly scrape along her arm, and both women appeared dirty and disheveled, as though they'd been in a scuffle of some sort.

"Argur!" Dala cried out. "Argur! They've taken the girls!"

"What?" he called out as she approached. It was the most intelligent response he could come up with.

"They took *Dele*! Dele!"

Argur's wife flung herself into his arms, buried her face in his chest, and wailed.

"They took three girls and ran for the hills," Birgny screeched. "So fast! So fast! You've got to get them back!"

Argur's blood ran as cold as a mountain stream as he asked: "Who took them? Who took three girls?"

"Trolls!" both women shouted, almost in unison.

And then Argur knew for sure just how bad a day it was going to be.

2.3

It wasn't hard to track back to where the attack had occurred; leaving Snar and Gouch with the women, the remaining ten knights took off at a run, following the trail to where ten women stood around—some wailing, some quietly weeping, some brandishing knives or clubs and looking furious. All ten of them startled when the men burst out of the undergrowth.

"Ha! Back!"

"The trolls!"

"Oh!"

"The Knights!"

"They've taken my daughter!"

Argur panted: "They've taken my daughter, too. And Timlin's. And Ronk's niece. Which way did they go?"

And it was a question that didn't need much of an answer, because the women had been standing in a grain meadow, and the trail the trolls had left across it, and through the woods beyond, might as well have been made by a boolis.

"How many of them?" Tom asked.

"Ten!" shouted one of the women.

And just as though that meant something to them, the men all nodded and tensed to launch themselves running again.

But Nortlan was shouting, "Stop! Stop! Argur, you've got to stop."

Impatient and angry, Argur shouted back: "You stop, boy. Stay here with the women. I'm going after my daughter!"

"Stop!" Nortlan said again, in a rudely commanding voice. "Argur, there are ten of them, and ten of us. But they're bigger, and stronger."

"No one is stronger!" Gower shouted indignantly.

But Argur stopped, if only for a moment, to listen.

"We've got shortspears and leverthrows," Nort panted. "You want to shoot into a mob that contains three human girls? We're dressed for *heezh*, not *bork*. Argur, you've got to get back to the castle. Get real weapons, get your armor, get your shield. Only then are you stronger. Humans are *faster* than trolls, you can get your stuff and still catch them."

"Trolls never get tired," Ronk said. "They just keep running."

"They could be raping Mog and Dele right now," one of the women said.

To which Nortlan replied, "They can't be running *and* raping. They can't. If they stop, we'll catch them. If they don't stop, then it means the girls are still safe. Either way, we've got to be *equipped*."

"We?" Jek sneered. "You're not a Knight of Ell, little rabbit."

"I mean 'we' in the sense of our people's—"

"He comes with us," Argur panted. "Nort's a *wise* rabbit. He uses his heart. He comes with us."

"I should ask my—"

"*You come with us*," Argur said flatly. "Your useless father can copulate with mud before I let him risk my daughter's..." Life? Virtue? Innocence? "...safety. I'll find you a spear and a shield. You're coming."

Argur watched the thoughts moving behind Nortlan's eyes. He'd already fought a boolis today, and lived to tell about it. Would he now fight trolls as well? For pride and honor, or a chance at Dele's hand in marriage, or simply because it was the right thing to do? Argur could not, in fact, compel him. That was the law: nobody in Nog La could compel anyone to do anything. He could only ask.

But what could Nortlan say? Just like that, right before Argur's eyes, Nortlan shed his boyhood, became a man, nodded to show he would join the Knights of Ell, and vomited into the grass.

And so they ran to the castle, and gathered up weapons and armor as carefully as haste permitted. A long armored shirt was thrust down over Nortlan's upraised arms, and a shield was thrust into his hands, along with a spear, and a pair of decent boots for his feet. All of it was careworn and too large for him, and Argur could scarcely drape a hunting bag over the boy's shoulders or cinch a belt around his waist without it all bunching up in funny ways. So Dala and Birgny solemnly stuffed linen rags into the toes of the boots, and when that wasn't enough, they swaddled more rags around his feet, and more still around his shoulders, like the top third of a heavy shirt.

Nismu, the Wizard of Sunrise Castle, came by to offer a hurried blessing with tossed herbs and a smoldering willow wand. "Strength for your journey. Courage for your journey. Wisdom for your journey. Keen sight for your journey." And then it was done. Nortlan was as much a man as they could make him on short notice.

"There. And now what?" Argur demanded of him. "Do you have any other bright advice?"

"Bring camping gear," Nort said at once, as though he'd been thinking about this for a while now.

"Camping?" Jek scoffed.

"In case we don't catch them," Tom said, grasping Nort's meaning. "If they're faster than we think, or they've had too much head start. Trolls don't fear the night."

And that made sense to Argur; trolls *were* the fearful darkness. Rarely all that active by day, they did most of their prowling around dawn and dusk. And sometimes around midnight if the moon was full, yes, because few things in this world dared attack them. They feared only human beings, who feared them right back. Masters of the world only so long as the sun was shining, humans retreated behind their castle walls, their village ditches and watchfires, when darkness slipped across the land. By night the monsters ruled, and really, if you thought about it, who ruled the monsters? The trolls.

"And we'll need to notify Sunset Castle," Nort added.

"Yes," Tom agreed. "They'll need to take responsibility for the boolis. The trolls are our problem. That's fair."

Argur nodded. "Yes. Unthinkably bad, but fair." To the other knights, Argur said, "Do it. Quickly! Max, will you go? And take a couple of strong hunters with you?"

And just like that, Nort had become one of Argur's trusted advisors.

Harv struggled to think for a moment here, because the knights were dressed in armor made of hardwood plates and knotted ropes, like something a cheap-ass theater company might try to pass off with a coat of silver paint. But it was real armor! The plates were less than a centimeter thick, but they ran two layers deep, interlocking so that no vulnerable areas were actually exposed, from mid-thigh to mid-throat. The shields were leather over wicker, nearly as tough as wood and yet lighter than a box of donuts. These defenses were skimpy by historical standards, but might very well deflect a spear, or soften the blow of a club or an animal horn. And in any case, the armor seemed to have a psychological value out of proportion with its actual stopping power. This was something most men didn't own and didn't have the time or the skills to make, or the knowledge to overcome. Something perhaps not widely found outside of Nog La. Something fierce.

Dala was shoving food into everyone's hunting bags: dried orr-ox meat and yesterday's roasted turnips, along with some precious *ogabred*—things they could eat without cooking, or even stopping. Birgny checking everyone's water skins, and trading the half-empty ones for full ones.

"Bring her back," Dala said to Argur. "We'll be fine here, just *bring her back.*"

"Bring all of them back," Birgny echoed.

Argur slapped his armored chest and roared. "Oh! Oh, we'll bring them back. These trolls don't know who they're messing with. They've *forgotten* who they're messing with. We'll teach them a lesson! This time, this time, *this* time we'll teach them so they *don't forget!*"

A cry went up among the Knights of Ell, and with that, a series of events was set in motion that, Harv somehow knew, would alter human destiny forever.

2.4

The trail was not difficult to follow; unless trolls were hunting and needed to move quietly, they had a tendency to club and trample their way right through the sort of undergrowth a human being might hold aside or step around. They also seemed to have followed the same track out of the valley that they'd made on their way in, and so it was doubly smashed and trodden, and yet also difficult to read.

"How many are there?" Nortlan asked, over and over again.

The easy answer was "ten," which was how many Birgny had claimed to have seen. But what Nortlan was really asking was, "Do they outnumber us?" And that was difficult to say. Where a human or an animal might leave clear tracks of one kind or another, the sheer destruction made it difficult to tell a footprint from a boot print from a club mark, or to tell any of it from the dragging feet of an unwilling human girl.

One thing was clear, though: as they approached the mouth of Ketlan Pass, the route of the trolls merged with that of the boolis, and where the two followed together, there were drop drop drops of blood everywhere. This left no doubt that the trolls had been the ones who drove the boolis down here and turned it loose. However, it left a *lot* of doubt as to how they'd controlled the monster up to this point. Ropes? Nets? A circle of spears all around it? This morning, Argur had felt that capturing a live orr-ox was such a dangerous project that only the Knights of Ell could be trusted to attempt it. This did not bode well for what they were up against now.

"Perhaps they're *tougher* than we are," Jek offered helpfully.

"Tougher than you, maybe," Tom jabbed back.

"Maybe they fed it," Nortlan suggested. "Boolises like carrots, I hear."

"Stop it," Argur told all of them. "We need your ears, not your voices."

When they quieted, the woods got *really* quiet—no birdsong except a single voice somewhere nearby, singing "Wow! Wow!" in the weirdly insistent voice of a smorkbird. The sound followed them as they traveled.

Not quite running, they maintained a fast walking speed that soon carried them to the stream running down out of the pass. The water eventually found its way down to Round Lake, but here it ran parallel to the edge of the valley, and formed its traditional border. The path of the trolls had now merged with a broader footpath and game trail leading down out of the pass, which crossed the stream at a bridge.

Harv couldn't believe his eyes. Or rather, he couldn't believe Argur's eyes, because this little wooden footbridge looked like something that might be found at a summer camp in upstate New York. The stream's ditch was perhaps four meters wide and two meters deep, and while the banks led down to a stony ford where the water was less than ten centimeters deep, someone had placed eight broad logs across it from highest point to highest point. These were lashed together with both rope and rawhide, and supported in the middle with a V-shaped truss fashioned from four logs on each side. The center of the V was anchored in the stream bed and surrounded by large stones that would keep it from sliding or buckling, and it was crazy to think something like this could have existed deep within the Ice Age. These "carpenters" of Sunrise Castle were clearly a lot smarter than Harv had given them credit for; the castle gate was a trifle compared to this.

The bridge also said something important about the nature of this society. Harv had imagined the whole valley of Nog La as a kind of fortress, walled off against outsiders, but the bridge said otherwise. It implied not only regular traffic between this valley and other valleys around it, but welcome traffic. Again, this failed so completely to line up with Harv's ideas that his mind basically stopped right there. Cave people didn't need—

✧   ✧   ✧

"No!" cried a shrill voice from underneath the bridge.

"What? Who goes there?" Argur demanded. "Come out here. Now! Come out here!"

"Stop! Pease!" the voice cried out again.

A figure emerged into the sunlight. Blinking, sneezing, cringing, more afraid of the sun than of Argur and his men. It was dressed all in brown, worn-out mammoth fur—fur boots, fur robe, fur bands around its arms. A necklace of what looked like chicken bones. Its own frizzy hair was *orange*—the color of a sunset or a campfire—as was its long, unkempt beard. Both hair and beard were composed of individual strands that seemed to move independently, like little blades of grass, rather than spiraling together like human hair. Its oversized ears were slightly pointed at the top, and its oversized nose was bulbous at the bottom, but most shockingly, its skin was such a pale pink that it was almost white—the color of mushrooms or maggots—and its eyes were like tiny lakes, as blue as the sky. As it pulled its lips back in a snarl of fear, Argur could see its teeth were as large and white as knucklebones. It was not quite as tall as a human, but its arms were as thick as Argur's legs, and its legs were as thick as the logs from which the bridge was fashioned. Its fingers were each nearly as wide as a baby's wrist. A dead rat dropped from the thing's grasp, landing wetly in the stream.

"Troll!" Nortlan shouted. Unnecessarily, for he was the only one here who'd never seen one.

The air—filled with birdsong just moments before—went silent.

"Load darts!" Argur said, more helpfully. In a blur, he and the other knights whipped out their leverthrows and balanced darts onto them. Halfway between the length of a shortspear and a knife, these could be sheathed in a slab of softwood and safely carried in bundles of five. They lacked the weight and impact of a spear, but you launched one hard enough it could still inflict a deadly wound.

"No!" the troll screamed, cringing and cowering. Argur realized it wasn't carrying any weapons, although that did not by any means make it safe to approach. A single punch from a troll could break an arm or a cheek or a chest. With a heavy stick grabbed randomly off the forest floor, they'd been known to human knock heads and limbs clean off. With a fire-hardened spear or club they could—

"No flying spear! Me Lug! Lug!"

"I should poke you full of holes," Argur snapped at the creature. "Where are the girls?"

"No!" the troll cried. "No girl here. Lug no fight girl! Lug
no fight man!"

Like all trolls, it had a shrieking voice all out of proportion
with its frame—high-pitched and sharp as a sewing bone stitching
through gravel. Speaking seemed almost to cause them pain, and
they could only squeeze out a word or three at a time, before they
had to gasp for breath. Like each word cost them as much breath as
an entire sentence. Not that they could speak in sentences anyway.

"You're a filthy creature," Jek said to the troll. Again, unnecessarily.

"Where are the girls?" Argur repeated.

"No girls! No Lug fight! Other *okor* fight!"

That was the word the trolls used to describe themselves:
okor or *okob* or something like that. Argur's grandfather had told
him that the trolls once spoke a language of their own—perhaps
more suited to their serpent lips and tree-trunk throats—but that
they had gradually replaced it with the language of humans.
Probably because of encounters like this one, where saving their
miserable hides depended on their ability to communicate. And
it had always seemed to Argur that their understanding was not
as limited as their speech.

"Other trolls took them? Not you?" Argur demanded.

"Not Lug! Lug stay here! Noga valley! Noga warm!"

"Where did they go, these other trolls?" Tom wanted to know.

It was another pointless question, because the path led only
one way: up into the pass, into the canyon and the mountain
valleys beyond it. Human beings lived in those valleys, but so
did monsters and, somewhere up in the mountains, the trolls
themselves. They were the last trolls in the area, as far as Argur
knew; the low countries had steadily driven them back toward
the sunrise and up toward the sky.

"We can't *safely* go on and leave *it* here," Jek observed.

"Are you saying it should come with us?" Nortlan asked,
disbelievingly.

"No," Tom corrected. "He's saying we should kill it."

The troll, Lug, reacted strongly to that. "No! No! No kill Lug!
Lug friend! Lug guard bridge!"

"From what?" Argur asked it. "Ten trolls and a boolis, coming and going as they please?"

"No kill!" the troll shrieked, holding its hand up in front of its face. Argur found it strange, to see such a powerful-looking creature reduced to such begging. "Pease! Pease! Sun burns. Lug hide. Pease. No kill."

And this truly did give Argur pause, because the trolls' hatred of direct sunlight was well known. And yet, this "Lug" was so afraid of Argur and his men that he'd willingly stepped out into the light, rather than risk being killed in the shadows. And these other trolls had nabbed human girls in mid-morning, and fled into full daylight, their skin probably reddening and blistering all the while. What had driven them to do it? Clearly because that was when little girls were outside and vulnerable, yes, but why travel all the way down here to nab them in the first place?

Argur had been raised on stories of heroism—his ancestors bravely killing monsters and driving away bands of armed, angry trolls. But Lug seemed neither armed nor angry nor part of any band, and Argur doubted this was any sort of deception. Trolls possessed a certain cunning—like humans, they hunted in packs and could drive an animal from safety to certain doom. But they fought their prey by throwing heavy rocks and stabbing it close-up, because slings and leverthrows and even a decently weighted throwing spear were beyond their feeble minds and fat fingers. They weren't liars or tricksters—just brutes.

Or, in this case, terrified cringing cowards? *Argur* was the one who was angry. Argur was *furious* over the safety of his girl. But was Lug responsible for any of that? There'd been a troll living in this end of Nog La for years, avoiding contact, never harming anyone. Was it Lug? Would it be...murder?...to kill the thing here and now?

"Don't hurt it," Argur told his men.

Lug brightened at that. "Oh! Thank! Oh! Thank! Lug no fight! Thank! Thank!"

But now all the men were looking at Argur strangely. Even Nortlan.

"Okay. What, then?" Tom wanted to know.

"We leave it here," Argur said. And then, when nobody reacted, he said, "I've seen this one before. It's not hurting anyone. Are you, Lug? Are you hurting anyone?"

"No hurt!" Lug agreed, with simpering enthusiasm.

"Wow," Jek said. "Reduced to *this*, are we?"

And that made Argur angrier. So angry that he lowered his leverthrow, lest he accidentally poke a hole through Jek in an unthinking moment. "Listen," he said tightly, "we have one fight, and it's to bring back our girls. We're not doing anything else. We're *not doing anything else.* If you want to slaughter animals, you can stay here with the hunters. The Knights of Ell are going that way." He pointed uphill.

Nobody seemed happy with that answer, and for a moment all eyes were on Timlin. His face, though no longer bleeding, was swollen and dark. He looked like mud, he probably felt like mud, and they would have left him behind if this weren't an emergency, and if Timlin's own daughter hadn't been one of the nabbed. More than anyone, he was entitled to an opinion about this. But Timlin just shrugged.

"Argur's plans have never failed me."

And then, unaccountably, all eyes were on Nortlan.

"What do *you* think, O wise rabbit?" Jek demanded.

Nortlan shrank back for a moment, afraid of saying the wrong thing. But then a thought occurred to him and he said, "They could be watching us right now. If we want our girls to stay safe, it matters what we do. It matters how we look."

That seemed to unsettle everyone. Now all eyes were on the forest, suspicious.

Finally, it was Tom who said, "Listen, we're wasting time here. I'm following Argur up into the pass."

"And me," echoed Timlin.

"And me," said Nortlan.

But Jek said, "Should we wash our *hands* first?"

This annoyed Argur greatly, because they were in a hurry, but the spirits did want human beings to wash their hands whenever they passed moving water. And now did not seem like a good time to be angering the spirits!

"All right," he said. "Make it quick."

This interested Harv, because he suddenly became aware of the smell of these men—a sort of peppery, chicken-soupy, vaguely shitty odor that implied it had been a long time since any of them had truly bathed. But perhaps dirty hands were a source of infection? These people accumulated a lot of cuts and scrapes and bruises over the course of their daily lives, so perhaps the tribes with handwashing customs lived and reproduced better than the ones without?

Harv also noticed the smell of the "troll"—quite clearly a Neandertal man—which was quite different. Shittier, for one thing, but also sharper and muskier—like the sweat of horses, or a dog's bed that had been cleaned, imperfectly, with vinegar. And through Argur's highly attuned senses he fancied he could even smell the creature's fear, like an undertone of hot copper plumbing.

And so they washed their hands, keeping suspicious eyes on Lug all the while, and then they were all moving again, their armor and weapons rattling.

"Thank! Thank!" said Lug, over and over again, his voice retreating into the distance as the ten of them marched over the bridge and on up into the unknown.

Trolls were capable of moving silently, but they were also capable of making a lot of racket—their shrill voices bickering as they crashed through bushes and the lower branches of trees, or splashed their way across the stream where it widened to fill the entire pass. And the stream, too, was capable of moving between its banks with barely a whisper or gurgle. At other times it growled and roared its way over rocks or down steeper slopes. And the mountain air sometimes carried sound well, and sometimes not, and sometimes the walls of the canyon were steep and close together and full of echoes, and sometimes they were far apart and gently sloping and full of pine trees. And sometimes the wind through these trees whistled or hissed, and sometimes it made no sound at all.

And so at times they could clearly hear the trolls up ahead of them, and it seemed the distance was quickly shrinking. At one point, where the pass was unusually straight and long, they could even *see* the *okor* rounding a bend up ahead. Close enough to see! But at other times there was no trace—not even smashed undergrowth—and it seemed the humans were falling behind. And at still other times the Knights of Ell had to stop and rest. To drink some water, to eat a bite of food, to catch their breath and take a load off their feet and shoulders for a little while. And this was a problem, because they knew full well that the trolls—strong and stubborn and tireless—would never stop. So the men urged each other onward, and Nortlan followed bravely, apparently too proud to admit his endurance was failing—which it very clearly was.

And then the sun itself began to fail—first slipping behind the wall of the canyon, then slowly dimming and reddening the bright clouds above it. And then the sky began to dim, and as far as Argur could tell, they were nowhere near the High Vales that were supposed to be back here somewhere. The fact was, the residents of Nog La were not travelers. Why should they be, when trading parties came to them? Although, now that he thought about it, there hadn't been many trading parties coming from this direction lately. In any case, not even the Knights of Ell had ever ventured back this far; they didn't really know how long it took to get anywhere. Not really.

And then it began to get dark, and then it *was* dark, and the canyon—which had seemed so empty during the day—began to fill up with animal noises. Was that howling wolf close by, or somewhere far up the pass? That yipping fox? That unfamiliar low-high-low shriek that was hopefully just some kind of bird?

"We need to stop," Tom said.

A minute later, when everyone was still walking, as a sliver of moon appeared over the canyon wall and the stars began winking open overhead, he said it again: "Argur, we need to *stop*. I already can't see anything, and we need to gather firewood and set up some fortifications."

"Fortifications?" Nortlan asked.

"To protect the camp," Tom said. "I'll show you."

"We can't stop," Argur protested. But that sounded wrong even to him, so he followed it with, "Not for long, not for the whole night. At dawn we need to get moving again. You know the trolls are still moving right now, and will be for some time."

"Probably not all night," Tom said.

"No," Argur agreed. "Not all night, but long enough to burn all the advantage we gained today. We're going to have to be faster tomorrow."

"Well, perhaps we shouldn't have brought the *rabbit*," Jek observed in his infuriatingly slow voice.

"He walks as fast as you," Timlin said, through swollen lips. "And complains less."

"All right," Argur said. "Let's find a flat spot. Gower and Snar, collect firewood if you would, please. Jek, if you dig a fire pit;

I'll gather stones to line it. Can you clear the area, Ronk? And Perry? Tom and Nort, I agree, you should fortify us. Timlin, you look like mud. Get your armor off and sit down."

As they set up camp, it occurred to Argur—not for the first time, but for the strongest time—that the knights were spread too far on this problem. Chap had run off to warn the lake villages, and both Pagel and Max had run to Sunset Castle. Gouch was home with a sprained wrist, and Timlin was here with a swollen face, not in much condition to fight. Nortlan had *never been* in a fight, and as far as Argur knew he couldn't even use a sling or leverthrow. And the entire complement of Sunset Castle was presumably dealing with the boolis problem—spirits knew what they were going to do about *that*. So, counting Argur himself, that left only... seven? He counted again and came up with six. Tried still again and came up with eight—a number so large he'd only counted to it a few times in his life. But then he realized he'd counted Timlin by mistake, and decided it really didn't matter. Point was, there were not enough knights here, and they were tired from hiking uphill all day.

It didn't give him a good feeling. The trolls had been greedy enough or desperate enough to attack in daylight, and also smart and brave enough to send a boolis thundering into Nog La as a distraction. If they also *outnumbered* the humans...

But while he fretted and gathered up rocks, other men did real work. Tom showed Nortlan how to cut and sharpen three chest-high green branches (not straight spear poles, but just ordinary crooked branches), and tie them together into a little tent structure with two points facing up and outward, and one facing down and back, buried into the soil. Camp fortifications looked silly, because a wolf or a troll or a hostile human being could leap right over. But Argur had rarely seen them do so, because tripping in the attempt could be extremely painful, or even fatal, and any time spent slipping between the fort sticks, or knocking them aside, would provide ample alarm to the men within. So, foolish or not, the fort sticks served their purpose. It made him wonder, for just a moment, how many things in life were like that: symbolic barriers that somehow worked. He should discuss it sometime with Nismu, for it seemed to him that wizarding must rely on a similar principle.

Or something like that. Once Argur had the firepit stones laid out, he started to help Tom and Nortlan with the pretend-yet-real fortifications. But oh! The panic of the day had worn him out as much as the walking, and by the time Ronk and Perry had shaved some kindling and struck a spark to it, he could barely keep his eyes open long enough to assign guard duty.

"Ronk and Gower, until the moon is *there* in the sky. Tom and Nortlan, until the moon sets. Snar and Me, until first light. Then we all get moving."

As he laid out his cloak and arranged his bed for the night, by the flickering light of a blossoming campfire that crackled with sappy green pine, his mind kept working on one simple thing: if the trolls weren't already home, to whatever hole or deadfall they lived in, they'd be stopping soon to set up a rude camp of their own. Either way, Dele would be at their mercy. He couldn't bear the idea, and yet still he somehow fell asleep almost before he'd closed his eyes.

Sometime in the night, he awoke to the sound of heavy breathing. And then the sound of kicking and grunting, and a yelp. He turned, and saw Jek lying away from the fire, in the jumping shadows, with his dick in one hand and a little hardmud woman in the other. Broad-hipped, broad-bosomed, and narrow waisted—the sort of figurine unmarried men liked to carry around with them as "good luck tokens" or "fertility charms." To please the sprits, yes, but these little mud women always seemed to be at hand when the bachelors emptied their balls. Argur had never seen the need, but of course he had Dala.

Gower was standing over Jek, threatening to kick him again.

"Hey!" Jek protested. "Private time!"

"Show some respect," Gower hissed, clearly trying to be quiet. "Our girls are being fucked by strangers right now."

"Private time," Jek said again, less emphatically.

"Respect," Gower answered, "or pain."

Grumbling, Jek put away both his little woman and his little man.

Argur's mind protested: there was no evidence that the girls were being fucked right now. Gower had no right to say that. His mind had a lot to say on this subject, but his eyelids were so heavy that he couldn't hold them up for long. They pulled closed, and dragged his face back down into the nestles of his blanket. Sleep was a mercy.

2.5

It was still dark when Argur was awakened by Tom and Nortlan, and once he'd shaken off the spirits he crawled out from his bedroll into night air that was unnaturally cold and damp for midsummer. He and Snar stomped themselves warm and then stood an uneasy watch, neither one talking, just listening to the owls until dawn began to break.

Hootoo! The owls said to one another, which in the language of Nog La was both a sound of derision and one of warning. You're in it now! *Hootoo! Hootoo!*

As the sky grew brighter, the walls of the pass became more visible, and something caught Argur's eye that, for a moment, made him raise his spear. Monster! But no, it was only the *bones* of a monster, jutting out from halfway up the hillside. His grandfather had once told him there was a dead dragon up here in the pass, and the ground had partially swallowed it up. But it didn't look like that to Argur. For one thing, it looked like the ground had been *washing away* from it, uncovering something that had previously been completely buried. And the skeleton wasn't emerging from dirt, but from the actual sandstone beneath it! For another thing, the bones seemed profoundly lifeless. Were dragon bones made of stone? There were no shreds or traces of hide or sinew or cartilage on any part of it. This thing had been dead for many years, at least. Probably a lot more than that.

"Dragon bones," Snar said, following Argur's gaze.

"Mmm," Argur agreed.

"I don't like it."

"Nor I."

The creature was on its side and still partially buried, but it looked to be taller than a boolis, and two or three times as long. The arms were short and thin, with knifelike claws, and might almost have fit onto the body of a cave bear, but the leg bones were as huge as a mammoth's. A long, snakelike tail projected out behind it. Its head was the size of a human being, with teeth the size spearheads. It could bite a man in half as easily as Argur could tear the flesh off a goose leg.

"I thought dragons had wings," Snar said.

Argur shrugged. "Not always."

"Not always? That doesn't make any sense."

And that was true; it didn't. But they had more important things to attend to this morning, so Argur drew out his flute and, after blowing a few melodic notes, leaned out over the sleeping Knights and blasted out a shrill tone.

"Arise, Knights of Ell! We have daughters and nieces to rescue!"

They awoke, startled and grumbling. And then, as they slowly got to their feet, one by one in the rising light of dawn, they saw the dragon as well.

"Oi!"

"Wow."

"Hmm."

"*Hootoo!* We've been sleeping under *that*?"

And then Nortlan: "Dragon bones! Oh mud, it's so *big*. I thought they were smaller."

"I thought they had wings," Gower added.

Then Nortlan asked, "Argur, have you ever seen a live one?"

"No," Argur answered curtly, gathering up his things from around the camp. "They've never been seen in Nog La. Or anywhere I've heard of, for many generations. Look at this one, buried in stone. How long would *that* take?"

"Interesting," Nortlan said, just standing there staring at the thing.

"Pack up," Argur told him. "You can look at it on the way down, once Dele and the others have been rescued."

The Knights rarely camped, but when they did they made a practice of cleaning up as completely as possible, leaving no way for possible enemies to estimate their numbers or their strength. The fire was thoroughly extinguished, its stones scattered. Piss and shit were covered with dirt to disguise their scent from predators. The fort sticks were disassembled and snapped in half and tossed in the stream, where they immediately began slithering and bouncing their way downhill, toward Nog La.

The men washed their hands, and then they were off, gnawing on *ogabred* as they hiked upward.

"We need to *move*," Argur told them. "We've lost too much time already."

But they made good progress, and soon came upon the place where the trolls themselves had camped. It was a mess; if the Knights preferred to clean up after themselves, trolls took the exact opposite approach: the ground was littered with gnawed bones and bits of raw animal pelt, turnip greens, and little piles of shit. Their still-smoldering campfires reeked of urine. *We were here*, the campsite announced, *and we don't care who knows it*.

"Argur, look," Nortlan said, pointing. On the ground was a little hardmud ball, somewhat larger than a sling bullet, with lines carved around it. "Isn't that Dele's?"

Argur stooped and picked it up. "Yes. I think it is."

"It's *someone's*," Tom said dismissively. "Trolls couldn't make that."

"Did she leave it here on purpose?" Nortlan asked. "For us to find?"

But no one answered. Did it matter?

"Let's keep moving," Argur said.

Before the sun was halfway to its peak, the pass finally flattened and turned downward, and then opened out into a much wider valley. They had reached the first of the High Vales. From the pass they could see the whole valley spread out in front of them, with a kind of footpath or game trail leading down through it, perhaps connecting to the pass at the valley's far end. The valley had its own roundish lake near the center, making it look like a miniature version of Nog La, though with a lot more meadow than forest.

"Does anyone see them?" Tom asked, looking down into the High Vale.

Nobody answered. It was a good half-day's march to the valley's other end, and not even Perry (who had by far the best vision of anyone in Nog La) would be able to see human-sized figures that far away.

"Or hear them?" Argur added.

Again, no one answered, but there was a general grumbling of assent: the questions were reasonable. The trolls hadn't marched all night, but had stopped and camped sometime well before midnight. This meant they must be down there somewhere, probably between here and the lake. And the view from up here was bound to be better than the view from the valley floor, so it made sense to pause here and really look and listen.

"I do see smoke," Perry said, "But it's not a camp. It's a village."

"A *human* village?" Jek wanted to know.

Perry shrugged. "I assume so."

"Humans must live closer to Nog La than the trolls do," Nortlan stated. "Or nobody would ever come to visit us at all."

Unconvinced, Argur said, "Let's check it."

So they made their way downhill, following the path toward whatever Perry had seen. In a while, all of them could see it, and before the sun reached its peak, they could see it *clearly*: a collection of ten round huts, made of bent wood and bundles of grass, with cured yellow leather over the top for waterproofing. They were nearly identical to the houses within Sunrise Castle, and the nearby lake villages. (The houses on the Sunset Castle end of Nog La tended to be oval shaped, with piles of stone at their bases, and a single straight log down the middle of each roof, but that was mostly because the wind spilling down from the valley and into the River Lands didn't let them make the houses quite as wide, so they were made longer to compensate.) Furthermore, the village was surrounded by larger versions of the fort sticks Tom and Nortlan had set up last night. Again, not foolproof—not nearly as reliable as a castle wall—but still a message to anyone who might think about raiding here: We're well equipped and well prepared. Do you really want to chance it?

"See? Humans," Nortlan said as they approached.

"Hmm. Well, perhaps they've *seen* the trolls." Argur mused, making a flourish in the air to emphasize the point.

Like Nog La, this valley really only had two exits. However, that assumed you were going to stay within the bounds of the valley and the pass. The hills surrounding this High Vale were low and smooth; if the trolls decided to cross them—if they lived back there somewhere, or if they were trying to throw off pursuit—then there wouldn't be much to stop them.

"Who goes?" a high voice demanded from inside the village.

They didn't have a gate, but they did have an opening in the fort sticks, with a single boy guarding it.

Annoyed, Argur called out, "Who do you think, boy? We're the Knights of Ell, from Nog La."

"The what of what?" the boy demanded in the same tone.

"What do you want?" Another voice called out, from a nearby hilltop outside the village. A woman this time, holding a little cabbage in each hand. She sounded, if anything, more suspicious than the boy.

"We're not staying," Argur assured them both. "We're in pursuit."

"Of what?" asked a third voice. This time a man, again from inside the village.

"Our daughters, nabbed by trolls."

"Oh," said the man. "That's the best. That's the *best*. You're going to get us all killed."

"Take me to your headman," Argur said impatiently. "Or bring him to us."

"He's hunting."

"Of *course* he is," muttered Jek.

Argur paused for a moment, wiped his mouth with his hand, and said, "Look, one of you is going to tell me which way those trolls went, or there's going to be trouble."

A growing crowd of villagers—both inside and outside the fort sticks—glared at the knights, but what could they say? What could they *do*? If they threw a rock or a spear, if they slung a hardmud bullet or leverthrew a dart, the knights would probably block it with a shield, or absorb the impact with their armor. And even if they didn't—even if one of them got injured—what happened next would be ugly and one-sided.

"They take our girls, too," someone finally said.

Someone else scoffed at that. "We *give* them girls."

Argur was brought up short by that. What did that mean? Why would anyone give human girls to a monster?

"To keep the peace," someone answered for him.

For a moment, nobody said anything. And then, suddenly, everyone was speaking at once.

"How could you do such a—"

"We have to keep our end of the—"

"They'll kill you, then our girls, and then—"

"Which way did they mudding *go*, you muddy mud—"

And then, a single voice piercing through: Nortlan's. "Heeey! Close your lips, close your lips, close your *lips!*"

That managed, somehow, to create a moment of general silence, so Nortlan followed with: "How many girls have you given up?"

"Two," someone answered after a pause.

"When?"

"Last year, and the year before."

"Last year and the year before? And what about *this* year? What about *next* year? How many more are they going to ask for? How many can you *lose?*"

Again, silence.

Argur was impressed. Nortlan had always seemed a rather feckless boy, not good at anything and not particularly interested in being good at anything. But most people were afraid to speak to strangers. Mud, some people were afraid to speak to neighbors and friends. But here young Nortlan had commanded the attention of an entire village, plus the Knights of Ell! Clearly, Nismu's blessing had given him courage. Argur was tempted to step in and take over from here, but with some effort he shut his lips and let the boy speak. He wanted to see how this worked out.

"I know you're afraid," Nortlan said in his squeaking voice, raising his oversized shield, causing his oversized armor to rattle around him. "*I'm* afraid. These trolls are frightening creatures, and they seem to have other frightening creatures at their command. They attacked Nog La! In the daylight! With a boolis! But nobody is asking you to fight them."

Again, silence.

"That's what *we're* here for," Nortlan said, now slapping a hand against his shield. And then against Tom's shield, and Argur's, and Jek's. "You see? You see? These men are the Knights of Ell, and they've been fighting monsters since, well, since the world was young. Just lift your arm and point. One of you, all of you, it doesn't matter. Just point to where the trolls live. Which direction do they come from? Which direction do they return to? Just point. Just point."

After all that fuss, Argur was disappointed when the people simply pointed up the trail, toward the other end of their little valley, where Argur and his men were going to look anyway. The Knights all chuckled nervously at that.

"The next valley," someone said.

"They moved in last year," someone else said.

"Nobody was living there. Too many monsters!"

And then a voice from the village said, "We sent them to you. They came to us again, and we told them there were *more* girls, and *better* girls, across the mountains in Nog La. If you attack them, O Knights of Blah Blah, be sure you kill them all. Because they will blame us for this, and *we're* the ones who have to live here. Not you."

Argur was tempted to murder whoever had spoken. In fact, he was tempted to murder all of these people. Had they really done that? Sent the trolls to Nog La, to save their own mudding daughters? But murder was worse than treachery. Murder would poison the whole valley of Nog La, turning spirits and human beings against one another.

So he was even more tempted to just turn and go, to leave these people to their own fate. They filled him with such rage and disgust that he honestly hoped they all would die. Killed by trolls or whatever. But instead he instead took a breath and told them, "If there were men here, they would form a Knighthood of their own. If there were women here, they would demand it. I see nothing but children. This boy"—he pointed at Nortlan—"is braver than all ten of you put together. Think about that. He's off to fight monsters in your name, while you, what, grub for cabbages in the dirt? Enough. Now hear me: you will give nothing more to *okor*. These lands are under our protection, and under our laws. Anyone who violates this will—" he paused to think of a threat, and finally settled on: "—answer to us."

"You also *smell* bad," Jek added.

The rest of the day was filled with frustration. They were told that the next valley over—the highest of the High Vales—was a full day's march away, and they had lost time arguing with the villagers. Not much time, perhaps, but any time was too much. The trolls were faster than they should be, with their short, thick legs. Again, there seemed to be some desperate need goading them along, driving them to work harder, and to do things no troll had ever done before.

Well, Argur and Timlin had a desperate need of their own, and so did all the other Knights who had daughters, or who were not yet married, or who had sons who were not yet married. Even a community as large as Nog La could not lose people without the loss being felt, one way or another, by everyone.

And so they marched across the valley and into the pass, which had no name that Argur had ever heard. Wary of ambushes, the men watched every direction at once, and listened intently for sounds like snapping twigs or birds suddenly changing their tune. But it seemed the trolls were not interested in attacking them here, and were still far enough ahead that all their immediate signs had died down. They did, of course, leave a visible trail—not just trodden earth but also turds and urine stains, the freshly gnawed bones of rabbits and goats and such. There were no bloodstains or entrails, though, which meant the trolls were subsisting on carried provisions. And that by itself was significant, because it meant (again) that they didn't want to be slowed down by hunting game along the way, and it meant that their simple carrying bags—made from partially cured animal hide with the fur still on it—must have been carrying a *lot* of food when they left their valley. Argur had always been told a troll required about twice as much food as a human, so to have enough to travel for four days must have been...well, a lot.

The day was also frustrating because the men were constantly tired. It seemed difficult to catch their breath, somehow. At first Argur thought he was imagining it, and then he thought it was just his own problem, but soon everyone was complaining.

"Perhaps it's *magic* placed upon us by the *villagers*," Jek guessed.

"Or by the trolls?" Nortlan said, a bit worriedly.

And that gave Argur pause. There were a handful of wizards in Nog La, like Nismu of Sunrise Castle, who could call upon the spirit world to accomplish strange things. Nismu could call birds with a block of wood and a stick, and heal sour wounds with maggots and mud. Maggots and mud! Other wizards could tell the sex of an unborn baby, or predict the arrival of a storm or an early winter. In Argur's childhood, a wizard had even been banished for placing a curse on a woman who'd spurned him. He claimed innocence, but she grew ill immediately after their argument, and died soon after. Argur had never doubted these wizards' magic was real, but there was a smallness to it—a quality immediate to their person. The banished wizard, Moget, was perhaps the most powerful Nog La had ever seen, but even he had had to *touch* Akka before she grew ill. He could summon birds, but could not command them. He could predict storms, but could not direct the lightning. Argur had *never* heard of a wizard who could tire out a group of strong men from across an entire valley.

Did trolls possess a stronger magic? They had somehow controlled a boolis, after all. They had somehow attacked in daylight, and carried away three girls and enough food to sustain them on the journey home. They were walking faster than they should be able to.

"Trolls are too stupid," Tom said.

"Perhaps," Argur said uncertainly. "They've always struck me as magical in some way, but it doesn't matter. Have they struck us down with lightning? No? This spirits of this valley are angry, that's all. These people are mud; what spirits would want to watch over them? Their ancestors are ashamed. It has nothing to do with us. We will catch these trolls today."

"And then what?" Nort asked.

It was actually the first time anyone had asked that question.

"And then we'll see," Argur answered, because what else could he say? That they would kill every troll? Certainly not because these idiot villagers demanded it. They would do whatever was necessary.

In fact, though, they *didn't* catch the trolls. The curse of weariness was simply too powerful; it *was* hard for them to catch their breath, and their packs and belts and shields and armor seemed heavier somehow. The sun seemed unnaturally hot, and the shade of trees seemed unnaturally cold. They had to rest frequently, to drink water frequently, so that by the time they had crossed this little valley and climbed partway up into the pass beyond it, the sun was behind the mountains and the light had already begun to fail.

"We can't fight them in the dark," Argur said bitterly. "Even if we catch them, they'd have the advantage."

"We should have brought Nismu with us," Tom said.

"We shouldn't have stopped for *armor*," Jek said. "We could have caught them at the bridge."

"Well, it's done now," Argur growled. "Let's set up camp. Same as yesterday."

This final indignity sat heavily in Argur's gut. Were they not strong enough to save their own daughters? Not swift enough to catch a band of lumbering trolls? Had his own failings as a leader left them soft and vulnerable and incompetent? The trolls would keep right on marching in the twilight, and would get to their home, and start doing whatever it was they did with nabbed girls. It didn't take much imagination to guess; their victims had all been close to puberty. Virgins, unlikely to be pregnant already, but easy to *get* pregnant in short order. It wasn't clear to him why trolls would want to put a troll baby in a human belly, but it was no hard guess that they would attempt it soon, if they hadn't already. As the sky turned dark and the stars came out and the Knights set up their camp, this idea brought Argur close to vomiting several times. And yet, still, with the curse of weariness upon him and hostile spirits all around, he slept.

2.6

They rose early again the next day, packed up their camp, and hurried over and down the pass, into the valley beyond it. This one was all grass and almost no trees. It seemed abundant with grain, which was odd, because as far as Argur knew, trolls didn't eat grain. They did eat meat, though—lots and lots of meat—and this Highest Vale was populated by a brown smudge that Perry declared to be a herd of woolly rhinoceros. Very dangerous, but very far away. He also pointed out several white specks that he said, worriedly, were boolises.

"We'll have to go *way* around those," he said.

"No," Argur told him. "That will cost us time."

"Running into a boolis could cost us more than that," Perry said. His tone was joking, but of course it was no laughing matter.

"Do you see where the trolls live?"

"No," Perry said. Then: "Wait, there's a little sinew of smoke. Oh, mud, they're *right down there*. We're almost right above them."

He pointed. Down below on the sloping hillside, away from the path they were on and nearly hidden among pine trees, Argur could see patterns of red and yellow—a troll's favorite colors. Squinting, he thought he could perhaps make out the forms of tents, and moving figures.

"Quiet your voices," Argur instructed everyone.

"They wouldn't live out there in the *grass*, exposed to the *sun*," Jek murmured, as though this had been obvious all along.

"We need to get closer," Argur said.

"Send someone," Nortlan whispered. "If we all go in, they'll see us."

"Oh, they *will* see us today," Argur agreed.

"No," Nortlan said quietly. "We need a plan. We don't know how many there are, or how they're arranged. We don't know where they're keeping the girls, or if they're tied up."

"He's right," Tom said. "I'll go."

Thinking for a moment, Argur said, "No, Jek is quieter. Will you go look for us, Jek?"

"Why me?" Jek complained.

"Because you walk quietly," Argur repeated. "And because you're brave and strong."

There wasn't much Jek could say to that, so he undid his belt and started sliding his armor off.

"What are you doing?" Nortlan asked, now clearly worried his planning was going to get someone hurt.

"Can't walk quietly in *this*," Jek explained, with considerable irritation.

Argur said, "Jek, if they see you, run straight back here as fast as you can. We'll form a half-circle and lead their fighters into a trap. You see, Nort? We do have a plan."

"I don't want them to see me," Jek said, looking down at himself. At the tan leather of his cloak, and the gray-green linen of his tunic. None of it matched the ground, or the trunks of pine trees. His brown skin would be harder to see, and so he shrugged out of his clothing as well, stripping down to nothing but a loincloth and sandals. He immediately began to shiver, although whether it was fear or just the accursed air, Argur couldn't tell. It didn't matter; approaching a village of trolls in just a loincloth, who wouldn't be afraid?

"Lucky for you I'm so *brave*," Jek said to Argur, then grabbed a little knife and set off down the hill.

Eager to get things moving—to get his daughter away from beasts!—Argur said to the men, "Load darts, but keep a spear handy. It's going to be close among these trees."

"No!" Nortlan whispered.

"No?" Argur asked, annoyed and somewhat incredulous. Did the boy now fancy himself an expert in combat?

Nortlan had a hardmud ball—a sling bullet—which he held up for Argur to see. "How about slings and clubs? Think about it: they didn't kill anyone when they were nabbing the girls. They didn't kill those villagers, either. Do we want to be the *first* to start poking holes?"

"I do," Argur said. Then: "Anyway, a sling's not reliable in woods like this. The bullet can hit a twig, or the sling itself can, and then your whole throw is off."

"But a *lot* of bullets," Nort insisted, "will hurt them, get their attention, even if they're not all on target. We'll let them know what they're up against, without starting a war."

The word he used was borkhuni, *which meant something like "big fight." It wasn't clear to Harv how this implied something different than a mere battle or skirmish, and yet the boy's meaning was clear: turning all of the trolls against all of the humans, everywhere. It also wasn't clear how he thought the news might spread to other trolls, if all the ones here were simply slaughtered. And yet . . .*

The creature back at the bridge had been very clearly a Neandertal. It had the heavy bone structure, the sloping brow, the thick jaw and broad nose with which Neandertals were always depicted in Harv's time. And dressed in furs! Finally, something like a real cave man! And that had pushed back Harv's estimate of the time here, to 30,000 or 40,000 BC. When had the Neandertals gone extinct?

He knew that modern humans of the Cro-Magnon type— Argur's people—had coexisted alongside ancient humans of the Neandertal type for thousands of years, and that did imply some sort of peace between them. Perhaps an uneasy peace, punctuated by violence as the Neandertals slowly went extinct, but certainly not an all-out war.

So perhaps Nortlan's concern was well founded; perhaps the humans—technologically superior but physically weaker—knew not to inflame their neighbors too greatly or too abruptly. Even the Knights of Ell had apparently taken generations—centuries, even—to wrest the valley of Nog La away from them. And still had not fully pushed them out!

But that creature, Lug—at once frightening and pathetic—had also very clearly been a monster from the storybooks of Harv's own time. From its fiery red-brown hair to its wicked-witch voice to its large, vaguely pointy ears and skulking manner, it was everything a troll or ogre or goblin was ever said to be. Could that possibly be a coincidence? Harv didn't see how. And yet, could stories like that persist for thirty thousand years? Was the cultural memory of these encounters that strong, that immutable, that . . . traumatic?

Or perhaps the quantome *memory? Harv was, after all, somehow*

*surfing his own genetic past with the aid of complex technology
even he didn't fully understand. But was that the only way to
access the quantome? Humans must have carried it with them for
a reason. And of course, in spite of Lug's crude voicebox and poor
command of grammar, he had very clearly been a human being. A
strange one, yes, but if you dressed him in khaki pants and a polo
shirt and a baseball cap, he could have ridden the subways of New
York City without drawing more attention than any other burly,
ill-featured man of uncertain intellect. Lug perhaps had more in
common with the under-bridge dwellers of Harv's own time—the
homeless and the abandoned—than he did with Argur's knights,
and* that *was a sobering idea.*

*These thoughts flickered through Harv's mind in the time it
took the clay ball to drop from Nortlan's grasp and into Argur's
open hand.*

Argur held up the sling bullet, examined it for a moment.
Softer and lighter than stone, it could rarely kill a man outright.
He had asked all the knights to pack them for the journey
because... Well, because his daughter was down there. Depending how things went, he didn't want her standing in the middle
of a storm of darts or spears.

"No," he said after a moment's thought. "It's not enough of a
threat. Darts and spears, people, but let's not kill anything that's
not trying to kill us. The rabbit's got a point."

He looked around at the trees, the path, the sloping hillside,
trying to figure out where the trolls would be coming up if they
chased Jek. Would he come straight up here, or would he zigzag
a little, either to dodge missiles or to put his feet on an easier
path? Argur didn't really have a way to know that.

Finally, he gestured. "Ronk, over there, please. Snar and Gower,
there. Perry and Tim, the same distance that way. Nort, you're
here with me. Tom, can you stand behind us, up the hill a ways?"

The men nodded and grumbled and took their stations, waiting. And waiting.

A smorkbird flapped down, settling on a branch.

"Wow!" it said to the men. "Wow! Wow!"

Annoyed, Argur threw a stone at it, hitting it squarely in
the chest. Not hard enough to kill—he had no intention of eating stringy smorkbird for dinner!—but enough to drive it away.

"Wow!" it scolded, then flapped off its branch and away. Down toward the troll camp.

"Wow!" they could hear it saying, somewhere down there.

"Bad," Tom said. "It'll give us away."

It wasn't a crazy worry; smorkbirds would often disrupt a hunt. They were curious creatures, and they knew humans sometimes dropped food scraps, whether intentionally or otherwise. And so they would often settle on a nearby branch and start squawking until every animal in the forest was looking their direction.

After what seemed like a long time, Jek came walking back up the hill. Not running, but just casually walking, with his arms hugged around him. At first Argur thought he must be hurt—perhaps badly hurt, and that brought a splash of fear and guilt. But as Jek approached, Argur didn't see any blood, and the look on Jek's face was more confused than anything else.

"Well?" Argur whispered tensely, when Jek was finally close enough.

"They saw me," Jek said, in a normal speaking voice. "Damn those blue eyes; they looked right at me. All of them. I was quiet, too, but a smorkbird gave away my position."

"Are they coming?" Tom demanded.

"No," Jek said, sounding surprised. "I don't think we have to worry about that. I think we can all just go down there."

"And what?" Tom further demanded. "Hold hands and drink a bowl of gargo?"

"Did you see Dele?" Argur asked, as patiently as he could.

"I think so. I saw *somebody*. It's not just trolls down there."

Nortlan said, "What do you mean it's—"

"Just come see," Jek told them all. The irritation was out of his voice for once, and he seemed genuinely at a loss. "I don't know how to explain it. Just come see."

The men looked to Argur, who thought about it for a moment and then nodded. They waited while Jek shrugged back into his pants and tunic and armor and then, still in their half-circle formation, they began to pick their way downhill. If they'd been heading into a normal battle, they might be bashing weapons against their shields, and groaning out the low war cry that had been known to frighten opponents into outright surrender before the first stone was hurled. But it appeared to be no ordinary battle they were heading to; everyone except Jek and Nortlan had their shields slung across their backs—a longspear dangling from one hand, and a loaded leverthrow raised in the other. Nort—looking more frightened than Argur had ever seen him—wore his shield on one arm, and a club in the other hand. Hard to mess up with either one of those. Jek himself was walking empty-handed, with all of his gear sheathed and slung. It was a bold statement, but one Argur wasn't ready to echo. Instead, he carried a longspear in both hands, held at his hip and pointed forward in what he hoped would be a menacing display.

But who knew what frightened a troll? Lug, back at the bridge, had been the lowliest example of the species that Argur had ever seen. Oh, they tended to skulk, to hide in shadows and to avoid a fair fight when they could, but they were also mammoth hunters! Argur had only been on three mammoth hunts in his life, and while nobody had died, very few had escaped without injury, and none at all without moments of terror. It was deadly serious business, and yet trolls wrapped themselves in mammoth fur like it was nothing at all.

As they approached the village, Argur could see canopies made of brightly pigmented animal hide, glistening with morning dew. Probably mammoth fur, yes, turned inside out and rubbed with spirals of red earth and dandelion. There was one large tent, probably twice the size of a Sunset Castle house, and open at the corners to let air flow through. Apparently, even this chilly air was warm to a troll. The second canopy was nearly as large and entirely open, like a spread-out hand hovering parallel to the ground. One end was supported by four interlocked mammoth tusks, twice as high as a human being. Each edge was propped up by a log that had been driven into the ground and lashed through holes in the leather, and the back side of it was attached to the hillside itself, by ten bone stakes driven deep into the soil. As they got closer still—now coming in from the side rather than directly above—Argur could see that this canopy projected from the mouth of a cave or den of some sort. As wide as a boolis is long, and high enough that a man could walk in without hunching over, it seemed to extend back into the hillside at least a another house length. Not a true cave, for its walls were hard-packed dirt, it was the sort of burrow a giant cave bear might dig.

Beneath the canopies, men and women and children lounged,

fanning themselves with bits of coarse-woven matting. No, not men: trolls. And women? The males had the fierce build every knight knew well, with long hair and beards ranging in color from flame-yellow to mammoth-brown. Eyes ranging from sky blue to thunderstorm gray to the deep yellow of honey. But there were *women* here with the same hair, the same eyes. Or *were* they women? Argur realized, with some surprise, that had never seen a female troll, never really considered what one might look like. Female orr-oxen and rhinoceroses had teats instead of a dong, but otherwise looked basically the same as the males. But these women... Aside from their weirdly pale complexions—some of them as pale as moonlight!—these women looked almost human. Thinner and lighter than their males, they had smaller ears and smaller noses, and could not properly be described as ugly. Some of them, not ugly at all.

And the children?

These were even stranger, because some of them *did* have black hair and brown skin, almost like a person. In fact, some of them clearly *were* people—the nabbed children of human tribes. But the funny thing was, they didn't look that different from the children who were obviously trolls. Oh, they were a bit less bulky, but they all had basically the same body and facial structure. What a fate! What dark magic had cursed this species, that their children might turn from slender little scoop-eared humans into hulking monsters? It was the same fate the boolises suffered, or perhaps the curse was the other way around: strong parents giving birth to frail, vulnerable children. But wouldn't that mean *human beings* were the accursed ones? *Never* growing big and strong and ugly? Was that what a troll would think?

And then he remembered why he was here, and called out: "Dele! Are you here? Dele!"

And a voice came back: "Father?"

"Dele?"

"Father! What are you doing here?"

And then she was there, emerging from the cave in a torn-and-mended blue tunic. Blinking at the sunlight, holding a hand up over her eyes.

Argur wanted to rush to her. He wanted *her* to rush to *him*, but she was surrounded by monsters, and half-monstrous women, and stayed where she was.

"What are you doing here?" she asked again.

"We're here to rescue you," Argur said, as though it were obvious. Wasn't it? Shouldn't it be?

Dele had a large, scuffed bruise on her arm, and a small one on her cheek, but otherwise looked basically intact. Two other young women came out and stood beside her: Timlin's daughter Maga, and a girl named Val whom Argur had never really gotten to know. Neither of them appeared especially damaged, either. None of them looked afraid, and none looked especially overjoyed at the sight of their rescuers.

What was going on here? He looked around again, more carefully now. The first thing he noticed—what he should have noticed right away—was that there were *wolves* nearby. A whole pack of them, sitting nervously off in the trees, as if unsure what to do. Argur could even smell them, now that he was paying attention! But the trolls were paying *no* attention to the wolves—no fear, no anything. Why not?

The second thing Argur noticed was that there were a lot more females and children here than adult male trolls. Taking a breath, he actually *counted* the males, and came up with a total of seven. All of their faces were pink and peeling, as if they'd been burned in a fire, and all seven had been lying down, as if exhausted. The sight of armed and armored humans, marching on their camp with loaded leverthrows, had persuaded them to grab weapons and stand, but they looked... well, neither afraid nor angry nor guilty nor particularly surprised. Just... resigned. Their faces were calm and a little bit grim, like they'd been expecting this, and were up to the challenge, but were really very much hoping to get out of it without a fight.

"Is this their whole village?" Nortlan asked Argur, as if he would know. "Did they send *every single man* down into Nog La?"

It appeared so. Now that Argur studied them, it also appeared that the eldest two trolls were afflicted with some kind of illness—their pale faces broken out in black, angry-looking welts. Some of the female trolls appeared to be afflicted as well. This band of creatures did not appear to be having good luck.

"Did they send *sick men* on a girl-nabbing expedition?" Nortlan asked, again as though Argur might know something he didn't.

"Will you close your *lips*?" Jek said to him.

Unable to bear it any longer, Argur barked at his daughter:

"Dele! Explain yourself! What the nameless spirits is going on here?"

Dele sighed, in a manner that suggested she couldn't easily answer that. "Father, will you put down those weapons? Before you hurt somebody?"

"These are *trolls*," Timlin said to his own daughter. "You were *nabbed*, by *trolls*. Get over here now."

"Father, you're scaring me," Maga said.

"This is complicated," added the third girl, Val. "It's true we were nabbed, but we've come to see these men and women are not true enemies. You need to put those weapons down. Please. *All* of us are in danger if you don't calm down."

For a moment, Argur had to admire the poise and confidence of these young women. Of *all* young women; where did they find it in themselves, to lecture men who were much older and much stronger than they were? When exactly did they become so certain they knew better? *Did* they know better? These girls certainly seemed to have more information than the Knights of Ell.

He paused for a long moment and then finally said to his men, "Unload darts."

Behind him, Tom stirred at that. "No, Argur, no. We don't know what's going on here."

"No, but *they* seem to. Unload darts, please. One at a time, and slowly. You can each hang onto a spear. Or club," he added, thinking of Nort.

Slowly, reluctantly, the knights did as he asked. Now what?

"Explain yourself," Argur said again to Dele.

"All right. Firstly, I know what you're thinking, but no one has touched us. Not that way."

Argur let out a huge sigh of relief.

"Nextly, these people have tried to talk to you. More than once."

"People?" sneered one of the men behind Argur.

"They can talk?" said someone else.

Dele glared at that, saying nothing.

"*Some*thing has touched *some*body," Jek said, pointing to a trio of what appeared to be red-haired human toddlers.

"Not without permission," said another woman. A human woman, a year or two older than Dele. "I'm Moti, a woman of the High Vale. What is that thing on your head?"

Argur reached up, and touched the bearskin hairpiece he'd been wearing for days.

"It's hair," he explained. "Now what are you talking about?"

"That's complicated," Moti said. "I was delivered here against my will, yes, traded for promises of safety. But these people have treated me well, and eventually it was my choice to bear the children of Nak, a man of this tribe."

Several of the Knights of Ell made sounds of unfeigned disgust.

"Ah, you think you're better?" Moti sneered. "Better than a 'troll'? Nak, call the wolves."

One of the trolls—apparently the one named "Nak"—responded with a very human look of annoyance at being told what to do. And yet, he placed two fingers in his mouth and emitted a piercing whistle. Then he began to, well, *sing*. His trollish voice was high and rough, but he made it work—the wordless notes rising and falling in his throat, formed into sounds by his circled lips, widening and narrowing. *Oh-Weh-oh-Weh-ohhhh! Oh-Weh-oh-Weh-ahhhh!* Truthfully, he had a better singing voice than a lot of humans Argur could name.

The ten wolves responded immediately; they had been sitting, on their butts, but now they rose to their feet, wagging their tails and whining slightly. They moved forward, slowly, out of the trees and into the midst of the trolls and women and children, who seemed unafraid.

Unafraid, of wolves.

The Knights of Ell didn't know what to make of that. Tensing, raising spears, stepping back a meter or two, they watched this display the way a cop might watch a drunken suspect, or a group of construction workers might look at a group of armed dancers frolicking in the street. Harv surfaced for long enough to understand, and appreciate, what it meant to make history, *to be the first person to see or hear or smell a thing that had never happened before. And have no fucking idea what to do.*

"You see?" Moti demanded.

"See what?" Tom flung back. "Animals living among animals?"

"Close your lips," Argur told him. "I need...a moment to think. Dele, come over here."

"No," Dele said. "Not until you make promises."

"*Promises!*" snorted Jek.

"You're strangers here," Moti said. "Extremely rude strangers. These men are magicians, not animals, and you've given them only this awful valley to call their home, where vegetables rarely grow. Where the sun burns their skin in half a morning. And now you invade here as well? How dare you."

"How dare *we*?" someone asked.

And then Nak spoke: "Talk! No fight."

That sent a stirring among the Knights. It was one thing for a miserable creature like Lug, cringing under his bridge, to request conversation rather than violence. But this troll named Nak appeared eerily calm; there was a sense of controlled violence about him, and something that was closer to disappointment than fear; *yes, I might get killed today. What a shame.* He was clearly more than capable of defending himself, of defending his tribe. Spirit's sake, he had *wolves* at his command!

Argur looked around at his men, and wondered if they could even win this fight. Maybe, if the troll women didn't participate. Were troll women fighters? He didn't know. But he didn't like the numbers in any case. "Maybe" was not a good way to begin.

"Pull back," he said to his men.

"What?" Tom hissed.

"Pull back. We need to think about this." To Nak and Moti he said, "Nobody touches those girls, or it's going to get ugly here. We're going to go speak among ourselves for a short while."

"Yes," Moti said, a bit haughtily. "You do that."

"Argur," said the protesting voices of ten Knights.

"Pull back," he insisted. "Downhill, down there. That clearing."

He pointed with a spear. It wasn't exactly a clearing; the hills surrounding this valley were covered in patches of forest, but the valley itself was mostly bare grass, and the spot Argur was pointing to was right at the edge—stalks of barleygrass rippling in the morning breeze, beside the hillside's whispering pines. It was a valley-sized clearing, all right, but he wanted to get away quickly, saying as little as possible within earshot of trolls and women. He wanted time to think, and to speak with his advisors, and to get over the idea that Dele—his own precious daughter—would rather stay with monsters at this moment than come away with her own father. What had they done to her? Or, alternatively, what did she know that he didn't?

There were things here that he was not understanding, and he didn't like that. The job of a Knight was to kill things, capture things, drive things away. The job of a *headman* was to talk and understand, and Argur realized he had always been a much better Knight than headman. But what did that even mean? That he'd killed and driven away things he should have talked to instead? Did one negotiate with a snow leopard?

He saw Tom whispering in the ear of Jek, and then, when they were safely out of trollish earshot, Tom said, loud enough for everyone to hear, "Are we circling back for an uphill advantage?"

"No, we're going down there. To talk."

"Talk about what? Argur, they have your daughter! And if they attack us downhill, from the cover of trees, while we stand around in the open..."

"They've had plenty of opportunity."

"They were outnumbered and surprised!"

"Hardly."

And then Nortlan said, "They have magic."

To which Jek replied, mockingly, "Ooh, magic."

"They have *wolves*," Perry said. "And strong women, maybe? If they're concentrated together like that, we don't have an advantage. It's better if they *do* come down and attack us on the grass. Pick them off as they come."

Clearly, no one was going to wait until they got down there to start talking, so Argur told them, "They've got our own girls taking their side. Our bruised, nabbed girls. I want to know how the trolls did that."

"Magic, obviously," said Nortlan.

"Maybe," said Argur, "Or maybe we don't have the whole story. We need to go back up there, sit down around the fire, and let somebody tell us what's going on."

"And drink *gargo* and hold hands until they slit our throats," Tom sneered.

"I think we can kill them all," Gower said, "and I think we should."

Tom nodded to him, punched him in the arm approvingly, and murmured something to him that Argur couldn't quite catch.

"They haven't killed us," Ronk said. "Bad luck if we're the first to draw blood."

"They nabbed our girls!" Timlin shouted, probably loud enough for the trolls to hear.

"*Quiet,*" Jek told him.

"Hey! Hey!" Argur whispered loudly. "Everyone close your lips! We can't all talk at once. Rabbit, what do you think?"

Nortlan paused, looking around at the men before saying, "I think those wolves could eat a lot of rats."

"Meaning what?" Tom demanded. "We should invite them all to Nog La? Trolls are cannibals, did you know that? They eat their dead. They eat *our* dead."

"Not often," Perry said.

"Everyone, be *quiet!*" Argur repeated. "You'll get your turn. Nort, speak."

Nort looked around again, uncertainly, before answering. "If they want to talk, we should talk. I think we could learn a lot from them. Their magic is...impressive. But we'd have to offer them something in return. Not our women! Right? Not our women. But something. It doesn't look like they're doing so well up here."

"Good," Tom said. "They don't deserve to."

Argur glared at him, and then said, "Your turn is now *last,* Tom. Speak out again, and your turn is never. Perry, what do you think?"

Perry looked thoughtful for a long moment, like there were many factors to consider, and one of them was not wanting to give offense to the men whose daughters and nieces were still up there.

"Speak!" Argur told him impatiently.

"You're not the only one who needs to think," Perry objected. "I...I think these are dangerous creatures."

"And?"

"And what? They're dangerous. Very brave hunters, but also sometimes thieves and poachers and scavengers and cannibals. Their skin is the color of worms, Argur."

"What's that got to do with it?"

Perry shrugged. It appeared he'd said all he needed to.

Argur sighed, then looked to Timlin, who said, "It would be dangerous to leave them alive. Also dangerous to fight them on their home terrain. But we can't leave the girls with them, obviously. Or the women they've cursed into loving them."

"Hmm. And?"

"Well, we should *threaten* them. I don't know why we haven't threatened them, Argur. Maybe kill one, as an example."

That sounded like a particularly bad idea, but Argur wasn't yet ready to start making statements of his own.

"What about the little children?" Ronk asked, when it was his turn. "They look human to me. What bad magic turns them into trolls as they grow?"

"What are you saying?" Argur asked.

"I don't know which ones we should take with us when we go."

"Hmm. Hmm, yes. It's a troubling question. Snar, you've been quiet. Do you have an opinion?"

Snar had a faraway look as he answered, "I think...I think... there's a boolis coming this way."

He pointed.

"Oh, mud," Perry said, following his gaze. "He's right."

Now everyone looked, and indeed, there was a little white blob down there on the grasslands, that was moving toward them rapidly. Argur squinted, and could see that it was, indeed boolis shaped. He even fancied he could hear the slamming of its feet against the ground as it ran.

"Hmm," he said, trying to sound calm. There was time. It wasn't upon them yet. "Let's put the troll camp between us and it, shall we?"

"My daughter's in that camp," Timlin reminded him.

"Boolises don't go in caves," Argur said. "The girls can hide back in there. I want the trolls and wolves to deal with this thing, not us."

"It could tire them out," Tom said approvingly. "Maybe even thin their numbers."

"We don't have much time," Snar pointed out.

"I agree," Argur said. "Run!"

Most animals had poor eyesight, and while most also had a good sense of smell, that was not a good way to identify the precise locations of things that were far away. Nevertheless, the boolis seemed to know exactly where they were. It charged toward them in bursts, stopping every so often to lower its head and paw at the ground in a territorial display, and then thundered into motion again.

The Knights were not at their swiftest right now, cursed with weariness and going uphill all loaded with gear. But still they ran, strung out in a line like knotted rope, and worked their way back up, to the right of the troll camp and then just above it. As the men arrived, one by one, they froze in place, grabbing trees and panting, trying not to give the boolis any moving targets to pick up against the background litter of the forest.

Annoyed shouts rose up from the camp itself; Argur's plan had worked. The boolis was now charging the trolls! However, the giant beast seemed to think twice about this. Its run slowed, and then stopped. It stood below the camp, breathing heavily and pawing the ground, just outside of stone-throwing range. Apparently, it knew *exactly* what it was dealing with, here.

"Fair's fair," Tom murmured, looking down with satisfaction. "Come on, charge!"

But one of the trolls stepped forward, holding a spear at waist level, making stabbing motions. And then sang in its shrill voice: *Ohhhhh-aaaaaah! Ohhhhh-aaaaaah!*

The boolis seemed to recognize that as well; it pawed the hillside for an angry moment, and then began to retreat. After a moment, it turned around and actually began, slowly, walking back down the hill where it had come from.

Argur eyed the troll and wondered about this magic of theirs. Did they learn it? Were they born with it? Were the animals born recognizing it, or did they need to be taught the meanings of different songs? Argur had fought against trolls five times in his life, had even killed one once. He had chased them away more times than he could count, and he had talked to them . . . once? Two days ago, when he spoke to Lug, at the bridge?

From the camp below, Moti called up: "Rude men! Did you think that would *work*? You send a boolis to trample these men, who command the wolves of the forest?"

Argur, panting for breath, called back, "Sorry! It chased us."

"Yes," Moti said. "They do that. Are you surprised?"

"It surprised us, yes," Argur answered carefully. Then he said, "Tom, we need to . . . Tom?"

Looking for his friend, he turned around just in time to see Tom's club swinging into the side of his head.

The world blinked for a moment, and Argur was on his knees, barely. One light breeze and he'd be on his side. He struggled to understand what had just happened: Tom stood over him with a club. For what? Attacking what?

"Tom?"

"That's going to hurt more than I intended. I was trying to hit you across the back of the skull."

But that didn't make any sense. Why would Tom hit Argur with a club?

Tom nodded, a sorrowful look on his face. "This, too."

And swung the club again. This time, Argur had a moment to comprehend that Tom's turn to speak had finally arrived.

"Oh, Tom," he had time to say, before the club connected and he went down.

The world blinked again (or did it?), and he thought he saw Nortlan standing over him asking what happened, what happened, and then a murky figure was swinging the butt end of a spear and Nortlan was down on the ground as well, and then somehow Argur was crawling. Did *that* make sense? He wasn't sure. And then he found himself looking out between the edge of the hill and the red-and-yellow rhino-hide canopy jutting out from it. Through this sliver he could see men and women and children, or perhaps trolls and trollettes and troll-lings, milling around in evident alarm. Like ants or bees or swimming ducks.

"Load darts," said a faraway voice. "Drop everything that doesn't look human."

And then there was a thumping sound, and someone was screaming, and blood somehow splashed across Argur's arm. And then the wolves here howling, and the trolls were screaming in their ugly-high voices, and then Dele was down there, holding her arms out and shouting no, no, and there was a rather delicate-looking female troll behind her and she was shielding it. It warmed him to see her acting with such foolish bravery, if only for a moment, but then (did the world blink again?) there was a dart sticking out of her chest. And that *definitely* did not make sense.

"No," he told the world. And then, as he watched his daughter fall, spurting blood from her chest and mouth, he explained it more emphatically: "No! Not that at all."

And when that didn't work—when she hit the ground in a pile of awkward limbs, her eyes staring blankly at the sky—he did the only other thing he could think of: he closed his own eyes and let the weariness send him to the spirit world.

✧　　✧　　✧

That night, beside the campfire, Argur slowly remembered how to count. There were one-two-three-*four* Knights of Ell: Snar, Jek, Timlin, and Gower. Or actually it was five, counting Argur himself. Tom, Nortlan, Ronk and Perry were nowhere to be seen.

There were one-two-three-four-*five* young women: Moti, Val, and Maga, plus two he didn't know. Dele, too was nowhere to be seen. Moti and Maga would not stop crying, but Val and the others seemed to be mostly all right.

There were no trolls here, male or female.

There were one-two-three-four-*five* young children: a girl and a boy with black hair, and a girl and *two* boys with orange. None of them had mushroom-white skin. These, also, would not stop crying.

Above him was a red and yellow canopy of rhino skin.

Argur could make no sense of any of this, and so he rolled over and went back to sleep.

2.7

The next morning, almost as soon as Argur had opened his eyes, the girl named Val came over and wordlessly offered him a skin of water. Sitting up awkwardly, he accepted it and drank quite a bit. His throat was dry, his skull a throbbing mass wrapped in painful, swollen flesh. He could only open his eyes partway, and although his arms worked, they seemed clumsy and far-off.

"How are you feeling?" Val asked him.

"Bad," he told her truthfully. He touched the side of his head, and felt bandages there. Bandages and a lump the size of a goose egg. About right, yes, for the hits he'd taken. And then he asked the question: "Dele?"

With immense sadness, Val shook her head. No, no Dele.

The answer hit him like autumn leaves, swirling and scratching and then gone. He was hollow, as if his gutted carcass had been sat up. He was pain wrapped around nothing at all.

Val looked him over for a few moments, and then asked, "Would you like some food? A nice bit of fatty ham?"

He didn't have an answer for that. He barely understood the question.

He looked around and saw his men packing things up, as if to travel. Around the edges of the camp there were five piles of stones and dirt. Fresh graves. There were drag marks everywhere, leading out to piles of dead trolls, dead wolves. Dead vultures, even.

"Trolls bury their dead," he tried to say to Val. It was wrong to leave them out like that, to rot. On the occasions when the Knights of Ell killed a troll, they always buried it, lest its spirit—or its living

184

relatives—seek vengeance. But his voice was slurred, incomprehensible even to himself, and Val just looked at him strangely.

"Can he walk?" Gower asked Val.

She looked at Argur. "Can you?"

That question made more sense, so he put a hand down and tried to lever himself off the ground. She bent to help him, and in a little while he was up. Leaning heavily on her, but up.

"He's going to need help," she said.

"I'll help him," Gower told her.

"We'll take *turns*," Jek said. "It's a long walk."

"Mostly down," Gower said. "But all right. Turns."

And so they walked. Not quickly, because the little children were even slower than Argur was, and they were too big to be carried by the young women for any great distance, and yet they refused to be carried by any of the Knights, whom they seemed to regard as terrifying figures. Argur didn't blame them. Their entire tribe had just been murdered, and they themselves were being nabbed. Maybe in the future they wouldn't remember this day. Maybe. But for right now they were on a forced march, among enemies.

"You missed quite a *battle*," Jek told him at one point, as he helped Argur up the rocky pass.

Argur only grunted in reply. A part of him wondered exactly what had happened: who had killed whom, and in what order. Who had fought bravely, and who had tried not to fight at all. Who had participated in his betrayal—was he also among enemies? But he was hollow, now, and couldn't really bring himself to care.

The woman named Moti seemed to be in a similar mood; mostly out of breath on their long hike, and occasionally overflowing with tears, she no longer appeared haughty or angry. She no longer appeared to be anything at all.

They must have passed the High Vale village somewhere along the way. Moti's village, and that of the two other women Argur hadn't met. And yet, these women walked on with the Knights, toward Nog La. Perhaps it was the best of their limited options: go home to the families who'd sold them, or go along with the men who'd tried—however badly—to rescue them. Who had in fact—however badly—succeeded.

The day was a blur to Argur, as though he'd spun himself dizzy and was wandering crazily not only across the ground, but through time. The group was headed downhill now, and each of his steps landed heavily, his sandals slamming and tugging at his feet. He was tired and in pain—every step and every moment were an agony beyond anything he'd previously imagined. And yet, he didn't seem to mind very much, and the end of the day seemed to come so quickly that at first he thought they'd only stopped for lunch.

But no, it was dark, and they were all sitting around a fire again. Or was it two fires? One for the knights and their daughters, and one for the women and children of the trolls. Enemy camps. Which one did Argur belong in?

"In all, we came out of this pretty *well*," Jek's voice was saying, distantly. "At the beginning we were *down* three people. Now we're down *five*, and up ten."

"Close your lips," Gower told him.

"It's like we've created some *people* out of *nothing*."

"Close them or I'll smash you."

And Snar was saying, "We lost knights and gained babies. You call that good trading?"

To which Gower said, "I'll smash you, too! Take watch, both of you. Lips closed. And Jek, if you make love to that hardmud woman tonight I'll jam her straight up your ass. Promise."

And then it was morning again.

Argur's spirit had been knocked out of his body, but not fully into the spirit world itself. It might have stayed that way until his body finally died, but instead parts of it began to return on that second day; he needed less help walking, and he kept better track of time. Better track of other people's conversations, too; when Jek told Snar that he'd heard a smorkbird up ahead, Argur actually answered with, "No, that's a spearsbeak."

"What?" Jek said, looking at Argur in surprise.

"Gloomier than a smorkbird," Argur told him. And then, after a moment's thought, "And lonelier."

"So," Jek said. "You're in there after all."

"Mmm," Argur answered, looking away. His attention had its limits.

And yet, it was not the only conversation he was drawn into that day, and when it became clear that the group could actually make it all the way back to Sunrise Castle before the sky grew fully dark, he actually exerted some leadership, saying: "No, let's not. Sad news is best delivered in the morning."

So they camped again, stopping early, setting up fortifications even though they all agreed this stretch of canyon had been quite well patrolled over the past few days, and was unlikely to contain any nasty surprises. "But we have toddlers," Argur said, to general agreement. With an open camp, it would take almost nothing for a snow leopard to slip out of the shadows and drag a child off into the brush, possibly without anyone even noticing.

"We didn't take the time last night," Gower said. "That was dumb."

"Mmm," Argur agreed.

He still didn't know which of these men were on his side. Any? All? He half-hoped they would murder him in his sleep, but of course they could have done that at any time. And perhaps the terrible consequence of acting rashly had affected their thinking; they all seemed happy enough to follow Argur's advice now. He thought again about confronting them, demanding explanations, but again, he didn't seem to care enough. One way or another, these men had either killed his little girl or stood by while it happened.

That night as the light was fading, he sat down by the fortification line and shrugged out of his armor. He then rolled it up and tied it into a bundle, which he stuffed in his bag. He wasn't going to let it tell him who he was anymore. And this, along with his general air of silence and confusion, seemed to render him less terrifying to the children, who did not shrink away when he settled down next to their fire.

In the morning, he found that one of the little girls had even curled up against the small of his back. Was she a troll? A human? A blending of the two, like red pigment mixed with yellow? Did it even matter? Perhaps Argur's brain or his spirit were damaged, but he couldn't remember why anyone had ever cared about this.

"Let's go deliver the news," he told everyone, with more confidence than he was actually feeling.

At the bridge, they stopped to wash their hands in the cold water below. Argur splashed water on his face as well, which felt good, and woke him up a bit. At first it seemed the troll, Lug, was nowhere around. And why would he be? The Knights of Ell were a band of murderers.

"You see the troll anywhere?" Gower asked no one in particular.

But nobody did, and so they climbed back up on the path, flicking their wet hands and wiping them together to dry them without touching anything.

Argur was not satisfied with this, and so he called out: "Lug?" Then sang: "Luu-uuug!"

There was no reply, which made Argur feel oddly sad. And so they headed back down the path again, into the valley proper, toward their sad duty. Spears and clubs clacked against rattling armor, but nobody spoke.

And then, to Argur's surprise, a shrill voice called after them: "More girls! Less men!"

Argur turned. "Ah, Lug. Were you hiding from us?"

Indeed, the troll was at the edge of a stand of trees, well outside the range of darts or even sling bullets. He appeared ready to flee, trusting nothing. And he was right: the numbers here spoke as clearly as any voice, that the knights had brought violence and death to his distant people, who after all had been nabbers and thieves and arguably rapists of a sort, but not actually murderers. When was the last time a troll had ever killed a human who hadn't specifically attacked it? Had it happened in Argur's lifetime at all?

Argur said, "I'm sorry you feel the need to hide from us, brother troll. Yes, we were in a fight—a bad one. We lost good men, and I think we killed good men as well."

"Bad," Lug observed.

"Yes. Bad. I prefer peace."

"Peace?" Lug called out, as if unfamiliar with the word.

So Argur told him, "If you do no harm, and if you obey the spirits of Nog La, then no one will harm you. You may stay in the valley, and even trade with Sunrise Castle."

"Trade?"

Argur sighed. This was the longest conversation he'd had since...well, since he got hit on the head, and he was quickly running out of energy for it. "We'll talk about it some other time."

And it seemed Lug had had enough, too, for he took off running into the trees, his strong, stumpy legs carrying him away. For a moment, there was only the sound of the wind.

And then Jek spoke: "Why do you *talk* to that thing, Argur?"

"Close your lips," Gower warned him.

And Argur, summoning the last strength of his spirit, said, "Do you see how much this fighting has cost us, Jek? A troll smiles at his children, same as we do." He might have said a bit more, but his throat closed on him and would make no further sound.

They resumed walking again.

When they finally came within sight of the castle, they could hear shouts from the watch towers. Excited at first, and then... concerned, as the boys on watch counted tall bodies and short ones, and realized something was badly wrong. By the time knights and children and young women had arrived in front of the gate, the two old men guarding it—Sower and Lancho—looked grim.

"Is this all?" Lancho wanted to know.

"This is everyone," Gower confirmed.

Lancho rolled his tongue in his cheek for a moment, then clicked it twice in reproach. "You should have caught them here. What did you do, follow them all the way home?"

"Close your lips," Gower said to him.

To which Moti added, "Things went badly. These men attacked everything in sight, including each other."

"*Close your lips*," Gower said to her, raising a hand as if to smack her.

Ignoring him, Moti told Lancho, "Don't worry, though: you won't be hearing from those trolls again. The Knights of Ell were quite thorough."

"Who are all these children? And women?" Lancho demanded.

It was too much for Gower, who cross-checked him with a spear, flat across the chest, pushing him back. "When you are young and brave again, Lancho, you may tell us how to fight. But I told you to shut them, and I mean it. We're in no mood to hear you."

Lancho, who used to be headman before Argur, visibly thought about pushing back, or at least about *talking* back, but appeared to decide against it. Instead he nodded his head and let the group pass him.

They were watched by girls, boys, old men, old women, and by the men and women who had not yet gone out to hunt or gather or fish or look for spearwood or knapping flint. They were watched by Gouch, who had stayed home with a sprained wrist.

"What happened?" he asked.

"Casualties," his brother Snar answered.

Argur asked him, "What of the boolis? Did Sunset Castle deal with it?"

"Yeah," Gouch said. "Drove it up the side of the valley and out into the mountains. Last I saw, it was running at full gallop. But they've got casualties, too. One of their men broke both legs, and maybe his back. And Pagel was there with them, and hit his head. He's been sleeping for two days now. Margle has gone there to be with him. I'm worried, Argur."

"Hmm," Argur said. More bad news. So perhaps the trolls *had* killed someone, but why? What drove them to it? The same thing that drove them out of Nog La: conflict. "Unfortunate. Perhaps this is what we get in trade, for leaving the trolls nowhere to live."

"Oh, the poor trolls!" Jek muttered, not quite loud enough to attract intervention by Gower.

"Yes," Moti said. "The poor trolls."

Ignoring them, Argur strode to the home of Nortlan's parents. They were standing outside, already aware that something was going on.

"Where's my boy?" the father, Pock, demanded. He was lazy and nasty and sometimes a thief—particularly of *gargo*, when anyone had it—but perhaps he loved his child as much as anyone else.

"I'm sorry," Argur said. "He was killed in the fight."

"No!" shrieked Nanka, the mother. She was also lazy, and a brutal gossip, and Argur had never observer her being particularly kind to her son. And yet, her eyes welled up with tears, and her throat choked with sobs.

"This is your fault," Pock spat. "You made him go with you. He was still just a boy!"

"That's true. I did. And I'm sorry. A lot of poor decisions were made, by everyone involved."

"Eat mud, Argur."

To that, he had no reply.

He delivered similar messages to the households of Ronk and Perry, his heart growing heavier, and his spirit fuzzier, with every word he spoke.

To Tom's wife, Birgny, he almost said, "Your husband betrayed our people and got my daughter killed. Along with himself, and Nortlan. And Ronk, and Perry. We lost *so much* because your husband insisted on fighting a strong enemy, when they wanted to talk. May your husband's spirit wander forever."

What he said instead was, "It was crazy up there."

"Crazy," she said back to him, the tears streaming down her face.

"I didn't see him fall, but I know he was brave."

"Brave," she said back to him.

"Yes."

"And what am I to do now, Argur?"

"I don't know."

"You don't know? I have babies to feed."

"No, I don't know. I suppose we'll figure something out."

"We'll *figure something out?*"

This conversation was making Argur's head hurt again, so he retreated, apologizing again and again.

And then he headed home to Dala.

Oh, spirits, what was he going to say? What could he possibly? He pulled aside the curtain door and stepped inside, somehow knowing he would find her there, right where she'd been on the last good morning of their lives.

And he did. She was.

"Hello, my love," she said, looking up from the embers of a fire she'd been poking with a stick.

"Dala..."

"I know. Argur, I know. You've been gone *four days.* I wasn't sure you were coming back at all. I wasn't sure anyone was."

"Dele had..."

"I know."

"I tried..."

"I know. I know you did. And I know *she* tried as well, to come back to me."

"I'm so sorry, Dala."

"I know that, too. My love, there's nothing you need to tell me. The world is full of monsters, and I watched a group of them nab my daughter. And as you chased after them, with such a late, slow start, I thought about it, and knew it couldn't possibly go well."

"They're not monsters," Argur said gently. "I saw them. I heard them. They're people."

"Hmm," Dala said, considering that. And finally she said, "Is that any better?"

✧   ✧   ✧

At this point, Harv's awareness slid and jumped and found itself in another person, a young man. A son born to Argur and Dala in later years, who saw his father in a very different light than Harv had. The older Argur, with gray in his beard, was a sorcerer or shaman of sorts. Having relinquished his armor and focused instead on leading the tribe wisely (along with some hunting, of course), he spent most of his time walking around the castle and its neighboring villages, dispensing counsel and judgment to those who sought it. He paid particular attention to those few young people who had red-brown hair and light-colored skin and vaguely pointed ears; where others might call them "trollman" or "knife-ear girl" or "fat fat fatty" (all of which rhymed in the language of Nog La), he considered these men and women to be vaguely magical and perhaps good luck, and often asked them to bless the weapons of hunters and the looms of weavers, and the houses of newly married couples. He also treated people's injuries and illnesses, performed weddings and funerals, and—most strangely, from the son's point of view—sang to animals.

The son, whose name was Nortlan, was mortified by all of this, and spent the majority of his time training to be a knight and large-game hunter. However, the need for knights had steadily diminished in Nog La, as many of the most dangerous animals seemed fewer in numbers, and less inclined to bother humans. Many in the tribe gave Argur the credit for this, as his singing really could soothe savage beasts, or at least confuse them, and when his own voice was not enough he would sometimes puff out a series of gentle notes on his flute. Or shrill ones; most animals would retreat from this, and he had more than once been observed chasing creatures out of the valley altogether.

(The recovered memories here were jumbled—more like previews of a movie than the movie itself—but Harv saw enough of this to wonder whether music might not perhaps be the second most important technology humans had ever developed, after fire. Argur would also sing to human beings, and although his voice was famously rough, his music nevertheless brought comfort where comfort was needed. There really was a kind of power in it.)

But Nortlan, like many of the knights themselves, believed the matter was simply down to their own diligent efforts to kill or drive out anything that was too dangerous, too hard to kill, or at least not tasty enough to be worth the risk. Snow leopards? Gone.

Hyenas? Gone. Wooly rhinoceroses? Only the smaller ones, with the least dangerous horns, were permitted to remain. The others were killed or driven away, along with the last few remaining mammoths.

And with this decrease in overall danger, the women started paying more and better attention to their grain and vegetable patches, and it occurred to Harv that civilization could very well have started right here, fifteen thousand years early. All of the ingredients were in place! But then the weather changed, and the summers got too rainy and the winters got too long, and he sort of lost the thread of it after that, except for a general sense that there were other good places in the world as well, scattered throughout prehistory, and it was only by a series of coincidences that Kingdom happened to be the first to really get out of the Stone Age.

But even they hadn't lasted. Perhaps nothing ever did.

University of Colorado Engineering Center
Boulder, Colorado
Present Day

"How many fingers do you see?" one of the paramedics beside Tara was asking.

"Three," Harv answered, finally lucid again. He was speaking through an oxygen mask held over his nose and mouth with a rubber band behind his head.

Strapped to a gurney in the hallway outside the lab, with Tara hovering over him nervously, he seemed strangely calm. She was afraid for his health and safety, and (truthfully) for her own reputation—both professional and personal. Uncertain of her role or status or whatever, she'd wept and held his hand and explained his condition to the paramedics as best she could. Thankfully, neither of them had asked her whether she was sleeping with the patient, or was on his payroll, or both. Neither had asked if she was a good Hindu girl or just some postdoc who couldn't keep her hands off the faculty.

"Oh, thank God," Tara said. It was one of many American phrases she'd absorbed over the last five years, until it practically leaked from her pores.

"Pupil responses look good. Can you follow this light for me?" the paramedic asked. He was a big man, buzz-cut and strong, with scissors and tweezers and tongue depressors sticking out from the numerous pockets in his short-sleeved uniform. His partner—a gray-haired, no-nonsense woman—was hanging a bag of saline on the gurney's IV pole.

"Good," the paramedic said. "Can you tell me your name?"

"Harv Leonel."

194

"And you work here?"

"Yes."

"Mr. Leonel, you've suffered an atonic focal seizure with loss of consciousness. Two of them, apparently. Do you suffer from a seizure disorder?"

"It's *Doctor* Leonel. And no."

"Can you think of any reason you might have gotten sick?"

Harv seemed to consider that for a moment, and then met Tara's gaze, and seemed to understand that she'd already told them everything. He answered, "We were using an experimental brain stimulation system."

"Magnetic? A TMS?"

"Yes."

"Are you on any medications?"

"Just low-dose aspirin."

"And have you had any of that today?"

"No."

The female paramedic took out some sort of handheld and started tapping its screen.

"How do you feel now?"

"Sleepy," Harv said. "I haven't seen this place for thirty thousand years."

The paramedics didn't like that one bit.

"Tara," Harv said, "were there wooden castles in Europe when the Neandertals were still alive?"

"What? I don't know." The question startled her, although she supposed it shouldn't have.

"I'd like you to focus on me," the male paramedic told Harv.

Ignoring him, Harv pulled back the oxygen mask and said, "I met sorcerers. My daughter died. We had cloth and pottery and beer."

"This can wait," Tara tried to assure him. She squeezed his hand, wondering again whether he was describing quantum memories or mere hallucinations.

Giving up on talking to him, the paramedics began wheeling the gurney down the hallway toward the stairwell.

"I need you to let go of his hand, ma'am."

For several minutes there was no chance to speak, as the two paramedics hauled the gurney through a doorway and up two flights of stairs. Its shopping-cart wheels were on some complex

armature that tilted and compressed and expanded with every
stair, giving Harv a smooth (if not quite level) ride.

The Engineering Center had been built before handicapped
accessibility requirements were a thing, and its lowest levels were
inaccessible by elevator. It was also built into a slope, so the "ground
level" on one side was lower than the ground level on the other. Like
an insane concrete castle, it narrowed into disconnected towers as it
went up, and the layout of the ground floors reflected this: a maze
of tiled hallways snaking around multiple service cores. Shadows
and daylight came from every conceivable angle, through purple-
tinted windows that seemed to confuse matters even further, but the
paramedics seemed to know their way. This was Boulder—a town
composed of aging hippies and professors and tech millionaires on
the one hand, and nitwit undergrads on the other. They probably
got called to campus a lot.

"Hold the door, please," the female paramedic called out to
a man passing through to the outdoors. They got Harv outside,
into the shadow of a massive tower supported by spindly-looking
columns at its corners.

The open ambulance was parked right there on the front, and
they puuushed Harv up into the back of it with hardly a bump.
Without asking, Tara got in to ride next to him.

"I had an armored shirt made of rope and wood," Harv said
to her.

"You're not making sense," she told him.

Thinking that over, he seemed to collect himself for a few
seconds before saying, "It was a mountainous region in Europe,
where Neandertals and, I guess, Cro-Magnons were living in
neighboring valleys. The level of social organization was high.
Even the Neandertals lived in painted tents. They had pointy ears."

"Try not to speak," the male paramedic said. It sounded like it
was aimed at Harv, but he was looking at Tara when he said it. He
and his partner were very busy, reading displays and writing on
handheld devices and injecting various substances into Harv's IV.

"Little bit of epinephrine here. Okay. This is a benzodiazepine.
You may feel a little floaty. Please keep that mask in place, sir."

But Harv remained alert, and kept right on pulling the mask
back, until finally they gave up and put some tubes in his nose.
He seemed to relax after that.

"It was real, Tara."

"Okay."

"Look, I know what you're thinking, but there was so much detail. Things I could never come up with. Why would I? It doesn't help anything if I sound crazy, or if my story doesn't add up."

"No," she agreed. And then, because she couldn't help herself, she asked, "Do you still remember the first seizure? Your years with Manu?"

"Vividly." He slapped the rail of the gurney. "It was real, as solid as this. But that wasn't his name."

"Okay," she said again, granting that for the time being, "but why would you still be receiving memories when you're not hooked up to the machine?"

"I don't know. It's worrying, isn't it? Maybe the brain can't process the information all at once."

"That's not good news," Tara said. "Are you going to keep seizing?"

"Who knows? Oh. Oh, I do feel floaty."

"That's to calm down the electrical activity in your brain," the paramedic said.

"It feels fine. It feels fine. But Tara, there's something you need to know: I wasn't a passive observer. I was able to influence events."

Tara snorted. "Um, no. Sorry. Is that the drugs talking?"

"No, no, is it so crazy? Think about it, Tara: entangled photons can affect each other instantly, even light-years apart. The qubit states in the Y chromosome have been entangled for a long time. A change in the present *should* be reflected in the past. Or vice-versa. It doesn't mean causality is violated; just that those two moments are adjacent in a higher-dimensional space."

"So you didn't . . . change history?" The words sounded outrageous as she said them.

"No. I don't think so. But I was part of it."

Tara was overwhelmed with all of this. She didn't know what to say, or think, and a really big part of her wanted it all to be the seizure dream of a half-fried brain. But there were just too many stacked-up coincidences here to ignore. *That* story didn't add up.

"Are you sure?" she asked feebly.

"No," he said. "We need to talk to some physicists. Cosmologists, maybe. And archaeologists. You're right to be skeptical—they certainly will be."

"What are you guys talking about?" the female paramedic demanded.

"Time travel," was Tara's answer. "Maybe."

"Oh," the paramedic said, and went back to what she was doing.

In the emergency room, Harv found himself tied to another electroencephalogram, along with an electrocardiogram and a pulse oximeter. The nurses and technicians cut off his clothes, and replaced them with a faded green-yellow-white hospital gown patterned like a stained glass window. They fussed over him, asked him a lot of the same questions the paramedics had, and rolled a portable MRI machine over his head and shoulders to take some buzzing, beeping images of his brain.

A female doctor Tara's age came and went several times, each time asking Harv how he was feeling.

"Tired," was Harv's answer every time. But his grip on Tara's hand was strong.

A technician asked him, "Do you have any family in the area?"

"No. My parents live in Texas. This is Tara, my girlfriend."

Harv thought he caught a glimmer of disapproval from the technician at that. And why not? Harv had committed the ultimate cliché of a sin: graying-at-the-temples professor bangs twentysomething postdoc. She wasn't *his* postdoc, so he hadn't technically violated any university ethics policies, but when he really thought about it—how it looked, how it felt—he couldn't summon much defense. Here they were, subject to a sudden wave of outside scrutiny, and what could he possibly have to say for himself? *She held my hand, sir. You'd do it, too, if you were me.* Harv did not make a habit of this kind of thing—not at all. The largest age gap he'd ever had in a relationship before was seven years, and even that had felt like a lot at the time. But all that was impossible to explain to these people. None of it was any of their business, and yet.

"Are you okay with your girlfriend overhearing your medical information?"

"Yes. And Gurdeep Patel, my grad student."

After restating that in several different ways, he thumbprinted an electronic release confirming it.

"What events?" Tara asked him, when things had settled down sufficiently. "What is it you think you...participated?"

"Well, for example, I spoke to Manuah. He heard me. He told his brother he heard me. I think it might be why he built his ark in the first place."

"Harv..."

"I know."

"What am I supposed..."

"I *know*. But this is an experiment, and that's one of our findings. It actually is."

"How... For God's sake, assuming *any* of this could be verified, how would we possibly write it up?"

"Good question."

"I mean, the subjectivity..."

"Yeah. But if we leave anything out..."

What a mess, Harv thought. Findings like these were every scientist's worst nightmare. Cold fusion? Extraterrestrial signals? Lamarckian evolution? Warm-blooded fucking dinosaurs? Being wrong meant never working again. It meant you'd wasted the best years of your life, and would finish out your time on Earth at the U of North Dakota, or behind the counter of a Starbuck's. And being right...

Hell, being right often meant your vindication arrived a hundred years after your death. If you were lucky, it meant decades of swimming upstream against stubbornly incredulous peers, waiting for them to die off or retire so the tide could turn in your favor. Either way, the rest of your life was laid out on rails, impossible to change.

"What have you done to us?" Tara asked Harv.

"Me? All by myself?"

"Fine. What have *we* done?"

At this point, Patel came in, looking worried. Harv had never seen him worried before.

"Hey, Boss," he said, at once too loudly and too gently. "How are you feeling?"

"Confused," Harv admitted. "Enlightened. Triumphant. This is going to be big."

"We need to nail down exactly what the machine did to you," Patel said, unnecessarily. So much of what he said was redundant or noncommittal or simply agreeing with Harv, and it occurred to Harv, for the umptieth time, to wonder what actually went on in Patel's head. He was unquestionably a smart guy, but he was two years into a PhD program, totally dependent on Harv for his future, and Harv wondered if he ever dared speak his mind–no matter the prompting.

"True," Harv said. And then, more thoughtfully, "Even the paramedics and hospital staff know that. Patel, you graduate next year, and we need to get you placed somewhere good. You need to learn to share more of what's going on in *your* brain."

"Okay, Boss."

Harv sighed. To Tara he said, "Could you talk to him for me, please? Find out what he really thinks?"

"Sure," Tara agreed, with that same whatever-whatever kind of tone.

He sighed again. "I suppose it's too much to ask, to have conversations like this from a hospital bed, while beset with seizures."

"Beset?" Tara asked. "That implies they aren't over."

He hadn't realized it until speaking, but he felt there *was* some kind of cycle going on here, and it was presently on the rise again. Hmm. Was that good or bad? Was any of this worth it?

He could totally understand the skepticism of Tara and Patel, and see it as a tiny shadow of how the wider world was going to react. But *he knew*. The machine had worked; its principles were sound, and his admittedly-kinda-crazy push to build it had been based on actual scientific insight. Forget Nobel Prizes; what really drove a scientist was blank space. Once you started glimpsing the gaps between the insights of other people, you soon realized there was a vast, blank wilderness behind them. Here be dragons! And in Harv's case, he simply wouldn't rest until he was out there on that vast, blank page, writing in his own contributions to human knowledge.

And here he was! Manuah and Argur were real people with real lives, and somewhere out there in the world were corroborating details. But would that matter, if Harv's own brain turned to mush? He'd also dragged two people into the blankness with him. Would they have cause to thank him, or curse him?

To Tara he said, "I think there's a...kind of a cycle, yes. I feel something coming, and I'm concerned that this is undermining the credibility of our findings thus far. It's important that the two of you take detailed notes. I don't think I'm dying or anything, but..."

"But you might be?" she asked.

"Any of us might be," he said. "But yes. I think it's... Wow. I think it's..."

Alarms started beeping, and then blaring. As Harv's eyes rolled back, he was struck by the realization that it wasn't an involuntary response. As the seizure came on, it simply *felt good* to roll them up out of the way. And he became aware of heat and dust and the distant sound of birds.

"I think I'm in Africa," he said in a clear voice, to no one in particular.

"Stand back!" someone shouted. "Back! Back! Visitors out!"

PART THREE

The Garden

3.1

"I want to see Father," Tik-Tik said again. He knew he had said it very much today, and Grandmother was becoming quite unhappy with him. But he did not understand, and she had not made the connection for him. Or else he only doubted what she was saying, or he disagreed with it—with the entire idea. Why had every adult agreed to journey from the old housing development, forever, and why had they gone in two different directions?

"Enough people, not enough food," Grandmother told him again. "Long commutes to work. People needed to gather and hunt, but food was far. That earth was finished. We needed new earth, to gather and hunt."

"But why one earth *and* another earth?" he demanded. "Why two?"

All around, men and women were setting up houses and placing stones in circles. There was much talk from the men and women, and Mother and Stepfather were laughing. Tik-Tik disagreed with that. Why laugh? Why now?

"Food limits people," Grandmother said. "Men and women make babies, and so people expand. But does food expand? No. And so people move here and there, until food is enough."

Tik-Tik understood that part, somewhat. But he did *not* understand why Father was *there*, while Tik-Tik and Mother and Grandmother were *here*. He questioned, again.

Now Grandmother was angry and said, "Mother and Father divorced, Tik-Tik. They argued much. Remember? Mother helped us, helped you, by divorce. Mother wanted new man and new house, with less shouting. Stepfather is good for Mother. Look: Stepfather is strong, happy, and peaceful. Stepfather hunts well. Stepfather makes cushions and plates and spoons for Mother, so Mother is happy. Stepfather's house is harmonious. Good? Good."

"Stepfather is Mute," Tik-Tik said, pointing and waiting. He watched Mother speaking to Stepfather, watched Stepfather nodding and laughing and speaking a few words. But his voice was not very beautiful, and he did not know many words.

But Grandmother only laughed at that. More laughter! She said, "Mute people may be warm, Tik-Tik. Mute people may say things with bodies, and with actions. Grandmother's man, Tik-Tik's Grandfather, was Mute, and loved. Very loved. Grandmother selected Grandmother's man, of many men."

She seemed lost in thought for a moment, and then said, "And Grandmother's Father was mute, and one of Grandmother's Grandmothers. More Talking People exist now, Tik-Tik, but so many people are Mute. Mute, Mute, Mute. Many beautiful people, many kind people, even many sensible people are Mute."

"I do not approve," Tik-Tik said. "The comparison with Father is bad. Father is strong and sensible. Father is not Mute. I do not approve of divorce, or of Stepfather. I do not approve of Mutes."

These were big words, and many words. Tik-Tik felt very sensible, talking like that.

But Grandmother looked unhappy again, and disapproving. "Do not be so certain," she said. "When Tik-Tik is bigger, and Tik-Tik's blood runs hot, Tik-Tik will find the body of a Mute girl as soft as the body of a Talking girl. And Tik-Tik may find the talking..." she seemed to struggle for words "...unimportant."

Tik-Tik didn't know what to say to that. Grandmother liked to say "when Tik-Tik is bigger," but Tik-Tik could not think that. He had never been bigger—had always been smaller. He knew in a vague way that small boys grew to be big boys, who grew to be men, but he had never seen it happen, and was not friends with the idea. Would he be out walking one day, and then suddenly be big, all at one time? Would he have to pick up a spear and hunt? Would he have to *make* a spear?

A distance away, there was some commotion: shrieking, and more laughter.

"You are funny!" Mother was saying to Stepfather, who had put down the house pole he was holding, and had begun whipping her with a long blade of grass, and grinning.

"Baaa," Stepfather said back to her, imitating the sound of a goat and grinning even more widely. Oh yes, very sensible.

"I want to see !Ibi," Tik-Tik attempted, hoping this argument might touch Grandmother's kindness. "And Uncle, and Cousins. And Moku."

Moku was his friend. !Ibi was his older sister, who had not come here with Mother and Stepfather. She was with Father, and traveling in a different direction, to a different place. Tik-Tik didn't know where. He didn't know when he might ever see her again.

"!Ibi and Father are harmonious," Grandmother said. "!Ibi and Mother are not. !Ibi and Grandmother are not. One big, inharmonious group becomes two smaller, more harmonious groups."

"!Ibi and *Tik-Tik* are harmonious!" Tik-Tik protested. And then suddenly he was crying, all at one time, and Grandmother was comforting him, saying, "Mmm, mmm, mmm, little one. Bitter tastes don't stay in the mouth. Rough stones don't stay under the feet. The future is green, and long, and Tik-Tik will be happy."

But it was a long time before he stopped crying, and by then Stepfather had made up a little bed for him inside their new house, and given him a drink of water from an ostrich shell, and Mother was giving him plants to chew on, and the tiredness of the day caught up with him, and he slept.

Tik-Tik soon discovered another thing that was different in the new earth: Mother went by herself to gather food and firewood, leaving Tik-Tik with other boys and girls in the care of three Grandmothers, and one Grandfather who didn't seem to do much except yell when his things were touched.

"Tik-Tik is very heavy for Mother to lift," she explained, "and Tik-Tik is very slow to walk with Mother. Staying with Grandmother is good. Grandmother will teach songs and stories. Grandmother will teach foods and not-foods, and running, and observation for danger."

"I do not approve of this," Tik-Tik said.

But his approval was not asked, or needed.

Another thing that was different was that the Grandmothers did not pay as much attention to Tik-Tik as Mother had done. This was partly because they had many boys and girls to watch over, but also partly because they simply took the task less seriously. And when the Grandmothers weren't looking, the boys and

girls would push each other and bite each other and pull each
other's hair. A girl named !Ey-!Ey hit Tik-Tik in the penis and
ran away crying, and never did get trouble from it.

"You shouldn't be running around with your penis out anyway," Grandmother told him.

And this led to another thing that was different: the loincloth Grandmother started making him wear. A strip of leather,
a cord, a knot. A knot! How troubling! Tik-Tik could not undo
it when he needed to give waste, and so he soiled the loincloth,
and himself, over and over. Soon the loincloth smelled so bad
that Grandmother could no longer wash it, and had to bury it.
Freedom!

But this gain did not last; Grandmother spent several days
teaching Tik-Tik to tie and untie knots, and then presented him
with a second loincloth.

"If this one is soiled, Tik-Tik will eat it," Grandmother warned.
"Tik-Tik also needs to learn to give waste outside housing development, not on the floor or street."

He took the warning seriously for a time, and when he finally
realized she was teasing about making him eat his waste, that it
was only a laugh to her, he had already made the change.

"Congratulations," she told him. "Now Tik-Tik is not a baby.
Now Tik-Tik is a boy, and will learn the ways of boys."

3.2

Rather suddenly, it seemed, Tik-Tik began to discover the world around him. When he used his senses, he found that the new earth was unpleasantly hot from the end of the afternoon through the early part of the evening. It was unpleasantly cold right before the sun came up. When rain came, it was unpleasantly wet, and when wind came, it was unpleasantly dusty. But most of the time, the new earth was very pleasant, and he could lie down in the grass, in the shade, and listen to the birds and bugs make their noises.

By comparison, he began to understand that the old earth had not been pleasant: hot and cold and dusty and muddy and full of thorns. He went back there sometimes when he slept, and rarely heard the sound of birds, or saw any people, although sometimes their muttering voices seemed to be somewhere nearby.

"Earths last some years," Grandmother told him. "Then plants die and animals go to new earths. And people go, too."

Tik-Tik wondered if this would also happen to this new earth. It did not seem possible. A stream ran through the new earth, a short distance from the housing development, and in places the sides were tall and covered in willows and raspberry bushes, and to get a drink of water was difficult. In other places, the sides were low and flat, and drinking was easy. Here he found frogs, and sometimes killed them with stones and brought them home for Mother or Grandmother to cook. His own food!

He ate the raspberries, too, and other foods Grandmother taught him to recognize. And soon he learned as much from other boys as he ever had from Grandmother. This grass is sweet! This leaf is sour! This flower is bitter! This larva (which will someday, somehow, turn into a bug!) tastes like meat, and if you put them all in your mouth at once, it is like eating dinner.

He learned to run from snakes and jump away from snapping turtles, and to climb for fruit, and to dig for yams with a stick. He learned to wrestle with the other boys—playfully at first, but then with growing force that let them understand who was strongest. They also learned who was quickest, nimblest, most sensible, and although Tik-Tik was not particularly aware of it, this process was slowly making his body and mind into tools that would do whatever was needed of them.

He learned *not* to wrestle girls, as this was forbidden, and *always* brought trouble. He once tried swatting !Ey-!Ey in her own private parts, and received a beating for it. But it was of little consequence; most of the time girls were no more than a distant screeching noise, easily ignored.

When he used his ears, he would hear the women say, "Hippos and crocodiles can not live in this small stream. It is good to gather water without fear." And he would hear the men say, "The game animals here are small, but they are stupid and easy to catch. And they do not attract lions! It is good to walk between the bushes without fear." And he would hear the girls say, "Ever there are beautiful flowers here, and coal and ochre to paint our faces." And the Grandmothers would say, "These bead stones are soft! We can drill holes in them without slipping and cutting our hands!" And the Grandfathers (of whom there were only two in the whole development) said, "When big birds sleep, I can hit them with stones. They are like fruit!"

And when he watched the Mute people grunting and gesturing, he understood that they also had reasons to like the new earth. It was quieter, and simpler, and there was less strife among the people. This meant that there was less to talk about, and so less comparison between the Mutes and the Talking People.

And in this way, Tik-Tik learned (if only indirectly) how to tell a good place from a bad one, and learned also that he lived in a very good place. When he slept, now, he rarely returned to the old earth, but remained in this one, wrestling boys and eating grubs.

"Is this best place?" he asked Grandmother one day.

"It is," she agreed. "I have lived many places, and this one is best."

✦   ✦   ✦

Harv surfaced for a moment here, muddled and confused. The memories and experiences of this time felt vague and jumpy and incomplete. At first he attributed this to corrupt data—thinking perhaps he was losing his lock on the transcranial magnetic signal as his awareness drifted further and further back in time. He didn't know when he was, but he could feel that it was more ancient than Kingdom or Nog La. But could the quantome data actually be corrupted? It seemed to him it should either be in a superposition of all possible states, or else collapsed into a single minimum-energy state. A row of two billion zeroes, essentially.

Perhaps the confusion was because he was experiencing the mind of a child? But as Tik-Tik grew older, nothing much seemed to change. It was as if these people actually experienced their lives in a kind of dream state, where later concepts of time and space and self had yet to fully develop. Tik-Tik had no ambitions, no plans, and rarely any detailed thoughts about the future at all.

And the language! Tik-Tik had several times burst into uncontrollable laughter—Harv's laughter—because when the people spoke, regardless of age or gender or status, it came out sounding like babytalk. Their vocabulary was built around perhaps a hundred word roots, which they happily stretched and mangled and smashed together to form complex concepts. And although the language included a wealth of sounds—clicks and groans and pops and whistles that occasionally sounded almost like birdsong—the words consisted mainly of repeated consonant-vowel pairs. The word for "mother" was actually "mama"! Father was "pfo-pfo," water was something awfully like "'glug 'glug," and most food was some tonal variation of "goo goo," "ki ki," or "nom nom."

As for grammar, well, that was toddlerish as well. There was an almost total absence of articles and pronouns, although these could sometimes be conveyed through gestures, such as pointing repeatedly to someone rather than repeating their name over and over. Nevertheless, words were repeated for emphasis or pluralization, or else simply spoken in a louder voice. A few words, like "Mmm," seemed almost infinitely versatile, and could mean almost anything depending on tone and context. Along with a small vocabulary of standardized gestures, this seemed to be the one area of communication where the Talking People were on the same level as the Mutes.

And yet, puzzlingly, the Mutes were not stupid. With clever hands and expressive faces, they seemed at least the equals of the trolls of Nog La, if not quite of the Talking People themselves. It was hard to say exactly what was wrong with them.

Tik-Tik also learned to hunt. At first it was just frogs and bugs hammered with stones, and then birds and squirrels felled by increasingly accurate, baseball-like pitches. And then he'd made a spear (little more than a sharpened stick, really) and spent hours and days and weeks hurling it at rabbits. These throws rarely struck the target, and even more rarely pierced it. He *never* made a kill, and so finally, in frustration, he went to one of the Grandfathers and asked,

"Why does Tik-Tik not spear rabbits?"

To which the Grandfather replied, impatiently, "With that thing? Wood points are for poking, not throwing."

"Why?"

"It is too light and too blunt. Boy needs sharp stone on end. Also, stick is crooked. Stick must be very straight."

"Mmm."

"Mmm? Does boy think boy is sensible? Show boy's throw."

Dutifully, Tik-Tik raised his arm and threw the spear, with approximately the same overhand pitch he would use for a heavy stone.

"Mmm," said the grandfather. "Make boy's feet like this." Getting up from the ground with great effort and fuss, he demonstrated, putting one foot farther forward and one farther back than Tik-Tik had done. "Make boy's hand like this:" He curled his wrist slightly inward, and the loose muscles of his arm tightened and bulged. "Make boy's arm like this:" and he drew his arm back low, holding his hand at the level of his ear. "Now *throw!*" he said, snapping his hand forward very fast. Faster than Tik-Tik thought the old man could move.

Tik-Tik tried to copy the movement, but his spear merely flipped around in the air like a frog.

"No," the grandfather clucked, shaking his head.

The noise was a tsk, tsk—*very similar to something Harv himself might make, never thinking of it as an actual word.*

"Not with that. Go get long stick, straight stick, and good stone for tip."

And so, grumbling, Tik-Tik spent the next several days scanning the environment for appropriate spearwood. The earth was green and flat, with bushes and trees. Tik-Tik understood that if there were lions in the area, this could be dangerous. You needed to be able to see lions from a long distance away. However, the only predators in this earth were jackals—too small to endanger anyone but toddlers, who were never allowed to wander far from adults. Tik-Tik knew that jackals could bite if he got too close, but in fact they were shy and never seemed to let him anywhere near, and so he patrolled the area alone, without fear, and without anyone else being afraid for him.

In his search for a spear, Tik-Tik began to realize there were different kinds of trees in the earth. Some had apples or figs or acorns or mongongo nuts on them, no two of which ever occurred on the same tree. The mongongo trees were light and breakable. The apple trees and fig trees were very crooked. The acorn trees were good, with straight, hard sticks. Other trees bore no fruit and had no names, but each type had its own leaves, and he learned that some had better sticks than others, but in the end he decided the acorn trees were best.

He tried breaking off green sticks from the body of the tree, but found they splintered and tore, rather than coming off in a clean piece. He tried collecting the dead wood around the trees, but found it was too light and breakable. Eventually he determined that freshly dead branches, still attached to a living tree, were the best sources of wood. Eventually he found a stick that was as tall and straight as he was, and he broke it off cleanly at both ends, and rubbed the ends smooth on a stone.

He then found another stone, and started knapping the two together, to form one of them into a spear point. He had seen spear points all his life, and assumed that making one must be easy. However, the stones refused to fracture. In a sensible moment, he went and found a softer stone, and hit it with the harder one. This time, at least, the softer stone broke. However, it crumbled into dust along the edge, rather than forming a sharp point.

Frustrated, he went back to Grandfather, showed him the stones, and asked, "Why does Tik-Tik not make spear points?"

Grandfather laughed. "With those stones? Boy can ask boy's Father to help find good stone."

"Man in house is not Tik-Tik's Father."

"Mmm. Boy can ask boy's *Step*father to help find good stone." Tik-Tik did not like that.

He did not particularly like Grandfather, either, but at least Grandfather had never done him harm. Grandfather hadn't replaced his real father, and taken him away from his sister and cousins and friends.

"Will *Grandfather* help Tik-Tik find stone?" he asked, with a timidity that surprised him.

Grandfather laughed a little, then sniffed, then mmm'ed. "Grandfather understands. Many boys do not like Stepfathers. But Grandfather is old; the wind no longer travels in and out of Grandfather's belly. Does boy think Grandfather stays here in the housing development, with babies and grandmothers, because Grandfather likes it?"

The old man looked away, then looked back, then away again. He said, "Grandfather was like you. Grandfather was boy. Boy was strong and fast. Grandfather was called !En-!En. Now Grandfather sits in dust."

This speech did not impress Tik-Tik, nor touch him emotionally. It was the sort of thing old people said, just as the sun gave light and the stream gave water. His answer was a complaint: "Tik-Tik's Stepfather cannot teach. Tik-Tik's Stepfather is Mute."

"Mmm," said Grandfather, thinking and nodding. "Grandfather understands even more. But Mutes can teach boy how to throw. How to find stone. How to shape stone. Grandfather knows Tik-Tik's Stepfather. Is good man."

"No," Tik-Tik said, although he wasn't sure exactly what he was saying no to. That Stepfather was a good man? That Stepfather could teach him?

But this made Grandfather unhappy with him. He said, "Then ask another boy, or another boy's Father. Grandfather can not help you. Grandfather is very busy, sitting in dust."

And that seemed to be the end of the conversation.

Even more frustrated, Tik-Tik waited around the housing development until the men started to return home from work.

These were the actual words that formed in Harv's mind—the closest equivalents to the words Tik-Tik was using to assemble his thoughts. The literal construction was something like, "Wait location house-build-build man man come house after work," and while that would not have meant much to Harv in its native state, Tik-Tik's own mind found it grammatical and sensible enough.

The houses of the "development" were larger than the houses of Nog La, and rather than domes they were triangular tunnels of tall sticks tied together with jute twine, and covered with thatch rather than animal hides, although hides were still used as "doors" at the open ends. A large opening at the center allowed smoke to escape. The whole assembly was dependent on friction and good luck to hold it together, and it didn't look to Harv like these dwell-ings could survive any serious weather. One strong gust of wind would collapse them into their own cooking fires. One cloudburst thunderstorm would wash the thatching off the sticks, and turn the jute strands soggy and weak.

However, this area (eastern Africa, perhaps?) seemed mild in every possible way, and stronger dwellings might simply be regarded as a waste of time and materials. During the day these were a busy people, and at night they were both lazy and bawdy; caring for houses would not be high on their list of priorities.

Interestingly, though, the spacing of the houses was quite similar to Sunrise Castle, as was the hard-packed look of the ground. But there was no wall here, and no sense of danger or foreboding about the outside world. Tik-Tik didn't regard his stepfather's house as a home, so much as a place to sleep and store things, and to eat cooked meals if he happened to be there at the right time.

There were no discernible seasons here—just days of sun and days of light rain—and so like a child on perpetual summer vaca-tion, Tik-Tik did not seem to hold himself accountable for much, or to depend on his elders for much. Needing something from his stepfather was a truly alien feeling, and one he fidgeted through with great impatience.

When Stepfather finally showed up, whistling, with a string of rabbits over one shoulder and a real, grown-up spear over the other, Tik-Tik pounced on him, as a jackal might pounce on a lion.

"Stepfather! Tik-Tik needs stone for spear points! Tik-Tik needs this now! Stepfather must help Tik-Tik find good stone!"

Stepfather listened to this, and then burst out laughing. "Muh, muh, muh!" he said, clearly doing his best to imitate Tik-Tik's voice. He laughed again, then held a hand up and said "Mmm" in a tone that very clearly meant "calm down, boy." He mimed the acts of eating, sleeping, waking up, and *then* going out to look for a stone with Tik-Tik.

"No," Tik-Tik protested.

"Noooo," Stepfather mocked. "Nowww!"

"Stay here for dinner," Grandmother said, emerging from the house with a scowl on her face. She shook a finger at Tik-Tik and added, "Tik-Tik does not eat enough real food. Tik-Tik eats bugs and apples and hard, uncooked yams, and cold leftovers. Tik-Tik drops into his bed as soon as sun is buried. Tik-Tik does not listen to stories around fire, and so Tik-Tik will grow up less sensible than Mutes."

"Tik-Tik is busy," Tik-Tik said.

"Tik-Tik will do as Tik-Tik is told," Grandmother said, with uncharacteristic firmness.

"Where is Mother?" Tik-Tik demanded, thinking he could appeal to her on both issues.

"Mother is working late," Grandmother said. "The ripest mongongo nuts are far, and Mother is filling basket with them for Grandmother to roast with rabbit meat, so that Tik-Tik can fill his belly with something that does not squirm."

Tik-Tik wanted to object, to nearly every part of that, but Stepfather grinned and held open the door, motioning for Tik-Tik to come inside.

"Talllk," he said.

3.3

Dinner was actually quite good, and as they all sat in the dust beside the fire, Tik-Tik was forced to thank Mother for collecting the nuts, and Stepfather for catching the rabbits, and Grandmother for putting the nuts inside the rabbits and roasting them on three rotisserie spits at the right height above the fire, for just the right amount of time, turning them at the right speed, so they tasted just the way Tik-Tik liked them.

Tik-Tik ate his fill, and more. "Mother grows fat," he said after this, noticing the way his mother's belly swelled out above her loincloth.

"Mother has baby inside," Grandmother said.

"Stepfather *put* baby inside," Mother said, to which everyone except Tik-Tik laughed.

Without getting up, Stepfather made a motion with his hands and hips that Tik-Tik did not understand, but that caused Mother and Grandmother to laugh even harder.

To which Grandmother said, "This new earth is good. Many new babies will find their way here."

"Yes!" Stepfather said, with a tone Tik-Tik could also not interpret. But again, the women laughed.

This annoyed Tik-Tik greatly, because he did not like thinking there was a difference between himself and the adults of the housing development. If they could speak things he did not understand—if a *Mute* could speak things he did not understand—then he wanted to be in on the joke.

"What?" he asked. And then again, more sharply: "*What?*"

Which only brought more laughter.

Finally, seeing his look, Grandmother clucked at him and said,

"Boys have no interest in babies, or where babies come from. But young men are *very* interested, as Tik-Tik will discover."

"Tik-Tik *is* young man," he protested, although saying it made him sound even more like a boy.

There were more jokes after that, some of which Tik-Tik understood and some of which he did not. Finally, impatiently, he said to Grandmother, "Tik-Tik is here for stories. Grandmother says Tik-Tik comes home too tired for stories, but Tik-Tik is here."

"Mmm," Grandmother said. "Perhaps Mother can tell us about her day."

Mother agreed, and launched into a story so boring it actually hurt Tik-Tik to hear it. Mother went here, Mother went there. Mother dropped her basket. Mother saw a bird. Blah blah blah.

When she was finally done, he said, "I feel sensible. Thanks for teaching. And now will Stepfather tell us the story of Stepfather's day?"

"Do not be rude," Mother said sharply.

But Tik-Tik persisted: "Why did Mother join with this Mute? This Mute can not teach. This Mute can not tell stories."

"Stepfather can sing," Grandmother said, nodding her encouragement.

And so Stepfather began a song that had only two words: "Love, harmony. Love, love, love, love, harmony." He could barely form the words, and yet he sang them over and over again, in rising and falling tones, putting as much feeling into them as any human voice ever could. Tik-Tik was annoyed at first—he hated it when Stepfather sang!—but gradually he found the music soothing him inside, and when Mother and Grandmother began to clap their hands and sing along, Tik-Tik hesitated and then finally joined them. And when the song was done, he couldn't think of anything rude to say.

"Important words," Grandmother said.

"Not many," Tik-Tik said, finding a bit of his anger again. Then, more seriously: "Why is Stepfather Mute? What is wrong with Stepfather?"

It was a question that had never occurred to him before, but suddenly it seemed very important. Had Stepfather ever been able to speak? Had he lost his words, the way a man might lose a spear point, or had he broken them, the way a man might accidentally smash an ostrich egg filled with water?

"Nothing is wrong," Mother said. "Mutes are born Mute."

"Mmm. But then where do they come from?"

Grandmother clucked. "Tik-Tik, almost everyone is Mute. Talking People are very few."

"Mmm," Tik-Tik said. "Then where do Talking People come from?"

Grandmother clucked again. "Tik-Tik does not know? All Talking People are boys and girls of Talking Woman, Grandmother's Mother's Grandmother. Talking Woman was different from Mutes. Talking Woman could sing like birds, and speak the thoughts that lived inside. All people could understand the thoughts of Talking Woman, even if people could not speak back to her. Talking Woman was lonely.

"Talking Woman often walked alone, even though there were snakes in the earth. Talking Woman often ate fruit of unknown trees, and dared scorpions to sting. Talking Woman often spoke to Sun, and sang to Moon, hoping for responses that never came. Talking Woman remained very lonely.

"To fill Talking Woman's heart, Talking Woman filled Talking Woman's womb. Talking Woman rolled in dust with many men who could not speak, and bore many boys and girls. But Talking Woman's boys and girls could speak! Talking Woman taught boys and girls all words, and some boys and girls knew other words and taught them to Talking Woman, and finally there was speech in the earth, and Talking Woman was not lonely.

"But still, Talking Woman walked alone in wilderness, speaking to animals, looking for animals that might speak back. One day, Talking Woman spoke with monkeys, and was scratched. One day, Talking Woman spoke with snakes, and was bitten. Talking Woman stumbled back home. Talking Woman told people what happened. Talking Woman died among Talking Woman's boys and girls.

"Boys and girls became men and women, but also brothers and sisters. Does Tik-Tik know? Brothers and sisters do not roll in dust together and do not marry. And so, Talking men and Talking women rolled with Mutes, and married Mutes, and produced more boys and girls, and some of these could talk badly, and some of these could talk well, and these were the Talking People. And when Talking People married Talking People, the boys and girls could speak, and when Talking People married Mutes, boys and girls could also speak.

"Talking People share thoughts, Tik-Tik. Mutes can not do this. This means what one person knows, all people can know. This made Talking People sensible, and clever, and hard to beat or trick. This made Talking People beautiful! Mmm, how Mutes wanted to join with Talking People! One Talking man may roll with many Mute women, and produce many new Talking People.

"And so Talking People grew, until earth was exhausted, and housing development split in two and was moved in different directions. Since that time, Talking People have split, and split again, and now cover many earths. But if Tik-Tik walks for many days in any direction, Tik-Tik will find only Mutes."

"And Mutes will want to roll in dust with Tik-Tik," Mother said, giggling.

Stepfather made his noise and his gesture again, and Mother and Grandmother laughed.

When they were finished laughing, Grandmother said, "All Talking People have this choice: marry one Talking Person, or one Mute. Or roll with many Mutes, many times."

"Some try to do both," Mother said. And then, after a long pause, she added: "This is why Father and Mother divorced."

In the morning, Tik-Tik woke up early and did not let Stepfather out of his sight, until he was very certain Stepfather wasn't going to go off hunting without him. The moment Stepfather awoke, Tik-Tik was speaking:

"Stepfather! Help Tik-Tik find good stones!"

"Mmm."

"Stepfather said Stepfather would help!"

"Mmm."

"Will Stepfather help?"

Stepfather nodded.

"Will Stepfather help *now*?"

Stepfather sighed, and glared, rolled his eyes, and voiced a single word: "No." He mimed the act of eating, then sat up and reached for some cold leftovers, and an ostrich egg filled with water.

"Will Stepfather help *now*?" Tik-Tik asked, when Stepfather had finished eating and drinking.

Stepfather shook his head, and mimed the acts of stretching, walking, and leaving waste. Tik-Tik groaned in frustration.

This went on for some time; Stepfather needed to watch Sun

bloom up over some bushes. Stepfather needed to check edges and tip on Stepfather's spear point, to make sure they were still sharp. Stepfather needed to bite off a hanging toenail. At some point, Tik-Tik finally realized Stepfather had run out of legitimate reasons to delay, and was simply teasing.

"Enough," Tik-Tik said. "Please."

And then finally they were off, to the unknown earth. Tik-Tik realized it was his first time going to work with an adult since he was a very small boy. Unfortunately that adult happened to be Stepfather, but at least Tik-Tik was going to get his stones.

To his surprise, they took off in a direction Tik-Tik rarely went: away from the stream. There were some low hills in the distance, and that appeared to be exactly where Stepfather was headed. Tik-Tik felt worms in his belly, for he had never walked so far from the stream and the housing development and everything familiar. He began to grow thirsty, but when he complained to Stepfather, Stepfather merely picked up a pebble off the ground and placed it in his own mouth.

"Mmm?" he said, gesturing to Tik-Tik.

Uncertainly, Tik-Tik picked up a pebble of his own, brushed the dust off it, and popped it into his mouth.

"Nng," Stepfather said, opening his mouth and showing Tik-Tik where the pebble was: under his tongue. Tik-Tik copied him, and to his surprise, found his thirst was satisfied. Stepfather nodded in satisfaction.

Tik-Tik's second surprise was that the earth out here was not empty. He had imagined the two of them walking alone through grass and bushes and trees, but instead they passed men and women busy at their own work: hunting miniature goats, gathering firewood, digging yams, smashing mongongo nuts. They waved or called out greetings to Stepfather and Tik-Tik as they passed by. Not so different from the children playing at the outskirts of the housing development! Was this work? Was this adulthood? Suddenly it did not seem so impossible or so distant.

His third surprise was that some of the people they passed were people Tik-Tik did not know and had never seen before.

"Who is that? Who is that?" he asked Stepfather several times. "Who is *that*?"

But Stepfather could not answer; he simply shrugged and croaked out the words, "Other people."

But the strangers became more and more frequent as they walked further and further from the housing development, and finally, it occurred to Tik-Tik that these might be the people of his father and sister, and of the childhood friends he could now barely remember. And when he asked this of Stepfather, Stepfather nodded.

"Is there another housing development?"

Again, Stepfather nodded, and pointed. That way.

Excitedly: "Can it be visited?"

Stepfather shook his head. "Busy."

Tik-Tik didn't know exactly what Stepfather meant by that. That *they* were busy? That Father was busy? Probably both. He didn't like that answer, but he *did* want to get stones today.

"Can it be visited another time?"

Stepfather nodded. And that was the day's greatest surprise: that at least some of the different earths and housing developments were within a day's walk of one another. Tik-Tik had always imagined that his development was isolated, that his Father and !Ibi were gone forever, that the people in his development were all the people he was ever going to know. But Grandmother *had* said there were other Talking People, and also that if Tik-Tik walked far enough, he would find nothing but Mutes. So it made sense, and made him feel insensible not to have thought of this before. But he resolved in that moment, that when he was a man he would be a great journeyer, and visit as many people and earths and housing developments as he possibly could.

They reached the hills, and there Stepfather helped Tik-Tik locate three different kinds of stone. It took a long time, and Tik-Tik became very thirsty in spite of the pebble in his mouth. Stepfather tried picking apples and pears for him, but that simply wasn't enough moisture, and so instead of going straight back to the housing development, they went out of their way to find a little watering hole. The water was muddy and smelled bad, but Stepfather drank it anyway. It had never occurred to Tik-Tik that water could be dirty, but he was so very thirsty that he drank, too.

On the way back, his feet hurt, and the stones were difficult to carry, and Stepfather began to look unhappy, and then angry, and then a bit scared.

"Rawr," he said, imitating the sound of a lion. He pointed at Sun and mimed it burying itself beneath the dust.

Tik-Tik became afraid then, too. This was another surprise: that lions or other dangerous animals might live within a day's walk of the housing development. All his life, he had been told the area was safe. But how big was this safe area? How many lions existed in the world, and how many of them were capable of getting between home and wherever Tik-Tik was now? This was a difficult concept for him; there were no words to describe it.

The sun fell lower in the sky, slipping behind treetops and then behind bushes, and daytime began to give way to twilight. Tik-Tik was often out in twilight, but (he realized now) always within a very short walk of the housing development. Never so far away. Never facing the possibility of anything unknown to him.

Sniffing the air, Stepfather urged him to walk faster. Tik-Tik did this, now without complaining, but whatever Stepfather smelled, it was not going away. And then Tik-Tik could smell it too: a smell like urine, like jackals, like the blood and meat of a freshly skinned rabbit. A smell like nothing else he'd ever smelled.

He heard a low growl, and turned to see an animal some distance away. The animal was much larger than a jackal, and it moved toward him and Stepfather with a grace and power Tik-Tik had never seen before. And again, his mind was unable to put these thoughts into words, which made them all the more frightening. Was this a lion?

Stepfather moved in front of Tik-Tik and brandished his spear, making loud noises. The creature paused, then seemed to think. Truly, it seemed to calculate the benefits of attacking this man and this boy, versus the risks of getting poked by that spear. It seemed to understand that although it was physically more powerful, this fight could be a dangerous one. It would have been smarter for the creature to pounce on Stepfather while his back was turned, but it was too late for that, and so with a cool, patient mind the creature weighed its chances.

Tik-Tik saw all of this in the creature's eyes, and interpreted it with a kind of frozen wordless horror. But finally the lion decided to find an easier dinner somewhere else. With a movement like a shrug, it turned and vanished into the bushes.

"Was that a lion?" Tik-Tik asked, his voice shaking.

"Yes," Stepfather confirmed.

They made it back to the housing development without further incident, but the sky was almost fully dark by then, and Tik-Tik had learned a new respect for the darkness, and even for the daylight, and believed he would never feel entirely safe again.

Finally, something that resembled long-term planning! Tik-Tik was now both worrying about his future and daydreaming about it, and although Tik-Tik was not aware of this, Harv sensed the first stirrings of adolescence within it. He knew, somehow, that Tik-Tik would be a great traveler, and that the primary motive of this would be swapping genomes with a wide variety of women.

Still, despite these developments, Harv found himself frustrated with Tik-Tik and his people. They seemed to be stuck somehow. Had they really just invented spoken language, a few generations ago? Or invented complex *language, at any rate?*

But perhaps "invented" was the wrong word. Was this "Talking Woman" the creator of a powerful new technology, or the beneficiary of a mutant gene in some neural development pathway? The evidence pointed toward the latter, or else why couldn't the Mutes be taught to speak? But was it really so simple? Could something as complex as language arise from a single gene, diffusing through an established population?

In any case, this stuttering babytalk put the Talking People light-years ahead of the Mutes; already they were developing a culture and a history that would previously have been impossible. Would this explosion in word power lead to all the complex tools and customs of all the future peoples of all the world? Were these the great-great-grandparents of everyone? *They did certainly resemble the people of Nog La, if perhaps a bit shorter and thinner and ruddier.*

And yet, there was something frightfully limiting about the babytalk as well. This primal Ursprache seemed not only to aid their thinking, but also, nearly as often, to get in the way of it. Tik-Tik's encounter with the lion had paralyzed him, in part because he couldn't think his way through it. He had the reflex of verbal internal dialogue, but not the vocabulary or the grammar.

And so, even as he teetered on the brink of adolescence, his mind was in many ways that of a toddler. He couldn't count higher than five, and it often seemed to Harv that he couldn't notice— couldn't see—anything he didn't have a word for. And that was a lot of things! He also seemed to draw little distinction between his dream life and his waking one, or to understand that everything in his world was connected to everything else in some way. And so, yes, Tik-Tik and his fellow Talking People seemed to wander in something like a drug trance or a cartoon, whose sketches of reality left large portions of the page blurred out, or sometimes completely blank.

In this way, Stepfather and the other Mutes actually seemed more advanced than the Talking People: more alert, more graceful, more at home in their skins and in their environments. If something couldn't be told in a gesture or a grunt or a single word, the Mutes didn't seem to conceptualize it at all. Rather, they simply let the experiences and sensations flow through them, and let themselves react appropriately.

It was no wonder the two groups were so willing to mate up with one another: the complementary splendors of brain and brawn, of storytelling and alpha-state vigor, were each deeply compelling in their own way. If the Talking People were vaguely magical, then the Mutes were vaguely animal. Or one was Yin and the other Yang. Or left brain and right brain. So many metaphors fit!

Harv knew very well that a few thousand generations from now, the Cro-Magnon people of places like Nog La would have fused these two aspects of their being back together again. Probably it took a lot less time than that. How long did it take for a pidgin trade language to transform into a regional creole, and thence into a fully differentiated language with its own clear rules and exceptions? Three generations? Five?

Of course, that was with the knowledge of real languages lurking in the background, informing the process. It was surely harder for the Talking People, with no linguistic traditions to fall back on except the grammarless calls and signs of the Mutes. But was it a thousand times harder? Was it even ten times harder? Would this foggy, sketchy Dreamtime last even another hundred years? Harv had no way of knowing. Still, for the moment, the Mutes and Talking People were what they were, and where they were, with largely complementary strengths and weaknesses.

"You would do well to stay close to your stepfather," Harv thought at Tik-Tik. Then, smiling to himself, rephrased it as, "Stepfather good sensible. Tik-Tik follow."

3.4

But Tik-Tik didn't listen to Harv, any more than he listened to anyone else. He went back to Grandfather to learn, impatiently and with much complaining, to make spearpoints. Stepfather had found him sizeable lumps of flint, chert, and quartz, and Grandfather taught him to shape these with a stone hammer, a wooden punch or chisel, a leather mitt, and a great deal of patience. The spearpoints of these people were basically equilateral triangles a bit larger than a quarter—quite unlike the long, leaf-shaped points of Nog La. They weren't particularly dense, either, but when fitted into a split at the end of a straight, heavy stick and then tied in place with sinew, they did somehow alter the aerodynamics and moment of inertia such that the stick could be thrown point-first with reasonable accuracy.

Grandfather also taught Tik-Tik how to make knives and scrapers, and then, as a sort of graduate-level coursework, how to fashion a hand axe.

"These are not very good for hunting," Grandfather warned, "but chopping wood, chopping bone, chopping meat are all easier with axe than with ordinary stone."

And so, suddenly, Tik-Tik was as well equipped as any man or woman in the housing development. It made him feel important, and it made the other boys his age jealous. Soon there were many fathers leading many sons on expeditions to the hills for raw materials, and Grandfather—who tired easily and did not have much actual time available during the day—began giving his lessons in groups.

Not to be outdone, Tik-Tik began hunting, for real. He could have let an adult teach him the ins and outs of the job, but

226

preferred to learn it all the hard way, through long trial and error. And in this stubborn way, he developed his own, unique tricks and practices, that would eventually be passed on to others. He still had a hard time with rabbits, but with increasing frequency he began bringing home large birds and miniature goats.

In the process he found he was journeying, by himself, farther and farther from the housing development. He was more and more wary of lions the further out he got, but he practiced his courage by chasing down and killing scorpions and snakes, and finally jackals, and bringing their bodies back as trophies. Although he was not the strongest or the fastest or the most sensible, Tik-Tik became known as the *fiercest* of the boys—a title which pleased him very well indeed.

Meanwhile, also not to be outdone, the girls that were Tik-Tik's age had begun constructing their own little houses on the outskirts of the development. Harv thought of them as playhouses, but to the girls it was serious business, and they set about trying to outdo one another by making bigger and bigger structures, and decorating the outer walls with leaves and flowers and rabbit pelts.

One of these girls, by the name of !Ey-!Ey, invited Tik-Tik into her house one day. Tik-Tik had not spared much thought for girls in a long time; they were neither good nor bad, in the same way that trees were neither good nor bad that gave no fruit and were not suitable for making spears. They simply existed in the earth as objects to be seen and steered around, and perhaps sometimes used for shade, but otherwise ignored.

However, on this day Tik-Tik felt a stirring within his loincloth, and for reasons he could not have explained or described, he consented to stoop down and crawl into !Ey-!Ey's little dwelling.

"Does Tik-Tik like this?" she asked, spreading her arms to point to the inner walls of the house, which were decorated with dried white flowers.

"Mmm," Tik-Tik answered noncommittally. He had no opinion about houses or flowers. However, when !Ey-!Ey spread her arms like that, he found his sight drawn toward her breasts. These had formerly been a pair of little brown spots on her chest, indistinguishable from those of a boy, but now they protruded outward, almost like those of a woman. When had that happened? He felt another stirring in the loincloth region. With no name for the feeling, he ignored it, but his body responded nevertheless.

!Ey-!Ey seemed to notice this, and shyly hunched over, covering her breasts with one arm, and her loincloth with the other.

"Does Tik-Tik's blood burn?" she asked warily.

"No," Tik-Tik answered. The question annoyed him. He'd never known what that expression was supposed to mean, and he hadn't asked to be in here with an insensible girl. "Why did !Ey-!Ey put flowers on walls?"

The question seemed to surprise her. "Flowers are beautiful. Why does Tik-Tik bring home dead snakes?"

"Snakes are dangerous," Tik-Tik answered. Then, realizing this was about as sensible as the conversation was going to get, he said, "Tik-Tik will not stay here. Tik-Tik will hunt today."

"Mmm," !Ey-!Ey said.

"Tik-Tik hunts well."

"Mmm."

"Tik-Tik is leaving now."

He got up and did so.

Over the next many days, though, he found the other girls pointing and giggling when he walked by. This irritated him, but he wasn't sure what to do about it. It was forbidden to strike or wrestle a girl, and he did not know anything to say to them to make them stop.

Finally, annoyed, he went back to !Ey-!Ey's little house to confront her about it. He had seen her go inside, so he followed her there, and yanked aside the little rabbit-pelt door.

Startled, !Ey-!Ey once again put her arms across her breasts and loincloth.

"Why do girls laugh at Tik-Tik?" he demanded.

She paused, then answered, "Girls know Tik-Tik was here. Girls know Tik-Tik was looking at !Ey-!Ey's body."

Tik-Tik felt the sides of his mouth and the center of his forehead pull downward. "How do girls know this?"

"!Ey-!Ey told them."

"Why did !Ey-!Ey tell them?"

"Mmm. Mmm. !Ey-!Ey doesn't know. !Ey-!Ey wanted to tell somebody."

Tik-Tik thought about this. He could not particularly imagine wanting to tell anybody anything, unless it had to do with hunting or spears or snakes or lions or walking long distances. He particularly could not imagine wanting to tell girls about looking at bodies. It was not sensible.

"Why does !Ey-!Ey cover !Ey-!Ey's breasts and loincloth?" he finally asked.

"Mmm. Mmm. !Ey-!Ey does not know."

"Do not cover them."

"What?"

"!Ey-!Ey hears Tik-Tik. !Ey-!Ey should not cover !Ey-!Ey's breasts and loincloth."

He waited to see if she would move her arms. Slowly, she did, although she was looking down at the floor.

"Why does Tik-Tik want to see !Ey-!Ey's body?" she asked quietly.

"Mmm. Tik-Tik does not know."

"Does Tik-Tik's blood burn?"

"No," he answered. But his hands reached out and touched her. He felt her neck, her breasts, her waist, her legs.

She gasped and then moaned, and then pulled away, saying, "Careful. Long time !Ey-!Ey has wanted Tik-Tik in !Ey-!Ey's house. But now Tik-Tik is here, and !Ey-!Ey's belly will not be still."

With more curiosity than lust, he reached for her again, and felt the knot that held her loincloth on. His fingers moved to untie the knot. His lips moved to kiss hers.

"!Ey-!Ey's blood burns," she said quietly, and reached for his own knot.

They remained in the little house for some time, and after that, Tik-Tik made a habit of visiting there every morning and afternoon. He had not asked for any adult advice about this, either, but he seemed to know what to do, and what he did not know, !Ey-!Ey seemed to. And what neither of them knew, they figured out by trial and error.

The other girls laughed and pointed, but now Tik-Tik did not mind. Other girls were insensible. Other girls wanted their own boys in their own houses, and one by one, they achieved this ambition.

Word got around in the housing development. One day, Grandmother asked Tik-Tik, "Is Tik-Tik doing something Tik-Tik should not? Tik-Tik is too young to roll with girls. !Ey-!Ey is too young to roll with boys."

"Tik-Tik is not doing anything," he replied. He did not care what Grandmother thought. He did not care what anyone thought.

However, one day when Tik-Tik had finally killed a rabbit, !Ey-!Ey said, "!Ey-!Ey likes rabbit. Tik-Tik should make fire and cook this rabbit for !Ey-!Ey."

This was another thing Tik-Tik did not know how to do, and so he went to Grandfather and asked, as quietly and discreetly has he could, how fire was made. Tik-Tik had seen the end of the process, when Mother rubbed two sticks together to create a flame, but the sticks were very particular in shape, and he did not know how they were created.

Grandfather taught him how to find a good, dry stick and split it down the middle with his hand axe, and then carve it out with his knife, and save the shavings in a little pile. Grandfather taught him to find a smaller dry stick and sharpen it flat with his knife, making a sort of wooden knife-spear out of it, and then push the larger stick into the dust and rub it quickly with the smaller stick until it began to smoke, and then dump the smoking ashes into the pile of wood shavings, and blow gently until it caught fire.

Grandfather made the procedure look easy, and Tik-Tik was deeply frustrated that he could not simply walk away and repeat it on his own. Instead, he studied with Grandfather for days to get it right, and for days more until he could perform it reliably every time.

But soon he was making fire sticks for !Ey-!Ey and teaching her to use them, and he was bringing her rabbits to cook, and the other boys and girls were livid with jealousy. Again, Grandfather was besieged with applicants. However, Grandfather suddenly died one day, and was buried out in the dust, away from the housing development, and the boys were forced to ask their own mothers and fathers for help. They asked Tik-Tik as well, but Tik-Tik would not help them. Why should he?

Then one day, Mother gave birth to a baby boy. It cried all the time, and Mother was constantly cooing and fussing over it, and Tik-Tik was having none of that, so he simply moved into !Ey-!Ey's little house full time. So did she, and for a time Tik-Tik and !Ey-!Ey lived almost as a married couple.

However, they soon began to fight. Tik-Tik would reach for her, and instead of rolling with him she would push his hand away and say, "Tik-Tik should tell !Ey-!Ey about Tik-Tik's day." Or she would tell Tik-Tik about *her* day, and it was even more boring than Mother's stories, because as far as Tik-Tik could tell, !Ey-!Ey never went anywhere or did anything more than a very short walk away from the housing development.

Tik-Tik began complaining about this, and demanding to roll with her, and when she refused or started into another boring story, he would yell at her, or she at him, and then they would be fighting again. "!Ey-!Ey should be Mute!" he told her more than once. "Tik-Tik would love !Ey-!Ey if !Ey-!Ey were Mute!" And she would say, "Tik-Tik *is* Mute! Tik-Tik does not talk, only shout. Tik-Tik only wants to hunt and touch and roll and eat and fart and sleep."

It got so bad that Tik-Tik began sleeping at Mother's house again, although he still spent as little time there as possible. Instead, he traveled. He gathered knapping stones from the hills, and spearwood from the trees, and he sometimes hunted monkeys and pigs by a very big watering hole. He encountered many people on his travels, both Talking and Mute. He encountered many *women*, and found that if he simply told them their eyes were pretty, or that their legs were smooth, or if he sang to them, then in many cases they would be drawn to him, and would roll with him right there in the dust, or invite him back to houses or playhouses, where he sometimes remained for many days before moving on again. He became known in many earths and housing developments not only as a fierce man, but as one who rolled with many women, never asking if they were married or whether any other man loved them. Never caring if they were older or younger than he was, or really anything about them.

At one of his increasingly rare stops at home, Grandmother gave him a necklace, with the brightest blue bead he had ever seen.

"Apparently Tik-Tik is man, now," she said. "Grandmother thinks Tik-Tik is too young to be man, but apparently other women disagree."

"Yes," he said to her. *Rather smugly, Harv thought.*

"Men wear adornments," she said, and placed the necklace around his neck, tying its leather cord securely in the back. Then: "This bead is soft. Do not treat it roughly, or it may crack and fall off. The cord may also break, or the knot may come undone. If Tik-Tik is man, Tik-Tik must be careful about such things. Tik-Tik should also dye Tik-Tik's loincloth with red ochre or black coal, or rub it in the green grass."

"Tik-Tik will do this," he told her, realizing that he would like to have a man's loincloth, rather than a boy's. "And Tik-Tik will be careful with this." He fingered the bead, and felt things for which he had no words.

But out in the world, he *did* treat the necklace roughly, never giving a thought to it as he climbed trees and chased through bushes and leaned hard against shovels and punch presses.

His travels increased, until he discovered, all on his own, the housing development where his father and sister lived. Neither of them resembled his memories. Father was remarried, to a Mute woman, and now Tik-Tik fully understood the appeal of that. Father and the Mute woman had no children together, though, and Father's skin was wrinkled, and his body was slow. He looked and moved like a Grandfather.

Tik-Tik's sister, !Ibi, was also not the same. She was not a girl, but a woman, who lived with a Talking man who never seemed to be quiet, even when it was time to sleep. They were not married, but had a baby girl and a toddler boy together, and the girl and boy were also never quiet, and Tik-Tik could not stand to be around them.

All of this made Tik-Tik very sad, for the family he remembered did not exist anymore, and what did exist was something he did not want, or did not know how to make use of. He visited many times, but then resolved to stop, because his visits were not making anyone happy. And what was the point of life, if not to be happy?

And so he continued his travels, and continued rolling in the dust with as many women as he could. This made him happy. Or at least, he *thought* it made him happy, until one day when he came upon !Ey-!Ey standing before an apple tree, with an expression on her face that Harv would describe as *pensive*.

"Why does !Ey-!Ey stand before this tree?" Tik-Tik asked.

She looked up, saw him, and turned away dismissively. "Why does Tik-Tik care what !Ey-!Ey does?"

Tik-Tik looked at the tree, and saw there was a snake in it.

"Do not touch tree," he said. "Snakes are dangerous."

"!Ey-!Ey cares nothing about danger. !Ey-!Ey wants apples."

"Do not touch tree!"

But !Ey-!Ey stepped forward, reached out a hand, and plucked an apple from one of the lower branches, not far from the snake's head.

"!Ey-!Ey does not listen to Tik-Tik," she said, and bit into the apple.

This puzzled Tik-Tik. He was finished with !Ey-!Ey, and had moved on to other women. Many other women. And !Ey-!Ey had moved on to at least one other man, that Tik-Tik knew of. How the girls pointed and giggled at him when *that* happened!

"What is wrong?" he asked her.

"Nothing," she said, taking another big bite and throwing the rest of the apple on the ground.

"Is !Ey-!Ey not happy with Cort?"

"!Ey-!Ey's happiness is no business of Tik-Tik."

He paused then. She seemed very angry with him, still. He knew he had caused her pain, but why would she still be feeling it? Tik-Tik was gone. Tik-Tik was no longer touching her, no longer yelling and sleeping and farting in her presence.

"*Please* do not touch tree," he said again, moving toward her.

"Not another step," she said. "!Ey-!Ey is not happy with Cort. !Ey-!Ey is not happy with Mik. !Ey-!Ey is not happy with *anyone*. !Ey-!Ey is especially not happy with Tik-Tik."

She reached for another apple, and was bitten by the snake. She pulled her hand back, but it was too late.

"No!" Tik-Tik cried out.

"See?" she said, holding up her hand for him to look at. Two spots of blood trickled out of it.

"No," he said again. "What has !Ey-!Ey done? *Why* has !Ey-!Ey done this?"

"Actions have consequences," !Ey-!Ey said, and collapsed into the dust.

Tik-Tik had to leave behind his spear, and the bundle containing his knife and his axe and his ostrich egg, in order to carry !Ey-!Ey back to the housing development.

"Why does Tik-Tik carry !Ey-!Ey?" she asked him at one point.

"Because Tik-Tik does not want !Ey-!Ey to die," he replied.

To which she said, "Whether !Ey-!Ey will die has nothing to do with whether !Ey-!Ey is carried somewhere."

Tik-Tik's belly would not be still. Tik-Tik's forehead would not be dry. There was light wind in the earth, and some dust in the air. Tik-Tik blinked, but could not rub his eyes. Tears ran down his cheeks.

At another point, she said, "!Ey-!Ey did not expect so much pain."

"No one knows pain of snake bites," Tik-Tik told her gently, "Except people bitten by snakes."

At still another point she said, "!Ey-!Ey thought !Ey-!Ey would have more time. !Ey-!Ey thought !Ey-!Ey could walk back home and go to sleep."

To which Tik-Tik said, "!Ey-!Ey should save !Ey-!Ey's strength. !Ey-!Ey can sleep in Tik-Tik's arms."

"Mmm. That is all !Ey-!Ey ever wanted."

It was a long walk back to the housing development, and she said nothing further.

3.5

Nothing was ever the same for Tik-Tik after that. Although at first !Ey-!Ey's parents and sisters did not blame him for what had happened, he could not help blaming himself.

"!Ey-!Ey's belly was sad," they said. "!Ey-!Ey had sadness inside before Tik-Tik ever touched !Ey-!Ey. She became sadder when Tik-Tik left, but this is not Tik-Tik's fault."

But he answered them: "Tik-Tik was bad to !Ey-!Ey. Tik-Tik has been bad to many people, and actions have consequences."

And this they could not deny. This they could not overlook, and so finally Tik-Tik did come to receive a measure of blame in their minds. But never as great as the blame in his own. He thought long and hard about what !Ey-!Ey had told him: that he never spoke, except to yell. That he might as well be Mute, for all the good his voice did anyone. Could his words have saved her? Had his touch somehow doomed her?

And he wondered: why did he miss her now? *Now*, when she was gone and buried and dust? Why *now*, did he begin to feel the stirrings of love that she had wanted from him so desperately while still she lived? Could a man love a woman who wasn't there?

For a long time, he stayed in Mother's house and did not speak. And then, when he emerged, he built a house of his own—a real one—and still did not speak. And then he went looking for his spear and knife and axe and ostrich egg, and when he could not find them, he set about replacing them.

He went to the hills for stone, to the trees for wood, to the bushes for pelts and cords. He made an axe with a wooden handle, and a knife with a wooden haft, and a spear with an oversized stone head, and he made leather sheaths to cover all of their sharp edges. He spent many days fashioning his tools, and received many compliments, for they were in some ways the finest tools the Talking People had ever seen, and were widely copied thereafter.

The ostrich egg was hardest, though, and required many days of travel to find a freshly laid nest. Once he found it he chased the furious mother away from it, and selected the strongest of the eggs, and brought it to a woman in a neighboring development who was expert at punching round holes in fresh eggs and washing the goo goo out of them. He went to another woman who was expert at fashioning wooden corks, to seal an ostrich egg when it was filled with water. He went to a third woman who was expert at fashioning pouches to carry things, with a loop of cord so that they could hang from the shaft of a spear.

However, he did not roll in the dust with any of these women, or with any other women he encountered on these journeys, even when they called out to him. Sometimes they called him out by name, for his face and his bead necklace and his red-and-black loincloth had become well known. But he did not go to these women who called to him, only saying instead, "Actions have consequences. Tik-Tik fears to act in this matter. Tik-Tik wishes everyone pleasant days."

He lived alone for a time in the house he had built, and then he finally began to feel lonely, and to feel a pressure of speech building up inside him. And so he visited the homes of his neighbors, bringing them rabbits and miniature goats, and birds and even jackals to eat. And he sat by their fires at night, listening to their stories, and attempting, finally, for the first time, to tell his own story, which was the story of Father and Mother and Stepfather and Grandmother, and even the Grandfather who had taught him to shape stones and then died.

And then his restless belly began to long for a different sort of journey, and although this earth was by no means exhausted, and there was no need to move or split the people, he began to say, "Tik-Tik wishes to find a new earth and create a new development. Tik-Tik has made many mistakes here. Tik-Tik has made mistakes *everywhere*. Tik-Tik does not believe Tik-Tik should live among people thus harmed, and wishes to begin again, with knowledge, and to do better."

At first such comments had little effect, for Tik-Tik was known as a man of fickle tastes and moods. But Tik-Tik persisted, and over time people began to realize he was serious. People began to realize he was asking if anyone wanted to come with him, to start their own lives again, with knowledge.

The first to agree was a Mute woman, who as a child had become friends with the double-click sound that meant "come here," believing it to be her name. Her birth name was Maya, but she could barely pronounce it, and no one called her that anyway. And so her name was Come Here, which brought much laughter to the people around her.

"Come here, Come Here," they would say, and she understood the joke and would laugh right along with them.

The second to agree was a Talking boy on the edge of manhood, whose Father had left and whose Mother had died. "There is no family here," he said. "Memories here are bad. There is no reason to stay."

The third was a Talking woman in the midst of an unhappy divorce, who said, "Dow-Dow thinks he owns wife, like spear or axe. Nobody owns. Nobody is owned."

Next was a childhood acquaintance of Tik-Tik's who at one time had been the strongest boy in the development. Even today, he was one of the strongest men.

After that, there were many, and one day they all left the housing development and moved to an earth many days' travel away, beside a big watering hole.

Life was not so easy there: hippos and crocodiles made the water dangerous, and antelopes (while excellent game animals and tasty meals) sometimes attracted hyenas that had to be killed or chased away. There were mongongo nut trees, but no longer any apples or figs, and the sky rained less often, so there were fewer yams to dig, and less grass for thatch. The people often complained to Tik-Tik, as though he were responsible for the weather here, and people sometimes expressed a desire to return to the old housing development.

"No one holds you here," Tik-Tik told them. "But going home again does not work like you think. Already, home is not same place. People move and die and marry and give birth. People *change*. How can home be the same? Home is in stories told beside fireplaces. Home is in here." He touched his belly, which for the Talking People was the seat of consciousness and the home of the soul, as they dimly conceived it.

As life became more established in the new housing development, Tik-Tik and Come Here were married in a simple ceremony, and in time she bore him several sons, and he learned that he was still capable of love—so much love!—for living people.

In the new development, each family had its own house, but there was also one big house where they would gather every evening to eat and sing and tell stories. And here Tik-Tik began telling not only his own story, but also retelling that of Talking Woman. And because his belly had never really settled over !Ey-!Ey, he frequently told her story as well. And having finally found his voice, he became known as a great storyteller, just as he'd once been known as a great toolmaker, and before that a great lover of women, and before that, the fiercest of boys. And he told the stories of both women so compellingly that in future generations they would twist together until nearly all the facts were lost, and the people remembered only that a woman who was mother to them all, had also been the first among them to speak, and that a snake in an apple tree had bitten her. And also that a man had failed to protect her, but had also loved her, in his own imperfect way, from a place of exile.

Foothills Hospital
Boulder, Colorado
Present Day

As Harv slept or seized or whatever was going on back there in the ER, Tara *did* hold Patel's hand. They were in the waiting room, sitting in uncomfortable vinyl chairs with uncomfortable wooden arms, with paper magazines strewn all around.

"I'm sure he's going to be fine," Patel told her, based on nothing at all.

"I know," she answered, just as pointlessly.

His hand felt good in hers, and although she couldn't bring herself to let go, she was aware of how ridiculous it must look to him. She was a walking cliché, a female postdoc who'd fallen for an older male professor. Would she now complete the cliché by flirting with the boys her own age? *Aiyo*, what a fool America had made of her.

Patel was the son of mustard-farm sharecroppers in rural Madhya Pradesh, the landlocked center of India. Hindu and yet Urdu-speaking, probably descended from the Sudra caste, he seemed on the surface to have little in common with a modern urban girl from Chennai. That her own childhood home had a swimming pool and three servants didn't make her anything more than middle class, but it was a world of difference nonetheless. She had no idea how Patel had found his way to CU, or how his education back home had been paid for, or anything else about him. And it didn't matter, because here in Boulder he was an academic, a sort of larval-stage Brahmin doing groundbreaking work. Here in Boulder the two of them were both simply Indian—all their differences collapsed and compressed into that single word, as if they'd come from the same small town.

"This day's going to define the rest of our lives," she said to him.

"Nobel Prize," he said, giving her hand a squeeze.

"Maybe. It's going to be hard, though. Nobody's going to believe him."

"Mmm. Do you?"

"I don't know," she said. "You?"

"Yes, indeed. I know every part of that machine. I know what it should do, and I always thought Harv was underestimating the effect it would have, to write the information straight into the hippocampus. That's the same thing as remembering it. He recruited me because I studied quantum mechanics *and* neuro-anatomy, but he rarely asks me any questions."

"Mmm."

In his slow voice, Patel said, "He's an impulsive person, Tara, but his theory is sound. It always was. Do you think I'd wreck my life, chaining myself to a crazy person? He graduates his students much faster than a lot of professors; I'd have no time to recover. Just three years of crazy, and then my PhD in craziness. No, thank you.

"The hard part is going to be finding anyone willing to replicate the results. I have to admit, this is not a promising beginning. Publication is not that big a thing; if we break it up into several papers, we can dole the shock factor out a little at a time. That should make it easier for people to accept. Yes, the Y chromosome is a quantum storage device. Yes, its contents can be read. Yes, its contents can be transferred into a human brain, with difficulty. *Then* we hit them with the details, with Manu and all that. It's doable. Harv will even let us be first author on some of the papers. He'll insist on it.

"But replication is another matter, Tara. It seems like we can't slam an entire quantome into somebody's brain like this. We need to find a way to divide it into digestible fragments, and even then it's pretty scary, given what's happened here. Also, when I think about the entanglements, it makes me think no one else is ever getting the same memories. No one else will be able to corroborate, you see? Even if two researchers share the same ancestral line, the wave function can only collapse at two different points in time."

"The past and the present?"

"Now they're both in the past, but yes. The hyperdimensional space can only connect that way, through . . . basically through a wormhole. One cave man links to one researcher, and that's it. But it's a shame that *these* memories came to somebody who wasn't trained to evaluate them. I never really thought about that. We should have set up the experiment quite differently."

Tara did her best to absorb that. She let go of Patel's hand, and rubbed her eyes. It was barely lunchtime, and she was already as tired as she'd ever been in her life.

"So all of this is real?" she asked.

"That's my opinion, yes."

After a pause, she said, "That doesn't make it easier, what happens next."

"No, of course not. But I have a crazy uncle, and he doesn't talk like that. Harv's statements are mutually consistent, and we've got the math and the biology to back them up."

"We'll need archeology, too," she said. "Someone to collaborate on the papers, and point out where to look for corroboration."

"Yes, anything to strengthen the case. When Isaac Newton published his theory of gravity, he wrote an entire book that answered every objection."

"Hmm."

For a while they said nothing. Finally she gave in to her fears and said, "These seizures are getting longer."

"For the moment, yes."

"That can't be good for him."

"No, but he got treatment early. I think they're giving him the right drugs to calm it down. Those brain scans are going to show inflammation around the hippocampus, as the brain tries to rewire itself, but the nurse said they're giving him corticosteroids. So it should all begin to improve soon."

Eventually, a dark-haired female nurse came and got them, saying, "He's awake again, and asking for you."

"Oh, thank God. Is he all right?"

"He's disoriented," the nurse answered.

"Is that normal?"

"It can be, but I'll let the doctor give you the details."

Through the double doors, around a corner and through a set of curtains, they found Harv with the young female doctor standing over him. She was Caucasian, with brown hair and pale green eyes, and over a cerulean blue sweater she wore a lab coat embroidered with the name "Dr. Steph." The overhead lights were off.

"It sounded like babytalk," Harv was saying. "The birth of language. I think it was literally Eden."

"Push five milligrams of diazepam," the doctor said to the nurse beside them.

"How is he?" Tara asked, ignoring Harv's rambling for the moment.

The doctor shook Tara's hand and answered, "Hi. Yeah, he's in what we call a postictal state, which just means post-seizure. He's exhibiting confusion and nausea, and he asked us to turn down the lights. That's all relatively normal. It usually lasts less than thirty minutes, although it can be longer with these kinds of protracted atonal seizures. Atypically, he was presenting with rapid eye movement for most of the event, almost as though he was dreaming. We don't normally see that."

"What does it mean?"

The doctor spread her hands. "I wish I knew. The brain can be a funny place."

"But he asked for us?"

"He has moments of lucidity, yes."

"Is he going to be all right?"

Here the doctor switched on a warm, professional smile. "We're doing everything we can. I've written a scrip for an anticonvulsant, which you can pick up at the pharmacy on the west side of the building. It could take anywhere from a few days to a few weeks to build up in his system, but it should limit further attacks, with minimal side effects. In the meantime he'll take sedatives, which I've also put in the pharma orders."

Then the smile drained out of her face, and she asked, "What exactly happened to him? He's got no sign of trauma, and no history of seizures."

Behind Tara, Patel answered, "He's a professor of electrical engineering, and he was experimenting on his hippocampus with a TMS rig, trying to implant memories."

"Hmm. Wow. *That's* troubling. It's consistent with our findings, though: microscopic hippocampal lesions. Do you know what the field strength was?"

"Four tesla."

"Ouch. That's quite high."

"You need that to reach the center," Patel said. "Where memories are formed."

Doctor Steph took a few seconds to contemplate that. Finally, she asked, "Did he succeed?"

"We think so, yes."

"Y-chromosome Adam was a *player*," Harv said, nodding. "That boy got some tail."

"Do you have any idea what he's talking about?" the doctor wanted to know. "Is it related to your research?"

"We think so," Patel acknowledged. "It will take some time to be sure."

"Implanted memories?"

"So it would appear."

"Hmm. Hmm. I had no idea that was possible. I mean, is it actually? It doesn't seem to agree with him." She'd been looking mostly at Harv while she spoke, but now she leveled her gaze squarely at Patel and said, "Sir, I'm going to have to ask you to suspend any further research. It's hospital policy to notify the police in cases of workplace injury, of which this certainly counts."

"Of course," Patel agreed. "We're working under an NSF grant, so we'll have to notify them as well. Any adverse event."

Finally, Tara said, "Will you two take it outside, please?" She pointed to a gap in the curtain. Then she settled down next to Harv on a chair identical to the ones in the waiting room, and took his hand.

"How're you doing, Baby?" She'd never called him that before.

"Going places," he said, meeting her gaze. "I saw a woman eating an apple, at the dawn of human language. I think it was Mitochondrial Eve."

Gently she said, "Mitochondrial Eve and Y-Chromosome Adam lived a hundred thousand years apart."

"Well, whatever. There was a serpent in the garden. How much more do you need?"

"Okay, Baby. Okay." She no longer knew any way to distinguish between facts, speculation, and pure bullshit.

"Tara, what if all our legends are true? I've met trolls, and seen the bones of a dragon. I've seen the Great Flood, and the Antediluvian ages that came before it. The voice of God, before the deluge. The people were just learning to speak in complete sentences. It was spreading to their children, like a mutation."

Tara felt a chill, because complex language *had* started with a mutation, in a gene called FOXP2. It controlled, among other things, the development of the left parietal lobe, where the language centers were located. Mice implanted with the human form of the gene could sing like birds.

"The birth of our species," he said to her.

And that wasn't right, either; depending on definitions, *Homo sapiens* might be as much as three or four times older than that. But she knew what he meant, and she feared (yes, *feared*) that he was right.

"Do you want something to write with?" she asked.

"How about a voice recorder?"

Obligingly, she got out her phone and opened the Record app, setting the handset down on the table next to his head.

And he began telling her a story that was too detailed, too jumpy, too jarringly consistent to be a dream or hallucination or on-the-spot fabrication. If this were a hoax, he'd been planning it for years. And Patel would have to be in on it. But the machine and the NSF grant were real. The seizures were real, and the brain inflammation in the exact right spot was real, so Occam's Razor left not much refuge for her doubts. This was really happening.

Time travel.

Time travel that mirrored the traveling of a Y chromosome to different points around the globe, its genome handed down intact from one generation to the next. That meant *Tara* was the expert from this point forward, and was going to have to get large portions of their story straight. The paleogenetics had to line up, or the whole thing fell apart! And the work promised to be challenging, to say the least. She hadn't had time to catch the details of Harv's last seizure, but if he was claiming to have been a Neandertal, then there was literally no way the puzzle was going to fit together. Neandertal Y chromosomes had never been found in any live human or excavated *H. sapiens* skeleton. The Neandertal haplogroups were all extinct in the modern world. Harv was a member of D-M174—very definitely a modern human haplogroup.

But it sounded more like he'd experienced memories from one of the European Early Modern Humans who'd been around at that same time—EEMH's as they were known on Tara's side of campus. Harv had several times used the term "Cro-Magnon," which was popular but had no formal taxonomic status, because it referred to a single dig site in France. But okay, the EEMH vector was still a problem, because it meant Harv's paternal line had to get from somewhere in Africa (which he was presently describing to her), to somewhere in central Asia where the haplogroup's defining mutations had occurred, and then to Europe, and then to somewhere in India or Pakistan, and then back to Europe again. It sounded absurd even to her, because ancient peoples simply hadn't moved around that much. Or if some of them had, the genetic signature of it was mostly overwhelmed by the vast majority who hadn't.

Too, Harv had never described being out of place in any of his visions. He wasn't a "Cro-Magnon" in Vedic India, nor a swarthy Indian in Scotland. The myth of racial phenotypes had been pretty thoroughly discredited at the genetic level, but even so, these movements would put quite a strain Harv's family's evolution and, more importantly, their cross-breeding with whatever locals they encountered.

She tried not to think about what this meant for her personally, because yes, trying not to think about something was so easy. So easy. Was she just one more in a long line of genetically compelled, xenophilic conquests? Would it matter if she were?

When Harv's account started to fizzle out, she said to him, "That's quite a narrative. Do you have any idea where it took place?"

"No," he admitted. "Or when. Somewhere in Africa, a long time ago. Or maybe the Middle East. Did ostriches ever live there?"

She sighed. "You know, it would be nice if you could've filled in some of these gaps. How about stepping backward a thousand years at a time? Or ten thousand? Give me some waypoints to follow."

"Sorry," he said. Then, "I don't think my brain could handle that."

"Yeah," she agreed, slumping. "We're not even sure it can handle *this*."

"There are a hundred things we could have done better," he admitted.

She both squeezed his hand and looked away.

"I was right there with you, Harv."

"Mmm," he murmured, apparently not sure what to say to that.

They sat in silence for a little while, until she asked him, "What do you think this means?"

"There were no cave people," he answered immediately, as if he'd been waiting for the question. As if he were already rehearsing all the perfect answers. "Not the way people think. Not ever."

"No, no, what does it mean for *us*?"

He shrugged. "Nothing changes for you and me. Not unless you want it to."

"Not *that* us," she said. "You and me and Patel."

"Oh. Well, yeah, we're going to be busy. Really busy, and not always in a good way."

"We'll need a lawyer," she said.

"We'll need a lot of things. It's going to get crazy."

"It's *already crazy*," she said, now feeling tears on her cheeks again. She turned off the voice recorder. "We took a lot of risks. That's going to come out, too."

"I know."

"It's going to reflect on all of us."

"I know."

"I'm furious with myself for helping you do this so ... sloppily. I know progress is messy sometimes, but this just looks *bad*."

"I know that, too. I'm sorry for all the ways this affects you."

They sat together for a while in the dim light, without speaking, with the beeps and voices and clatters of the emergency room wafting over them. The air smelled of bleach and floor wax, of polymer bags and tubes and basins and fixtures slowly outgassing. Like new car smell, she thought vaguely.

In the absence of conversation, Tara felt her anger turn inward. Harv was only four centimeters taller than she was, and his white skin, black hair, and dark brown eyes were nondescript at best. He wore sneakers and T-shirts to work, and carried a backpack over one shoulder, like a man less than half his age. The only truly remarkable thing about his appearance was the silly pink lenses he wore in his glasses. How exactly had she fallen so completely into his orbit? How could she explain that to other people, in a way they'd understand?

And yet, when her head was on his shoulder, she felt as relaxed as she ever had. In his company she felt *cool*, and that was a strange thing, because even when he was boozing and vaping and driving too fast, he was quite visibly a dork. But that was the thing about very smart people: what you saw on the surface was all ripples and reflection, giving no information about the depths below, the rays of sunlight shimmering on treasure.

After a while, Patel stuck his head back into the curtained area around the bed. "Boss, I'm going to talk with the police. Is that okay?"

"Yep. When you're done, you can send them in here. If I'm awake."

Tara sighed. "If you're *awake*? Jesus, Harv." Then: "How are you feeling?"

"I have a headache," he said.

And somehow they both laughed at that.

"I think I have one too," she said.

"I'll buy you a really nice dinner when this is over," he said. "Anywhere you like. That Thai place, or whatever."

That sounded fine for a second, but then she thought about it and said, "It still isn't over?"

He paused for a few moments, as if listening, and then shook his head.

Well, *that* was demoralizing. She asked: "Is another seizure coming?"

"Uh-huh."

And that raised all kinds of questions: how did he know? What sensations were flowing through him? Why was any of this happening, and why wouldn't it stop?

"Have we *killed* you, Harv?"

The question seemed to rock him back for a moment. *Had* they? *Would* he? All he could do was shrug and say, "I dunno. I certainly hope not."

And the girlfriend part of her didn't know what to do with that, so she let the scientist in her ask, "What's the sensation like?"

"It's like a pressure, building behind my eyes."

"The headache is increasing?"

"No," he said, "it's separate from the headache. It's more like a push. Or a pull. It's like gravity. It's a big sine wave rolling in and out, and right now it's trending stronger again. But it's building more slowly this time."

His hand felt suddenly clammy in hers. Sweat had begun to bead up on his forehead. She tried to imagine what was happening inside him, and came up with nothing except a vision of cartoon lightning bolts crackling through the inside of his head, louder and brighter.

"Oh, gods, Harv," she muttered, squeezing. "Stay with me."

"It feels different." His voice sounded woozy. "Maybe it's the drugs. Something different is happening."

The alarms stared up again.

"This is going to be bad," he noted calmly. "I feel like I'm falling."

The memories of the Talking People, none too clear even while they were happening, fell way from Harv's mind, and he felt himself skidding farther and farther back in time. But now history had a slick, yielding quality that was difficult to anchor against. He caught glimpses—a million glimpses!—of life on the beach, life in the forest, life on the open grasslands. People active in the daylight, or in the moonlight, or in the twilight between. Human history was definitely not some linear progression, but a restless fucking around from one place to another, an endless adaptation to new problems and circumstances.

And yet, without language, Harv's mind seemed to have nothing to attach to. Feelings of love and lust and joy and fear washed through him but didn't take, and it began to feel like he was falling through time, with nothing to arrest him. And now Harv felt his own fear, because none of this was supposed to be happening. Nothing at all was known about this process, or what it might be doing to his brain, or to his soul (if such a thing could be said to exist), or to the delicate quantum states that defined his own natural memories. These had become entangled with equally complex states from other times and places, but what if that entangling mechanism had ceased, or saturated, or decohered?

The images flickered by, faster and faster. And other sensations: heat and cold. Rain and wind. Pain of a thousand different types. Exactly like a falling man, he felt a need to scream. He thought perhaps he did scream, but was there air enough in his lungs for another thirty thousand years? Another million?

His sight began to fade into a gray tunnel that blackened and shrunk around the edges, withering down to a single spot of light, and then winking out entirely. If he'd been screaming, he stopped then, believing himself dead or worse, and in any case beyond hope of rescue.

And then, suddenly, his memories found something to latch onto—something big—*and with a kind of buzzing-scraping-thudding sensation, he felt himself collapsing into something so far back that his mind—his mind, the mind of a chrononaut-scientist!—could not conceive of the distance. And then he opened his eyes.*

PART FOUR
The Voyage

4.1

Light glinted off the water and into the eyes of a creature called Ba. Ba blinked and grunted, feeling a spike of pain and pressure and dizziness through his head, quickly subsiding to a dull ache. Closing his eyes, Ba kicked his feet, twisting around in the water to face away from the setting sun. Then he opened his eyes again, and felt better.

For a moment, Ba thought he'd hit something, or that a wave was flipping over the raft on which he lay, stomach down, with his head and arms dangling off the front. But no, the water was calm, and the raft beneath him was sturdy. In fact, with the light now behind him he could see there was a *beautiful* fish almost within arm's reach. Collecting his wits, he raised his right arm and, with the forked wooden gaff in his hand, stabbed the fish right through the middle, despite the optical illusion that the gaff was bent at the water's surface.

And that's how we do that! he thought to himself. Ba was good at what he did, and could be a bit of a smug prick about it at times.

He sat up on the raft, hauling in the wriggling fish, then jabbed it down on the timbers in front of him, scooped up a raindrop-shaped hand axe, and smashed the space between the fish's head and body. Its struggles eased after that, and soon it was dead.

Ba sometimes felt sorry for the fishes he caught; they obviously didn't want to be stabbed or axed or eaten. But neither did most things, and his tribe did have to survive. Of course, this was his third big fish for the afternoon, and the sun would be down soon, and the other man and woman who'd been out here fishing today had each caught a single big fish of their own and then gone home. There would be plenty to eat, so perhaps Ba would go home now, too, and let the rest of the fish continue living their little fishy lives for another day.

Looking toward the beach, he tried to gauge the surf he'd have to paddle through as he landed his raft. The height and strength of the waves wasn't always easy to judge from out here past the surf line, but right now it didn't look too bad, or sound too bad. Still, he tied his three fish together with a length of jute twine, and then tied them to one of the timbers of the raft. He'd lost more than one meal to the breaking surf, and wasn't prepared to lose this one. When he was ready, he stowed the gaff and axe under his body, paddled around with his arms until he was facing the land, and then began kicking toward shore.

His raft was a miniature version of something Huckleberry Finn might recognize: eight tree trunks lashed together, each as wide as Ba's upper arm, and chopped at the ends to about two-thirds of his height, with a pair of stabilizing bars lashed crosswise underneath. Of course, Ba could neither speak nor count (not higher than three, anyway), and had no cultural reference points for his engineering marvel. But his father-figure, Kaa, had taught him well, and so the tribe continued to eat its fill of fish even after Kaa had disappeared one day on a fishing trip, leaving not so much as a washed-up body.

Everything was food for someone.

Ba kicked and paddled and kicked some more, until he felt the surf-line waves begin to lift and push him. Then he gripped the edges of the raft firmly, and kicked a couple more times until a wave lifted up beneath him, catching him on its front and *heaving* him forward.

And for just a flickering moment, Ba was reminded of Manuah on his reed boat, as the wave lifted higher beneath him, tilting his face down toward the water and his feet up toward the sky. He loved this part—the fear and joy and power of it. And the speed! As fast as a man could run, and faster! He was good at this, but it was not easy, and wipeouts happened all the time. And then, yes, the fear began to win out, as he realized this wave was going to be bigger than he'd thought. Soon it was as tall as the raft was long, and then it was as tall as Ba himself, and then it was a blue-green tube through which the red sunlight shone, and Ba's feet were getting sucked up into it.

And then it was breaking on top of him, and underneath him, and he'd neglected to steer with his legs, so the raft spun sideways and *tumbled* in a pounding confusion of water and foam, wet beach sand and smooth rocks and seashells as sharp as hand axes. And then the water was retreating, leaving Ba sitting on his wet ass amidst a yard sale of fish and twine and tools and expertly chopped logs.

Ba was nude and covered in wiry black hair, less like a chimpanzee than like some hirsute movie stars he could think of. The hair on his shoulders and upper back was as thick as the hair on his head, but he had the rounded, naked buttocks of a human being, and so the water tickled his nether regions as it pulled back into the sea. He had only a moment to appreciate the sensation before he saw another wave about to curl and crash. This one was higher than the last—a *problem* wave—and so he gathered up as many of his things as he could, got to his feet, and trotted up the beach, laughing like a drunken sailor.

Well, he thought, *that was fun.*

He was lucky not to have impaled himself on the fishing gaff, but all life was luck, yes? Until it wasn't. At least he'd *saved* the gaff, and the three fish, and about half of the raft. The rest he could gather up once he'd caught his breath. The waves were coming in, not out, so the sea would not suck away the timbers. Unfortunately, he *had* lost the hand axe, which kind of blew ass. Now he was going to have to spend the next day or two making another one.

But rather than moving, he instead looked up at the fiery spectacle of the setting sun. The air was clear today after an afternoon rain, and the rays of the sun shone brightly through clouds that looked like goats and snakes and bushes. And to the right of the sunset, across the water, he saw a distant land.

Ah!

It certainly wasn't the first time he'd seen those hills and beaches, but he never got tired of the sense of wonder they inspired. What was over there? Were there animals? Vegetables? From the color of the hills, he was pretty sure that some of them were made of bare stone, and others were covered in trees, but that was all he knew. And it struck him, not for the first time, that the distant land wasn't *all that* distant. If the ocean were solid, he could walk there in a fraction of a morning. Ba knew how to swim, but he had a general idea that this was a slower mode of transportation than walking, and a lot more tiring, and it carried a significant risk of drowning if he tried to do it for too long. Swimming short distances was tiring; long distances were out of the question.

So yes, when he was out on the water he preferred to use a fishing raft, even though this was slower still. The purpose of a raft was not to go anywhere; it was to *not* go anywhere. Just to float out past the surf line where the big fish were. And to hold your stuff while you did it.

But he wondered suddenly: *could* a raft go somewhere? It might need to be a bigger raft, that could hold his entire body. Sometimes Ba would get surprised by *really* big fish that tried to eat *him*, raft and all. He'd always successfully fended them off—sometimes by kicking them really hard, if they were behind him. Sometimes by jabbing their faces with his gaff, or stabbing them in the back with a hand axe. They did *not* like that! But anyway, he was no fool; if he was in the water and saw big fins, he headed straight for shore. If he was on the shore and saw fins, he skipped fishing for the day, and went hunting for eggs or birds or honey instead. But out in the middle of the ocean, these choices would not be available to him.

Wouldn't he be safer on a larger raft? Couldn't he just pull his arms and legs out of the water and wait around until the danger had passed? He could even sleep on the raft, if the journey lasted that long. He could bring food with him. Thirst might be a problem, though; ocean water was not drinkable, for some reason. He got sick every time he tried, and every time he accidentally swallowed a wave. But if he brought melons or berries, then perhaps he could go without drinking for a day.

I'd be like Christopher Columbus, he thought. Wait, what?

The thoughts dissipated. Perhaps Ba had spent too much time out in the sun today, but in any case it was time to get home and feed his tribe. Shaking his head, he dropped his pile of things well up above the high water line along the beach, and then went back down to the water to gather up the remaining pieces of his raft.

The hand axe was an annoying loss he'd have to deal with in the morning. He couldn't do much of anything without that.

4.2

As sunlight faded and twilight gathered, Ba returned to camp and dropped his fish next to the fire. His favorite woman, Mar, hugged and kissed him as he tossed his other things aside in a rough pile.

"Mmm?" she asked.

"Mmm," he replied, sharing with her the annoyance of his lost hand axe.

"Mmm?" she inquired again, seeking clarification.

He mimed the act of chopping, then looked at his empty hand in feigned surprise. Putting a hand over his eyebrows as if to shield against the sun, he looked this way and that way, then gave up and shrugged.

Mar laughed.

"Har har," he mimicked back to her.

She hugged him again, as if to say, *it'll be okay, darling.* Then she sat herself down by the fire pit, scooped up the little blade she kept there, and commenced scaling and gutting the fish.

"Mmm?" she asked, pointing to the fire.

"Mmm," he said. *Yes, I'll get some more wood.* Unlike many of the tribe, Ba and Mar both knew how to make new fire. It was one of many, many things Kaa had taught. But it was time-consuming and very tiring; one had to build a fire nest out of dried grass, and then fill it with kindling, and then find smooth sticks of just the right size, and then rub them together vigorously inside the nest, without slipping and smashing it apart. If you did it just right, then eventually the nest would burst into flame, and you could start feeding it sticks and soon you'd have a decent fire going. But it was a lot easier to keep the fire going all the time, and so that was what the tribe nearly always did. Right now it was a low smolder of coals barely larger than the palm of Ba's hand, but with a little love it could be brought back to life.

"Ba!" said another woman, whose name was Cheek-click. She was holding some yams.

"Mmm!" said a young boy named Popping-sound.

And suddenly the whole tribe was converging out of the bushes and weeds, many people. An older man named Guh was among them, swaggering and pushing, carrying over his shoulders the gutted carcass of a young gazelle he had somehow managed to kill.

"Naah!" Guh boasted, tossing the carcass on the ground in front of Mar as though she were supposed to deal with it. He then grabbed Cheek-click around the waist and pulled her in for a not-quite-consensual kiss. Guh was big and strong, and enjoyed being an asshole about it. He never did any work, other than hunting, and he sure didn't know how to build a raft or start a fire. Why bother, when smarter, more responsible people could be counted on to do it for him?

Cheek-click squirmed in his grasp, trying (though not very hard) to get away. Guh would mate with all of the women all the time, usually right in front of everybody. Ah, but when Guh was out throwing rocks at things, whom did the women turn to? Ba wasn't every woman's favorite, but he did all right, and he was certainly Mar's favorite and Cheek-click's favorite, and that was more than enough for him. How many women did one man need?

"Niiih," he said to Guh, a bit mockingly. He pointed to his three big fish, which together probably had nearly as much meat as that gazelle.

"Mmm?" Guh demanded, then released Cheek-click and pushed Ba lightly on the chest. Not enough to really start something, but enough to let Ba know there could be a beat-down at any time. Then, to compound it, he picked up one of Ba's raft fragments— the forward underside crosspiece—and snapped it over his knee, tossing the two pieces into the fire contemptuously. See?

Then, in a move that was one hundred percent classic Guh, he spread his arms wide, offering Ba the opportunity to hug him. Sighing, Ba stepped in and did so. He wasn't proud of it, but hell, it was just easier than fighting and losing all the time. He'd get back at Guh later, by fucking Cheek-click or something.

Guh's smell—like sweat and blood and sex and hair—turned Ba's stomach. But even he had to admit there was something vaguely reassuring about Guh's strong arms. Asshole or no, Guh was a good provider and defender, and all the predators were scared of humans—even of the little children—because Guh had taught them over and over again what a hard-thrown rock could do to their bones and guts. Humans were dangerous!

"Mmm?" Guh asked him. *Do you surrender to my awesomeness?*

"Mmm," Ba agreed, reluctantly.

Satisfied, Guh released him.

"Rrr," Ba said then, pointing to the fragments of his raft.

Guh just smiled and shrugged at that (*hey, these things happen*) and plopped his ass down beside the fire pit.

With that out of the way, Ba set about gathering wood, while Mar cleaned the fish and Cheek-click smashed her yams between two rocks, so they would cook faster. Other men and women and even children set about various tasks, so that the camp felt full of homey bustling. Lo's baby—the only baby in the tribe at the moment—cried briefly and was silenced when she began to nurse him.

All was right with the world.

All except for Ba's lost hand axe, and his daydreams about ocean travel. Was that a crazy/stupid thought? Would he simply get himself killed, or disappear like Kaa had done? As he built up the fire and helped the women cook and then tried to wolf down his dinner without burning his fingers or his throat, as he watched the twinkling stars come out and felt the first cool breeze of evening slither across the land, as he poked at the fire with a stick and watched people—singly and in pairs—slinking away from the heat of the fire to sleep or mate... Ba wondered. Was it really possible? Was that land across the water something he could really get to? What would he find there?

One of Ba's unofficial jobs was to bury the fire for the night, to protect its embers while the people slept, and as he did this he started really thinking about the kinds of things he would need to make such a journey, and although he was unaware of it, this was actually the hardest anyone on Earth had ever thought about anything. At some point he nodded off, without noticing, and dreamed he was fishing again, with those cool green hills looming larger and closer every time he looked up.

✧   ✧   ✧

In the morning he lounged around for a while, and then when people started to filter out of the camp on their assorted jobs and hobbies, he mated with Cheek-click, as he'd promised himself he would. And then, because Mar looked a bit jealous, he mated with her as well, and then lounged for a while longer, until the morning sun cleared the tops of the bushes, leaving shadows nowhere to hide. Then he got to work.

First and foremost, he needed a new hand axe, which for Ba's people was the equivalent of a whole garage full of tools. In hills behind the camp there was a good deposit of the kind of flint he liked, so he went there, and selected a nice spar that jutted out from the rock face. Picking up a hunk of heavier stone, he smashed the spar a few times until it broke free and landed at his feet. Then, with a mixture of tedium and craftsmanly pride, he gathered up some appropriate stones from the ground, sat down, set up a little work area around him, and began knapping the stone.

Ba's people were well adapted to the sunshine; through his body hair and leathery brown skin it neither burned nor overheated him, and while he did sweat a bit, and slowly grow thirsty, he did not attach any great urgency to this. Ba often went all day without a drink, allowing his mouth and throat to dry out without feeling any particular distress. He knew where to find the water when he really needed it, but right now he was busy.

But before he'd really gotten very far in shaping the new axe, something strange happened: the stone fractured along a face, peeling away a large flake and revealing...

A seashell?

No, not a seashell. It was stone—it was *flint*, specifically—but it had the shape of a little spiral, just exactly like a sea snail or a nautilus or any of a myriad other mollusks he had caught and cooked and eaten in his day. It seemed, improbably, as if some sea creature escaping danger had crawled all the way out of the water and then, unsatisfied, crawled up into the hills and then right into solid rock to find its safety. Was such a thing possible? Ba had certainly never seen anything like that, but here it was.

For a moment he was unsure what to do. Throw the stone away? Keep it as a decoration? (This concept was very hazy in his mind, for his people did not live in houses or wear jewelry, so what was there to decorate?) He sniffed it, and detected no fishy odor or whiff of salt water. Whatever this thing was, it had died a long time ago. Finally, shrugging, he decided to go ahead and make a hand axe out of the stone around it.

The work went quickly—this was good stone, and he was motivated not to waste any time. He would need the axe to chop down trees and shape logs and cut jute plants, and green branches to make a wicker nest. Nests weren't used for much, as Ba's world lacked anything to store or anyplace to store it, but if a wicker nest were weighed down with stones in a salt marsh, it could hold jute plants for a few days—long enough to dissolve away the stems and leave behind the fibers, which he could roll and braid into twine. Making a fishing raft was the work of many days, and making an oversized *voyaging* raft would be the work of many more.

When he was finished, he had arguably created one of the very first works of art. The little spiral sat just below the hand-grip and just above the blade, so it would be clearly visible while the hand axe was in use. And it was also a good axe! Kaa had taught him well, and this one fit just perfectly into his hand, with sharp blades and a sharp but sturdy point. He could not have been more proud.

When he was done admiring, he returned to camp, drank his fill from the stream there, relieved himself in the nearby bushes, and waited for people to return.

"Mmm?" he said to them one by one as they arrived, trying to show them the axe, trying to point out, specifically, the little seashell in its handgrip. "Mmm? Mmm?"

One by one they looked at it with confused expressions and shrugged. *So? So?* They either didn't understand what they were looking at, or didn't know what to make of it, or really actually didn't have the sense to appreciate its symmetry and form. Or they understood it but just didn't care.

When Mar finally arrived, he showed it to her and *she* oohed and aahed over it. Well, that was why she was his favorite: she knew how to *do* things, and how to appreciate the things others did. She was fully present in a way that even Cheek-click was not.

But then Guh arrived, and saw Mar and Ba looking at the hand axe, and he immediately needed to make it all about him. So he stepped up, forced his way between them, and peered down at the hand axe.

"Rrr," Ba said, pulling it away, fearing what Guh might do. Break it? Throw it in the ocean? Claim it for himself? But Guh grabbed his arm, and when Ba tried to pull away, Guh grabbed harder and *twisted*. "Ah!" cried Bah. "Ah! Ah!"

He managed to free himself, and then, before he quite knew what he was doing, he brandished the axe at Guh, as if threatening to chop him with it. This startled Guh, and Mar, and several other nearby people; it was a major breach of social protocol.

"Mmm?" Guh said, genuinely confused. *Here now, brother, what's all this? I'm just trying to look.*

Ashamed, but also worried, Ba opened his hand and held out the axe for Guh to examine. Guh peered down at it, squinting, and to his credit he actually did seem to understand that there was something special—something quite out of the ordinary—about this hand axe with its impossible seashell in the hilt.

"Mmm," he said, still confused.

Not knowing what else to do, Ba, dropped the axe in the dust and spread his arms, offering Guh a hug. Guh accepted, stepping forward into Ba's embrace, smelling like every gross thing that had ever happened to him.

4.3

Ba's people lived on a northward-projecting peninsula, and so the sun both rose and set over the water, and to the extent that Ba thought about this at all, he believed the sun was an enormous bonfire, and that the ocean was needed to quench it so that night could fall. Or something like that. Anyway, some sixteen days after the destruction of his fishing raft (not that Ba could count, or would care very much if he could), the tip of the sun blazed to life over the waves of what he thought must surely be the Straits of Gibraltar, on the western edge of the Mediterranean Sea.

"Ba?" Mar called out. She was leading Guh by the hand, dragging him down the beach toward where Ba was loading supplies onto his brand new voyaging raft.

In a little wicker nest lashed down to the center of the deck, Ba was piling melons, which would be both his food and his water supply. In the nest he also stored his wonderful hand axe, to handle his chopping and hacking and smashing needs, and a couple of stone flakes, for finer slicing and scraping work. Across the top of the basket he'd tied a crisscross of twine, like a spiderweb, in hopes of keeping things from falling out. Beside the basket, secured through loops of twine, were a pair of fishing gaffs, and two extra logs about two-thirds the size of the raft beams, each with its own length of twine spindled around it that was much longer than the span of Ba's arms. Rafts had an unfortunate tendency to come apart when you least expected it, and it seemed prudent to have some extra materials on hand to effect repairs.

"Ba?" Guh echoed, looking with some alarm at what Ba was

doing. Nobody had ever done anything like this before, and Guh didn't know what to make of it.

"Mar," Bah said, nodding to his favorite. "Guh," he said, nodding to his least favorite. Then he shrugged. *What can I do for you?*

"Mmm?" Guh said. He was holding a sharpened stick, and with it he pointed at the raft and raised his eyebrows at Ba. "Mmm? Mmm?" *Explain yourself.*

Guh had grown increasingly contemptuous of Ba these past two weeks, as Ba's fishing yield dwindled to almost nothing and Ba's time was increasingly spent on this sort of inexplicable business. Wicker nests? Giant rafts? Long spindles of twine that could not be used to fish or hunt? But now that it was all together in a purposeful assembly, Guh's contempt had given way to confusion and a sort of vague, unfocused fear.

"Iiiih," Guh said, voicing his displeasure.

"Ba?" Mar repeated. "Ba? Mmm?"

Feeling some need to, yes, explain himself, Ba pointed to himself and said his name. Then he pointed toward the distant hills across the water and said, "Uungh. Uungh." Then, to further explain, he pointed to himself, and then to the raft, and *then* to the distant hills. He made a ripply gesture with his hands, like ocean waves.

"Uuungh."

Mar understood right away, and looked horrified. She began shaking her head. "Ba, iiiih."

Ba actually wondered if he were observing, right here at this moment, the birth of some primitive form of language. Perhaps people had never had anything this complex to talk about before, but with certain tones and gestures apparently already coded into the DNA, it was not so great a step to string them together: *No, Ba, I don't like it.*

But Ba just shrugged, nodded, and pointed to the hills again. *What do you want me to say? Yes, I'm going.*

Not liking that answer, Mar turned to Guh and said, "Mmm? Guh, mmm?" She grabbed his hand and started pulling him toward Ba.

But Guh just looked confused and afraid. He seemed to have figured out the *what* of Ba's plan, but was baffled by the *why*, and he wanted no part of any of it. He pulled his hand away from Mar and, with a look that combined all the best aspects of a sneer and a grimace and a plea, he backed away, pointing his stick at the raft and saying, "Iiiih." Then he turned and, with a dismissive wave of his other hand, walked away. *Whatever. Go ahead and leave. Go ahead and get yourself killed. I'm not going to watch.*

Now Mar had no one but herself, and so she grabbed Ba's hand and said, "Ba. Ba. Ba."

She, too, understood what he was about to attempt, but she did not seem to understand that he intended to come back. Ba tried to convey this to her with gestures, but here he fell short. He could not seem to make her understand.

(Ba knew somehow that the hands and bodies and emotions and facial expressions and body language of his people were very nearly human, with brains were larger and more complex than those of the gorillas and chimpanzees and orangutans who had learned to use sign language in the modern era. He'd never seen any of these animals, but he could picture them in his mind. And yet, that was a sign language invented and taught by *Homo sapiens*—by weird, hairless, childlike people with high, flat foreheads and tiny lower jaws and, very often, skin the color of fishmeat and eyes the color of sky or sea or leaves. Ba's brain was even capable of representing something like words, in a sort of "mentalese" he used for thinking, but it simply lacked the wiring to connect these mental symbols with the noises and gestures he made, in any sort of systematic way. He was not capable of spontaneously inventing complex words or signs that Mar could understand, and for a moment, this pained him.)

Gently, Ba pulled his hand away from Mar, and then set about triple-checking the knots that held his raft together. They looked pretty good.

Then there was nothing left to do but launch, which he did. Getting down on his knees, setting his hands between the chopped and rounded ends of the logs, he *puuuuushed* the raft down the beach, over pointy shell fragments and smooth sea gravel, past clumps of seaweed and driftwood, and down to the waterline. Protected by brown body hair—nearly within the range of what you might find on a modern human, but still quite thick—his knees felt the scraping and abrasive sensations, but weren't bothered by them.

Just before it was in far enough to start floating, he stopped, pulled it back slightly, and got to his feet. Brushing the sand off his knees, he approached a heartbroken Mar and hugged her, and brushed his lips lightly against hers in a gesture of reconciliation.

"Ba—" she tried to say, but before she could get her own arms fully around him and probably try to restrain him, he spun her around and bent her over, brushing his flaccid genitals against her rump in a moment of symbolic mating—his people's equivalent of a romantic kiss. It was all he could do. It was all he could say.

And then he was off, pushing the raft into the water until it was up to his knees, then his waist, and then his navel. Then he was lifting his torso up onto the raft, again letting body hair protect his skin against the roughness of the chopped log ends, and using his legs to kick furiously through the surf zone. An experienced belly-surfer in a culture that valued the ocean, Ba timed it well, so that one wave broke in front of him rather than on him, and all he had to do was kick through the churning mess it left behind, and the next wave broke behind him, and then he was through the surf and out into the open sea.

And a daring ocean voyage—every bit as consequential as a powered airplane flight or a trip to the moon—had begun.

Ba had been more or less ready to go for two and a half days, but he'd waited until the conditions were right: an early morning with few clouds, with the surf low and the tide going out and a gentle wind at his back—though not enough wind to kick up any serious waves. He had no names for any of these concepts, and they were more intuitive than analytical. Today just felt right.

The raft creaked and popped beneath him, settling into itself, but the knots held firm, and the structure moved like a single object. He kicked and kicked, occasionally looking over his shoulder at the shore where Mar stood looking forlornly after him. Already he was farther from shore than he'd ever been (truthfully, than anyone had ever been), and while he'd expected to have to deal with some problems (even *Homo erectus* were acquainted with entropy), he was nevertheless surprised to find that as he kicked farther out, the water became colder, and the raft was suddenly moving east as well as north. The effect was subtle at first, but Mar was definitely dwindling faster than she should have, and in not quite the right direction. He compensated by cutting a diagonal, heading more directly toward the hills on the other shore, because he could see that if he didn't hit the right area, the water got a *lot* wider on both sides, and his journey could become very long indeed.

And here he felt his fist real glimmer of fear. Not the theoretical fear of attempting something unprecedented, but the more literal fear of spotting an actual danger whose scope he had no way of measuring. He responded by kicking faster and harder, which seemed to work.

His next problem came when the wind picked up. No longer quite so mild, and no longer blowing in quite the right direction, it tore the tops off of the sea's gentle waves, turning them to froth and spray. This got into Ba's eyes, where it stung, forcing him to blink rapidly. Waves that had been no taller than his hand were soon as tall as his shinbone, and then taller, and while he knew perfectly well how to steer a raft into an approaching wave, he found he was spending more and more of his energy on this. And whether it was because of this wind or simply because the water out here was more restless, he began to feel that he was being drawn eastward more quickly.

His heart beat faster, and it became hard to tell how much of that was from exertion and how much from fear. Still another problem came when his legs and his heart and his lungs began, yes, to feel tired.

Among his people he considered himself the most accomplished swimmer, which mostly meant that he was capable of treading water for a short time with a gaff in his hand, and swimming short distances without a fishing raft, and also capable of holding his position on a fishing raft for a substantial fraction of the day, just beyond the surf line, neither being swept in nor swept out by the ocean's fickle tides and currents. He was also capable of walking all morning and all afternoon, and indeed he enjoyed a good walk, and the explorations that came with it. And he could run! He could outrun half the tribe, sprinting until they dropped back or even fell over with exhaustion. But this kind of endurance swimming was like nothing he'd ever attempted before; it was like walking really quickly through mud, with a heavy load in his arms, without ever stopping. It was strange, and strangely exhausting.

Still, he was making visible progress as he went. Already, the beach he'd started from was so distant that he could no longer

tell if Mar was still standing there or not. He allowed himself
a brief rest before continuing, and soon allowed a longer one
where he actually hauled himself up fully aboard the raft and
chopped open a melon with his hand axe. He hadn't eaten very
much of it, though, before he began to get alarmed at how far
off course he was drifting.

And so, with that same blend of exertion and fear, he rolled
back into the water. He then experience a moment of real terror
when he felt the raft drifting away from him, and realized that
if he didn't have its buoyancy to support his weight, he wouldn't
be able to avoid, for very long, sinking and drowning out here
in the empty ocean, far from his people. He kicked his legs and
paddled his arms furiously, closing the distance and then grabbing the raft firmly with both hands and hauling his torso up
onto it. That wasn't a mistake he'd make again!

Wearily but with little choice, he simply resumed kicking.
The sun rose higher in the sky, becoming hotter. This would not
ordinarily have been a problem for Ba, but the wind had died
back down again, and even with the cold water on his legs and
buttocks and genitals, he found the combination of hard work
and sunlight was roasting his head and shoulders and back. He
paused several times to splash cold water on them, which did
provide some relief, but never for long enough.

Then the sun began to sink lower in the sky, and because
he was drifting eastward, and compensating by kicking in a
northwesterly direction, this meant the sun was glaring directly
into his left eye. Ugh. He tried closing both eyes for a while, but
this quickly resulted in his veering off course, and when he tried
closing only the left one, he found it only added to his sense
of fatigue. So this was another thing he simply had to endure,
squinting and blinking his way across the ocean.

And yet, the far shore was now looking distinctly closer than
the near one. He was more than halfway across! Significantly more!

Overcome with thirst, he climbed back onto the raft and
resumed eating his melon, now warm and partially dried out in
the sunlight, and vaguely salty from the ocean spray that had
gotten onto it. Nothing had ever tasted so good. He dared to eat
a second melon, and then take some additional time to check
his knots again.

The only knot he knew—the only knot that existed in all

of the world—was what future generations would refer to as a "granny" knot. And as those future generations could tell you, the granny was a knot that readily worked itself undone. They could also tell you that jute twine wasn't particularly strong when it soaked in water for too long. Especially if it was crude twine spun together by hand! Ba knew these things as well, and so he had compensated by knotting each strand of twine many times, and then wrapping it several times around a log, and then knotting it several times more, and wrapping it around another log, and so on. For redundancy, he had used nearly twice as much twine as he would have for an ordinary fishing raft, and yet he still had good cause to worry. Fortunately, for now things appeared to be holding together.

Taking a bit more precious time, he unlooped a bit of twine from one of his spindles, cut it with a stone flake, and then tied his own left hand to one of the raft's logs. The horror of floating free in the ocean had been dogging him ever since it happened, and here was something he could do to minimize the chance of it happening again. Then, finally, he lowered himself back into the water again, and resumed wearily kicking his way toward shore.

At one point he began to hear clicking noises, and then moments later a cloud of flying fish (or bird fish as he sometimes thought of them) swarmed past him, and moments after that there were gray, man-sized, smooth-skinned fish leaping out of the water all around him. These bore a passing resemblance to the man-eating fishes that had probably killed Kaa, but their tails and faces were different, and when they briefly cleared the water they almost seemed to be smiling or even laughing.

But then they were gone, and shortly after that a flock of seagulls arrived in all their shrieking, squawking glory. Some were grabbing bird fish out of the water—no doubt separated from their school as the bigger fish tore through it—and some were simply settling down onto the raft as though Ba had brought it here for their benefit.

One landed right in front of Ba's face and turned its head this way and that, eyeing him curiously. Ba's people had been known to eat seagulls when they got hungry enough, but mostly the birds were considered a nuisance, harassing fisherpeople and shitting on picnics. Ba reached out to swat the bird off his raft, but it simply hopped back out of the way, joining several others on the far side of the raft, and still eyeballing Ba as if trying to figure out what he was, or why he was so far from shore.

"Nnngh!" he said to the birds. They ignored him, preferring to cluck and squawk among themselves, and so he decided to ignore them as well. The shore was getting *close*, and he could now see individual trees and bushes. The shore was mostly rocky, but he angled toward a stretch of beach where he could comfortably land the raft, and as he altered course he could begin to pick out the pale spirals of seashells lying in the sand, just above the line where the surf was breaking.

With a final burst of effort, he kicked toward this foreign beach, reaching the outer edge of the surf zone and then angling his way onto a decent-sized wave that could carry him in without breaking over his head. And then suddenly his feet were kicking wet sand down beneath the wave, and then his knees were dragging, and the birds were noisily scattering, and then he was crawling, pushing the raft forward up onto the beach as the wave retreated behind him with a faint sucking sound. Another wave came from behind, pushing him further up the beach, and then he was on his feet, hopping around to the front of the raft and grabbing it by the birdshit-stained twine wrapping, and he was pulling and pulling until it was above the stripe of seaweed and driftwood that marked the high water line. There was a big, frondy tree here, just at the base of some grassy sand dunes, and with the last of his strength he pulled the raft into its shade.

And then he collapsed, rolled onto his back, looked up at the sky and called out, "Wooooooh!"

He'd done it. He'd traveled across the ocean to visit an unknown land. Now it was time to get up and explore the place, if only he could move.

4.4

Ba rested deeply and then napped lightly, with the sea breeze blowing over him, and with one arm on the raft and the other thrown across his eyes to block the daylight. He was hot and sticky and sand-covered, and his dozing had a feverish quality for a while, until the breeze and the shade finally began to cool him off. But then the sun emerged from behind the tree, and he snored himself awake.

He sat up and looked around: it was late afternoon—almost time for the sun to begin igniting the clouds in fiery color.

He quickly realized he was fiercely hungry and even more fiercely thirsty, so he grabbed a melon from his wicker nest and bit straight through the rind, sucking the juice and pulp right out of it and then swallowing and taking another huge bite. The structure of Ba's vocal cords made choking unlikely, so he munched and munched, stuffing most of the melon into his mouth and swallowing great gulps of it.

When he was done, he grabbed another melon and did the same thing, and then he grabbed and ate the final one. Only then did he feel like getting (unsteadily) to his feet. Standing on his legs was like trying to balance on two blades of grass; they wanted to buckle and collapse underneath him. The ground seemed to slither and move and shift its mass beneath him. He was no stranger to landsickness, though, so he fought his way to a sort of rhythm, and started getting his land legs back.

Across the water, he could see the place he'd come from. The place he'd lived his entire life. The place where Mar and Guh and Cheek-click still went about their normal business. Were they thinking about him? Did they wonder if he'd made it across? If he'd died? The place didn't look like anything special; in fact it looked a lot like *this* place, which Ba had seen across the ocean nearly every day of his life.

The beach here was fairly small as such things went, with sharp, rocky ridges coming down into the water on either side. The middle led straight back into a mess of grassy sand dunes, and behind that a waist-high sand cliff. Sighing, Ba climbed the dunes and the cliff and crawled up onto grass.

"Aaauglhh!" said a human voice, and Ba looked up to see he was surrounded by hairy people.

"Maaahh!" he said back to them, stepping away and then, to his dismay, falling backward down a sand dune. He got to his feet as quickly and as gracefully as he could, and then loped toward the raft, where he stooped and retrieved one of his fishing gaffs, then spun back around to face these humans.

Ba's people sometimes encountered strangers, and he knew enough to be wary. Strangers sometimes wanted to eject you from your fishing spots or camping spots. Sometimes they wanted to mate with your women, whether or not the women agreed. Sometimes they just wanted to push you around, or break your things.

Of course, sometimes strangers were perfectly friendly, and shared their food and their tools. If they were women, sometimes they just wanted to mate with somebody new. If they were men, sometimes they also just wanted to mate with somebody new, the polite way, or sometimes they were just passing through on their way to somewhere else. Exploring their world, always searching for good places. But Ba had learned to be careful, and to expect nothing in particular from encounters like this.

"Maaawrgh!" he called out, waving the gaff in an arc in front of him, defining his personal boundaries.

Cautiously, heads began to peek over the edge of the cliff. Two woman and a man.

"Mmm?" one of them said to him.

And then they were stepping over the cliff, walking slowly down the dune face, making soothing gestures with their hands. *Easy, friend. We didn't mean to startle you.*

These gestures would still be in common use a million years hence, and from them Ba suddenly realized these people had seen him sleeping. Curious, they'd retreated to a respectful distance and, apparently, waited for him to wake up.

One of the women was holding a half-finished wicker nest. Now she pointed to the middle of her chest and said "Nga." She pointed again, and repeated the sound.

Ba, beginning to calm down, introduced himself in the same manner.

"Mmm?" asked Nga, pointing now toward Ba's raft. She'd clearly never seen anything like it, and wanted to know what the deal was here.

Thinking hard, Ba pointed to himself, and then to the hills and beaches on the far shore of the ocean, and then to the raft, and then spread his arms to encompass this beach. *I came from there to here, using this raft.*

Nga took a moment to drink that in, and then she gestured toward the far shore.

"Ba?"

"Mmm," he agreed.

"Mmm," she said, thinking that over. "Mmm."

"Joh," said the man, pointing to himself.

"Lih," said the other woman, gesturing similarly.

And now that they all knew each other, Ba tossed aside the fishing gaff, slightly embarrassed with himself. Even in a fight, he wouldn't ever actually jab a person with that, any more than Guh would throw actual hunting stones at a person. It could cause a terrible injury! But he'd found it could intimidate bullies, far better than a hand axe or his fists.

"Uuuh," he told Nga and Joh and Lih. *Sorry.*

"Mmm," Nga said, accepting his apology. Then she gestured for him to follow her. "Mmm?"

"Uuuh," he answered uncertainly. He'd come here to see what there was, and he supposed he should have expected there to be people here. What had he imagined—a whole empty country waiting to be walked and fished and camped on, by just himself?

Finally, he shrugged and nodded. *Yes, okay. You seem like nice people.* And although he left his fishing gaffs behind, he did go to the raft to pick up his hand axe, because to an *H. erectus* man, going around without a hand axe—especially among strangers— would be a source of embarrassment. Like announcing he didn't plan on doing any work or helping anyone out.

"Ooh," said Lih when she saw the axe in his hand. Then: "Mmm?" *May I take a closer look?*

"Mmm," Ba assented.

She peered at the spiral imprint of that impossible little sea-shell, making appreciative noises, and then she waved over Nga and Joh so they could have a look as well. They all seemed quite impressed, which was a relief to Ba, after the indifference of his own people. This axe was *special*, and he enjoyed being among people who understood that.

When they were done looking, they led Ba back up over the dune and the cliff, across a pleasant stretch of grass and trees, over some rocks, past another somewhat larger, somewhat hidden beach where Ba could see a man and a woman fishing in the waist-deep water of a small cove or lagoon. The fish were big and slow enough, and the water clear enough, that Ba could see them from up here. This looked like much easier pickings than raft fishing beyond the surf zone, though not nearly as much fun.

Interestingly, although these people's fishing gaffs were about the same length as Ba's—slightly longer than a human arm—they were not as straight. Perhaps they didn't know where to find good wood here, where the baby trees crowded together in the shade, growing straight up, with few branches. Ba had always thought that isolated saplings were lonely, and spread their leaves out instead of up, in the blind hope of touching another of their kind. By contrast, the crowded ones grew straight and fast, as if racing one another.

The fishing gaffs here also had four prongs instead of two. Ba couldn't count that high, but he could certainly tell the difference between a stick that had been split at the end and propped open twice instead of only once. This made sense to him, as each prong improved the chances of stabbing a fish. The prongs were also jagged (or *barbed*, as the thought suddenly occurred to him), which he immediately understood would make it harder for wounded fish to wriggle off the tip and get away. Of course, *Ba* didn't need that kind of assistance, but still these were good ideas that he might just bring back home with him.

On the other hand, the gaffs did not appear to be twine-wrapped or fire-hardened, which meant they were not going to last very long. One false jab and the whole thing would crack into two long pieces. Or even four! How much time did these fisherpeople spend chopping and splitting fresh wood? Sheesh.

The fisherpeople, intent on their task, did not look up, and

Nga led Ba and the others past the beach, over another hill and into a little depression with a stream running through it, emptying down over rocks and gravel and into the sea. There was another man there—a short, stocky one with a balding scalp, and graying hair on shoulders and the sides of his head.

"Orr!" Nga called out. The man looked up and saw Ba, though he didn't seem particularly surprised.

"Ba," she said to Orr, pointing her finger in Ba's direction.

"Mmm," Orr said, only mildly interested.

Nga paused for a moment, holding her hands up and trying to gesture something. Then she pointed across the water, at the hills and beaches Ba had come from, and said his name again.

Orr shrugged and shook his head, not getting it. Nga looked briefly frustrated. She thought it was really interesting that Ba had crossed the water in his oversized raft, but she had no way to convey this. Not without the actual raft in front of her. Perhaps not without Orr actually seeing the landing for himself. Did these people even know how to make rafts?

"Oh!" Nga said, as if something had just occurred to her. Gently, she reached out to grab Ba's wrist, and with his acquiescence she lifted the hand that was holding the axe. "Mmm? Mmm?"

She pointed at the little seashell.

Orr peered and squinted.

"Mmm," he said, nodding as he noticed the seashell. "Mmm." He held out an axe of his own, which was made from some multicolored stone. Jasper or agate or some other quartz aggregate, Ba thought to himself. He had seen such stones before, but who would have thought to make an axe out of them?

"Mmm?" Ba asked, holding out his hand.

Ba and Orr exchanged axes. This was interesting, because while every axe Ba had ever seen had a fairly sharp point on it. Orr's came to a *line* instead. Hand axes were a particular thing in Ba's mind, and it literally never occurred to him to vary the design even slightly. But he could see at once that this rounded point would make the tool more effective at certain tasks, like beheading fish or shaping logs, and less effective at other tasks, like punching holes in gazelle bones to get the marrow out. However, Ba didn't do that kind of thing very often, preferring to leave such chores to Mar and Cheek-click. And the elongated point probably worked a *whole lot* better for cutting down trees and splitting apart fibers from a jute plant, which were things Ba did fairly often.

How had this shape occurred to Orr? Was it like Ba, deciding to make a larger raft, because he needed one and could see the shape of it in his mind?

Ba daydreamed for a moment, about what it would be like if people could really share their thoughts with one another. Not just grunts and pointing and grimaces and smiles, and not just physical demonstrations of how to do something or make something, but actual complicated thoughts, like how he hoped Mar would start having babies soon, and how he liked his fish roasted with the skin on it, so it was crunchy on the outside but soft and flaky on the inside. If two people could share their minds, they could tell each other *why* and *where* and *how* a thing was done, or could be done, and wouldn't *that* be interesting!

But the thought was fleeting, and vague. Ba's ability to think about the past and future was impressive by primate standards, but his grasp of abstract concepts was slippery at best, and so in another moment he was simply admiring the color of the axe, and the heft of it in his hand.

"Mmm?" Orr said, spreading his arms. Shall we hug? Shall we be hand-axe buddies?

Ba consented, and the two of them shared an embrace.

"Aah!" said Nga, now spreading her own arms, revealing her naked breasts, projecting out from a hairy chest. She seemed jealous, like *she* was the one who'd discovered Ba, and so *she* should be the one hugging him.

And so Ba hugged her as well, and then Joh and Lih. Then Joh and Lih and Orr all hugged one another for good measure, and then Nga had to hug everyone, and then she hugged Ba again, then kissed him and turned around, offering her rump.

"Mmm?"

Ba laughed. *That* didn't take long.

"Mmm," he agreed, then also nodded at Lih. *I'll mate with you, too, if you like.*

Lih also seemed to find it funny, and in another moment they were all laughing. *Look! Everyone wants to have sex with the new guy!*

Finally, things settled down, and Nga beckoned Ba to follow her. They brushed past Orr and down into the depression, where they found several young children playing. This tribe also had a little campsite set up there beside the stream, with woven reed mats laid out around the firepit. This was another thing Ba had never seen before, but grasped immediately: it kept their fur from getting damp and dirty while they slept. Hmm. And again, while Ba couldn't count, he could see from the number of mats that this group was smaller than his own. Maybe that was why the women were eager to mate: the poor dears were *bored*.

Ba did what he could for them, as the sun set and the whole sky turned to fire.

Yeah.

And then the two fisherpeople returned with dinner, and since the tribe's fire seemed to have gone out, Ba politely picked up a pair of dry sticks and said, "Mmm?" *May I light the fire for you?*

They agreed, and soon Orr was using a stone flake to peel strips of wood and build a fire nest, and Nga was gathering kindling, and Joh went off to get some driftwood from the beach. As he'd promised, Ba rubbed the sticks together. He was pretty good at starting fires, and although he had no particular conception of time, he was able to rub some little smoldering embers into the fire nest in only a couple of minutes, which was not bad at all.

And as the stars came out, they all ate fish together and groomed each other, and farted and laughed and drummed out rhythms on their thighs, and no *Homo sapiens* ever did attend a better party.

4.5

In the morning, Ba awoke early, drank from the stream, and waited for the others to stir. When they did, he set about asking them where he could find melons. He held an imaginary round shape in front of him, and bit into it with gusto.

"Mmm!" Nga said, comprehending. She pointed in a direction, and then with a series of gestures, managed to ask Ba whether he wanted her to show him personally to the spot where the melons grew.

"Mmm," he agreed. He was having fun here, but he was worried about Mar. She'd looked *so sad* as he paddled away, and he wanted her to know he was still alive and well. Unfortunately, the only way to do that was to go back and tell her. His legs groaned at the thought—they were sore and tired from all of yesterday's exertions—but a man had to do what a man had to do.

And so, yes, he would need melons.

Just to be safe, he went back and retrieved one of his fishing gaffs from the raft. He didn't know what sort of dangerous animals might be in the area, and while a gaff wasn't necessarily a better defense than a hand axe or a pointy stick, or even an ordinary rock plucked straight from the ground, he felt it *looked* more intimidating, perhaps even to an animal.

Nga came with him, and they mated again on the gritty sand beside the raft, before setting off in search of melons. These turned out to be not very far away, growing in a clearing in the sunlight a little ways upstream from the camp. They looked strange enough that Ba might not have recognized them on his own; they were smaller than the ones at his home, and instead of having smooth green rinds, they were coarse and sand-colored, blending in with the stony ground. Seeing his skeptical look, Nga took the hand axe from him—Orr's hand axe—and cut one of the melons from its vine. She then sliced it open and handed half to Ba. Inside, it had yellow flesh and black seeds instead of red flesh and white seeds, but when he bit into it, he found it was sweeter, and had a pleasant flavor not quite like anything he'd ever tasted before.

"Mmm," he said, smiling and nodding.

Nga proceeded to cut several more melons for him, and together they carried the load back to his raft. As she watched, he tied the spiderweb of twine back in place over the top of his melon basket, securing his food and water supply in place.

"Mmm," he said again, thanking her for her help.

She looked at the twine with such curiosity that it finally occurred to Ba that she'd never seen such a thing before. Did her people not know how to make it? This actually would not be that surprising, as Kaa had been the only one in Ba's tribe to know and pass on the art, and the only ones to really learn it from him were Ba and Mar. He realized such things must have been invented and forgotten and relearned from strangers, many times over as the generations ticked by. In fact, knowledge and ignorance of all kinds probably diffused in waves throughout the *H. erectus* population, with only a very few individuals creating any real innovation.

Individuals like Ba himself? Was Ba the *very first person* ever to think of journeying by water? He found the thought intriguing, but difficult, and it didn't remain in his mind for more than a passing moment.

And on its heels came another fleeting thought: how *peaceful* these people were. Even when they were fighting, even when they were afraid for their lives, they seemed relatively unburdened by complexity or worry. If they were the first primates with a complex sense of past and future, well, they didn't spend a lot of energy on it.

Had some horrible mistake been made, somewhere along the way? Had humanity traded *this* for billions of lifetimes of pointless strife? For quantum computers and single-malt whiskey and ugly divorces? Ba had everything he would ever need in a square mile of coastline. Had this journey been a mistake? Was it the first step in a much larger, much stranger journey whose final destination was still unknown?

That thought *really* didn't stick in his mind, though, and he shrugged it off as easily as he might flick a spider off his arm.

And then it was time to leave.

Aware of the technological shortcomings of Nga's tribe, Ba handed her the fishing gaff. He figured she, or some other member of her family, could figure out how to copy the design, if only they had twine to wrap it with. So he also gave her one of his twine spindles. This would be harder to replicate, but Kaa had shown Ba several different ways to make twine. Brine-soaked jute fibers were the best, but almost any plants could be used, including ordinary grass. Braiding and splicing the fibers together was not much more difficult than building a fire nest, and he hoped that with an example to work from, Nga would be able to figure it out.

Besides, Ba himself would come back here soon to check up on her. Now that he knew the crossing was possible, there was no reason he couldn't make it again—perhaps even more than once.

"Mmm?" he asked her.

"Mmm," she confirmed, nodding.

Goodbyes were not customary among Ba's people, so he did not walk around looking for any of his other new friends. He did hug Nga, however, and give her a friendly kiss on the lips. She hugged and kissed him back, and swatted his rump as he leaned over to push the raft out to sea.

At the water's edge, he paused for a moment to wash his hand axe, and his hands, which were still sticky with melon juice. And then he was off.

However, this time he hadn't given much thought to the wind and the tides. Distracted by Nga and a bit cocky from yesterday's success, he simply walked out into the sea, pushing his raft through the surf and then mounting it, kicking hard against a headwind and a rising tide and, as he moved out into colder water, a stronger eastward current than he'd faced the last time. None of this was apparent to him at first, and to the extent that he noticed anything at all, it was how tired and sore his legs still were.

Still, by midmorning he began to realize he had not made much headway. The land behind him hadn't shrunk as much as it should have, and the land ahead remained far off and shrouded in haze. His first response was to kick harder, but this wasn't particularly sustainable. Once he began to tire out, his second response was to grow increasingly afraid. What if he couldn't find his way back? Looking across at the shoreline, he didn't even know which beach he should be aiming for, and if the current carried him too far he'd be facing a *very* long swim to reach any land at all.

Frustrated, he pulled up onto the raft for a rest and a quick brunch of melons. The salty sea air was cold against his fur, and he realized the wind was against him, so for both of these reasons he instinctively flattened himself against the raft for a short while, until he felt ready to plunge back into the water again.

But then he saw the fin: a gray triangle slicing through the water like a flint blade. Over a period of minutes it circled the raft twice at long range, before spiraling in almost close enough to touch. Ba was only dimly aware that other animals might be conscious beings like himself, so he didn't attribute much malice or even agency to this behavior, but he did understand very clearly that this was a hungry fish, investigating the raft (and Ba) as a possible meal.

Leaning over, he could see the outline of the fish through the blurry water. It was much too large for him to catch and eat, but at the same time it seemed much too small to eat the raft. Perhaps it was after Ba himself? No doubt he still reeked of the guts and blood of the fishes he'd eaten last night, and perhaps during his swim he'd laid down a scent trail of coppery hemoglobin and fishy trimethylamine that the shark had followed. In any case, the thing was easily big enough to take a fatal bite out of Ba, who could not and would not go back in the water until this threat had been dealt with.

He tried reaching out and poking the dorsal fin with his remaining fishing gaff. Unfortunately the shark was too far away for him to reach. He tried poking with the twine spindle / spare log, and this worked a little better, since the log had slightly longer reach. However, the ends of the log were rounded, and did not seem to cause the shark more than momentary distress.

So, thinking furiously, he lashed the gaff to the spindle, double-checking and triple-checking the knots before jabbing the whole assembly at the shark's dorsal fin, and the sensitive gills just below and in front. That worked, and the shark thrashed away in confusion.

However, in another minute it was back again, and he had to jab it even harder to get the same response. It returned again, and still again, until Ba could see it bleeding from its gills. He jabbed it harder and harder, leaning out farther and farther over the water. And then the unthinkable happened: he lost his grip on the spindle as the shark wrenched away from him, and it fell, with the gaff still lashed to it, into the waves. He reached out for it, but it was drifting away, and there was *no way* he was going in after it.

Fortunately, the shark chose that moment to vanish from sight. Ba had no idea how deep the ocean was, but he certainly thought there was enough room down there for it to be hiding, following along underneath the raft somewhere. Noon came and went, and it was a good long while after that—twenty minutes or so—before the fear of getting lost at sea began to outweigh the fear of being eaten.

Finally, finally, he lowered himself back into the water and resumed kicking. The wind had died down by this time, and he was able to get clear of the area and, he hoped, outrun the shark and any of its friends and family that might be following along with it. The fear made him strong, and he was able to reach the midway point of the crossing without tiring noticeably, and then to keep on going.

However, another problem eventually became apparent: all his stabbing and jostling had loosened the lashings of the raft, which had begun to flex along with the waves that passed under it. This was not good. It meant that at least one of his cross-braces had come undone, and was no longer stiffening and stabilizing the structure. Sighing nervously, he climbed back up onto the raft and did what he could, hunting for the ends of the loose strands and threading them back around the logs. This was normally accomplished on dry land, with full visibility, and with the option of flipping the raft over multiple times as he worked on it. Doing it blind and wet and rolling in the waves was something entirely new. One of the strands broke as he was tugging on it, and then broke again as he tried to splice it, and finally floated out of his reach and drifted away on the current.

In the end, the best he could do was sacrifice one of the outer logs of the raft, pulling it up onto the deck as cargo and using the liberated lashings to reinforce the rest of the raft. He had lost the forward stabilizing bar, so while he had a reasonably firm aft end to grab onto, the forward part of the raft was loose and floppy and kept trying to splay itself out like the spreading fingers of a hand.

Sighing again, he slipped back into the water and resumed kicking, his body afire with nervous energy. He needed to get back to land as quickly as possible, but the harder he kicked, the more he seemed to be straining the lashings!

As the afternoon wore on, he had to climb aboard several more times to tighten things down, until finally he ate up the last of his melons and tossed away the nest that had held them, using its lashings to hold the front of the raft together, sparing only enough string to tie down Orr's hand axe. Things were better after that.

And yet, while the hills and beaches of home were drawing ever closer, he had to angle hard against the current, and he began to realize he was not going to make it ashore before sunset. This filled him with fresh terror, because the night sea was full of mysterious lights and sounds, and slimy things that wrapped and grabbed and bit. Ba's people almost *never* went swimming at night.

For a while he was propelled by fright, and for a while longer he coasted on the realization that he was *almost* there. He could even see little trickles of smoke rising up here and there, possibly from human encampments! But then the sun was igniting the clouds, and light was streaming through the gaps in the sky, and the vast blue expanse was turning yellow and orange and red, and finally purple.

Darkness and exhaustion caught him at almost exactly the same time. He stopped kicking. He breathed heavily, and then deeply, wondering what to do. His legs were nothing more than lengths of floppy twine, and the surf zone was still so far away, and as the light failed he could no longer even tell the difference between beaches and rocks. If he managed to make it to shore, would he be smashed to death on a reef?

He began seriously considering the idea of heaving his body up onto the raft and just spending the night there, letting the current take him wherever it was headed. It was a bit like death, that idea, and yet it contained enough hope to be seductive.

But he was so close to his goal! He scanned the coastline, and to his surprise he saw a pinpoint of orange light. A campfire? Something to aim toward? He didn't know how big it was, or how far away, but it gave him hope of a different sort, and so he began kicking again, ignoring the protest of his muscles and the pounding of his heart.

He kicked for longer than he thought was possible, and then he kicked some more, and finally he was able to see the fire clearly enough to make out the individual logs that were burning. Someone had built and ignited a smoky cone of sapling trunks, each about the size of his raft timbers, and indeed he could make out a human figure on the beach, lowering yet another sapling onto the cone and then dashing away into the darkness.

Ba felt a final burst of energy then, and kicked hard and steadily until he'd reached the surf zone. He even found it within himself to time the waves, and catch the right one, and ride it in toward the beach.

As the wave curled and broke, the front of the raft finally came apart altogether, but it hardly mattered, because Ba's feet were on the sand. He was chest-deep in the water, in the still moment between crashing waves, and with a grabbing, sawing motion he managed to pluck Orr's hand axe off the timbers and stagger forward, until the water was at his waist, and then his knees. And then the sea was pulling back, draining away beneath him, and he was ashore, leaving the world's first ocean-going vessel behind him as the world's first bit of floating garbage.

Ahead, the human figure was back again, feeding another log to the fire, and Ba could see it was a woman. In fact, Ba could see that it was Mar herself! And then Mar caught sight of Ba and rushed toward him with open arms, squawking in amazed delight, and the two of them were embracing on the beach, with the waves lapping and breaking and shushing behind them.

Mar kissed him and squeezed him and joyously turned around to offer her rump, and although Ba could barely stand, much less mate, he found he could stay upright by leaning on her, in the warmth of the beacon fire she had lit to guide him home.

Foothills Hospital
Boulder, Colorado
Present Day

The seizure lasted over an hour, which the doctor said was not a good sign, given the high level of medication Harv was on. They switched his IV from something called Balanced Salt Solution to something called Lactated Ringer's, and injected a drug called carbamazepine into the feed. When he finally started to show signs of consciousness again, they added *nine grams* of something called fosphenytoin.

"That's all we can give him," the doctor warned.

"I'm fine," Harv said, rather suddenly.

He didn't look fine. He was curled on his side, his eyes closed.

"Harv?" Tara asked.

"Yeah. I'm here."

"Can you open your eyes?"

"No. Not yet. The light hurts."

"The lights are off," she told him.

"Still."

She took his hand again, and sat quietly with him until he finally blinked and looked at her.

"Hey," he said gently. "How are you?"

She coughed out a laugh. "You're asking *me*?"

He smiled at that, and closed his eyes again.

"What happened?" she asked.

"I invented boats," he told her. "A *long* time ago. I'm pretty sure I discovered Europe."

She snorted unhappily. "These results would be better if you weren't loaded to the eyeballs with psychoactives."

283

"Sorry."

"I'm *so worried* about you."

"I know. Thank you. I'm glad you're here."

Doctor Steph said, "I'm sending him up to Intensive Care. He's going to have to stay there for a few days, and if he has another seizure, it could be life-threatening."

"I think it's over," Harv said.

The doctor paused, pulled her hair behind her shoulders, and leaned forward to peer into Harv's eyes with a penlight, propping the lids open with her fingers.

"Your pupils do look better," she said. "EKG looks better. Why do you say it's over? Tell me how you're feeling."

"Different," he answered. "Quieter. There was a kind of . . . buzzing sensation that I didn't notice, but it's gone now. The headache is also getting better. I think I reached the end of the tape. I'm not sure the quantome goes back any farther."

At the doctor's look of incomprehension, he added, "There are no more injected memories to process."

Steph looked at Tara. "Did that make sense to you?"

"Yeah."

"He sounds lucid?"

"Yes."

"Well, that's a good sign, given his present drug load. He's not out of the woods yet, but I'm going to back off the fosphenytoin and see what happens." Then she looked at Harv and added, "You're still going upstairs. Even if the seizures are over, you're going to need massive supportive therapy. Your neurons have been highly stressed, and they're going to start dying if we don't intervene."

"Hmm," he said, sounding rather embarrassed at that.

"Is he going to be okay?" Tara asked.

"It's definitely too soon to tell," Steph replied firmly. "But he looks better than when he came in."

"I feel like a million bucks," Harv said weakly. "And a Nobel Prize."

They ended up keeping him for three days, and discharging him with firm instructions not to drive, mow lawns, or operate any other sort of machinery. The police interviewed everyone and, with Patel's help, made a cursory inspection of the lab. After ascertaining that no obvious or significant crimes had been committed, they referred the matter to the Occupational Health and Safety Administration. The OSHA rep, of course, issued numerous citations ("Unsecured Cables, Multiple Trip Hazard," "Emergency Stop Activated," "Emergency Stop Not Tied To Main Power," "Magnetic Field Related Injury" and "Workplace Injury Requiring Hospitalization"), along with a ten-thousand-dollar fine, and orders to correct the defects within thirty days, and cease all use of the equipment until that time. He also tried "TMS employed with no licensed TMS operator on site," but that turned out to be only in the draft regulations, not the current ones, and had to be dropped.

"I'll pay it out of my own pocket," Harv said. "It's not the university's fault."

"Mmm," the OSHA rep said. Then, half-jokingly, "I don't take cash. By the way, I didn't turn anything off in your lab, for fear of damaging the equipment. You'll need to send someone in there to shut it all down."

"Do you feel up to it?" Tara asked.

"Sure," Harv said. "As long as you're driving."

So she drove and parked, and they walked to the Engineering Center and down the stairs to the lab. In the darkened subbasement corridor, he touched her on the small of the back, and she drew close to him, and they kissed, *really kissed*, for the first time in days.

"Wow," he said. "I needed that."

"We both did."

He unlocked the door and flipped on the lights, then picked his way over loose cables to the operations console, where he leaned over and keyed in the commands for the shutdown sequence.

"There," he said. "What a week, eh?"

"Yeah," she agreed, then added, "There's something I'm still wrestling with, though. Statistically, Manu should have carried a Y chromosome from haplogroup F, which dominated India at that time. It's ancestral to ninety percent of Eurasians and indigenous Americans, and even some Australian Aborigines. But it couldn't have come from a 'Cro-Magnon' person in Europe. That would be haplogroup I or R1. And *yours* is group D-M174, which ought to make you Tibetan. Or Ainu, from Siberia and northern Japan. Or Andamanese, I guess. The Andaman islanders have their own global flood myth, by the way, and so do the Ainu. But they're *not* related to the European early modern humans. Not closely."

He worked his way back over to her, pointing at the NMR target receptacle and nodding. "Yeah, okay, but who says that chromosome stayed put? It appears to come from a long line of adventurers. I have to say, I'm quite proud to be part of their legacy."

"It *is* impressive," she allowed. "And there is some D-M174 in India and Eastern Europe. So, maybe. If your genealogy goes back any farther than Scotland, it might tell us something."

And Tara knew, in that moment, that she and Harv were destined to break up. Not today; she didn't want to ruin what could well be the most important week of both their lives. Not next week, either. Hell, she wasn't through *fucking* him, or curling up to sleep with his her hand on his hip. It might not even happen this decade.

But she wanted children someday, and she realized she didn't want *that chromosome* passed on to them. And that meant all this heat and drama had been a glorified summer fling all along, and couldn't last. And perhaps that was okay. Perhaps a good Hindu girl from Chennai could forgive herself that much.

"I love you, you know," he said to her in a gentle voice. He touched her hips with both hands.

"I know," she answered. "I love you, too."

"We traveled in time together."

"I think so, yes. I think we did."

"There could actually be a Nobel Prize in our future."

"Indeed."

With the power-down sequence activated, the green status lights winked out one by one. Harv turned off the overheads and closed the door, saying, "You know, this technology has a lot to teach, and a long way to go. For all we know, someone from the future could be watching us right now."

"Oh. I hope so!" she said, and kissed him hard. "Let's make it worth their while."

Postscriptum

In the decades since Harv Leonel's historic journey, few researchers have attempted to replicate the result, and none have unambiguously succeeded. However, no genetic, linguistic, cultural, archaeological, or quantum-mechanical evidence has emerged to refute any of his claims, and considerable supporting evidence has been uncovered in nearly every year since then. His Y chromosome (of the D-M174 haplogroup) is certainly the most studied in all of human genetics, and its wanderings are consistent with groups that can still be found in these same locations today.

Thus, scientific opinion has gradually shifted from general incredulity toward a broad consensus, that the past occurred more or less exactly as Leonel claims it did. His reports of backward influence remain controversial and, one fears, unfalsifiable, although it must be admitted that the laws of physics permit (if grudgingly) such temporal interconnects.

Time will tell if the human quantome has been irreversibly scrambled by Leonel's experiments, or whether the tape must restart from scratch with every reading. Or indeed, as many have speculated, whether the Y chromosome is only one of many quantum repositories in our collective lineage. And if it happens that these words are being read by humans or hominins from our own distant future, let me say, we thank you sincerely for your attention, which permits us to live again, if only briefly, through eyes of which we can only dream. Adieu.

Notes on Part One: The Deluge

The Neolithic comet impact was a real occurrence, as was the permanent (though gradual) flooding of the coastline as the polar caps melted at the end of the Ice Age. There's no evidence these two events overlapped, but if the myths of Manu and Noah were based on real events, then there would have to be not only massive and rapid flooding, but also some significant warning that disaster was about to strike. If water levels were already rising, then the comet impact would have been particularly devastating, so the scenario outlined in the story seems to fit with both the legends and the known facts.

The Comet Impact: For purposes of this story, I've assumed the impact site is 7000 kilometers northwest of The City—close enough for the effects to be catastrophic but not immediate—and occurs at 6 p.m. Since the speed of compression waves in rock is around 5000 m/s, the first ground shock would then take twenty-three minutes to arrive. The speed of *shear* waves in rock is around 3000 m/s, so the second, bigger ground shock should arrive sixteen minutes after the first one. The only route for shockwaves to travel through water would be around Africa, a distance of roughly 27,000 km. Since the speed of sound in water is 1550 m/s, a series of reflected and refracted compression waves should begin arriving after a total of 4.8 hours, or shortly before midnight.

Of course, the real danger is from tsunamis, which are *transverse* waves, and the soonest one could arrive directly from the impact site would be about thirty-four hours, with numerous reflected and refracted secondary waves arriving in the hours after that. However, the passage of compression waves through both the ground and water means that numerous undersea landslides are likely to occur, triggering tsunamis of their own that could arrive almost anytime. In the story, I have the first tsunami reaching The City twelve hours after impact. Tsunami wave heights of up to 30 meters have been reported in modern times, and unlike normal ocean waves, tsunamis have extraordinarily large wavelengths of up to 100 km. This means they don't simply break on the shore and then roll back, but travel inland for significant distances. The weight of all that water has to slide back into the ocean eventually, but with additional waves arriving before the first ones begin to retreat, the resulting flooding could well reach tens of meters in depth and hundreds of kilometers in reach. Literally the end of the world, for anyone living within a few days' travel of the coast.

Words and Names: The language of Kingdom (aka, "The Language") is a loose amalgam of Sanskrit, proto-Indo-European, and other ancient languages, with an attempt on my part to match the sounds to words that occurred in later history. For example, in the Old Testament, Noah's boat is referred to as an *ark*, which is derived from the Latin for "chest" or "receptacle" (literally "curve"). In the Torah, it's referred to as a *tevat*. One of the Sanskrit words for raft is *tarka*, and one of the words for boat is *tari*. Putting it all together, the word *tavitarka* (raft of boats) is a plausible enough precursor for fictional purposes.

Similarly, the three sons of Noah are named Shem, Ham, and Japheth, while the three sons of Manu are named Sharma, Charma, and Yapeti. Here I've rendered them as Sharama, Hamurma, and Jyaphethti. Manu's wife is Saturupa, while Noah's is either Naamah or Emzara; the name Emzananti doesn't fit all of these, but it sounds nice.

Noah figures appear in myths throughout the world, with diverse names like Ziusudra, Utnapishtim, and Fuhi. Manu's story in the Hindu Rig Veda appears to be the oldest of these myths, but around the world there are a suspicious number of Noah-like heroes with Noah-like names, including the Hawaiian Nu-u, the Arabic Nuh, and the (female) Chinese Nüwa, that likely have common origins. Thus, I opted to combine these names with Manu's, yielding Manuah. Yes, I know it sounds like "manure," but I think that may be pretty close to a real person's real name, and I didn't want to bastardize it any further. There are dozens of such reconstructions in the book, including place names, character names, and basic vocabulary words, but truthfully my notes are a mess, and some of them were foolishly thrown out along the way. But I think you get the idea.

By naming the city The City, I'm echoing the Sumerian city of Ur (once thought to be the world's first city), from which we derive the modern word "urban." Similarly, the name Kingdom is intended to reflect that this is the world's first kingdom, at least in the sense we understand it.

The ancient Akkadian Epic of Atra-Hasis is old enough, and a close enough match to the stories of Noah and Manu, that I slipped its protagonist in as Manuah's brother, and borrowed several of its details. I'm sure I've gotten a lot wrong here, but if all these myths mutated from a single story that predates the Rig Veda, then its broad outlines could well be similar to what I've scribbled here.

Kingdom and The City: Yes, there really are two drowned cities off the coast of the Indian subcontinent, that are tens of square kilometers in size, feature megalithic stone architecture, and prove conclusively that civilization is substantially older than our histories have taught us. Anyone interested in this should look for Graham Hancock's excellent *Flooded Kingdoms of the Ice Ace* and *Magicians of the Gods.*

Present age estimates put the destruction of these cities about 9,500 years in the past (9.5 kya), which is not a match for the suspected time of the Neolithic comet impact at 13 kya, or the end of the Ice Age at 12–15 kya. I suppose I'm guilty of artistic license, but were there really *two* disasters, either of which could trigger worldwide flooding, and also a pair of flooded cities that vanished in yet a third, unrelated cataclysm? That all seems a bit suspicious, given that our myths describe only a single flood of global proportions.

Also, the drowned cities are located off the northwestern coast of India, over 400 kilometers east of the suspected course of the Sarasvati River in Pakistan. However, the cities are located in the Gulf of Cambay, 40 kilometers from the present-day coastline, and that coastline has changed a great deal over the past 13,000 years, with the water being at least 120 meters deeper. The Gulf of Cambay is separated from the Indus River by the flat ground of the Indo-Gangetic Plain, parts of which are now submerged, and large rivers like the Mississippi are known to wander in their courses over time. Given all of this, I do believe it's plausible that before the Deluge, the deltas of the Indus and Sarasvati rivers were farther south and east, and significantly wider, than we see them today.

In any case, most large cities are constructed near major rivers, not in the middle of nowhere, and as far as we know there aren't any drowned cities where these two rivers end today. Again, disagreeing with current scientific theories could be considered artistic license, but if the Rig Veda holds any truth, then I do think my timeline and geography may be consistent with it.

Ancient Astronomy: Amazingly enough, the Vedas really do reference the speed of light, placing it at 2,202 yojanas in half a nimisha. How this was derived is unknown, but modern translations of these units imply an error of only two percent. At the time of this writing, an analysis can be found at http://nirmukta. net/Thread-Speed-of-light-in-Vedas-can-you-prove-it-wrong. Weblinks don't tend to be very stable over time, but Archive.org may retain a copy of it, and in any case the basic terms should remain searchable.

The first modern estimate of the speed of light was made by Danish astronomer Ole Römer in 1676, based on telescopic observation of the moons of Jupiter, whose eclipses varied in time based on the distance between Jupiter and the Earth. In other words, this calculation relies not only on telescopes, but on accurate measurement of celestial distances, and the orbits of Jupiter *and* its moons! Is there a simpler way to measure the speed of light, using only tools that would have been available in the ancient world? If so, we have yet to rediscover it. The simplest explanation is that the ancient proto-Hindus understood telescopes, measurement of distances by triangulation, and also Keplerian dynamics. Incredible? Yes. But apparently true.

In fact, the Vedic peoples measured units of time in everything from microseconds to gigayears, and distance from angstroms to A.U., so if anything I've underestimated the sophistication of their society. What did they need with all these measurements? And by the way, I'm offended by suggestions that this information must have been handed over by aliens visiting the Earth. Ancient peoples had the same brains we use today, and we know they maintained a healthy interest in astronomy. The Vedas contain no reference to the speed of sound, but that's a much easier measurement, so yeah, they probably had that, too.

Boats: The boating details in this section are mostly drawn from the modern (and ancient) sport of dragon boat racing, which is surprisingly popular in my landlocked city of Denver, Colorado. True aficionados of the sport will realize I've altered some of the basic commands to be, perhaps, more consistent with the way ancient peoples would have viewed them. Reed boats of the sort described here are made throughout the world, and probably rely on designs handed down since well before the dawn of civilization. Coating their hulls with bitumen is described in the Epic of Atra-Hasis, which (if the legend is true) implies this technology was known in the Antediluvian world.

Notes on Part Two: The Monsters

The Trolls: Neandertals were slightly shorter than their Cro-Magnon or European Early Modern Human (EEMH) cousins, but more heavily muscled, with more robust skeletons and larger, heavier skulls. In straight-up unarmed combat, a Cro-Magnon without modern aikido skills would not have stood much chance against a Neandertal, although he could almost certainly outrun the fight. Neandertals were slightly less intelligent, despite larger brains, and they had heavy brow ridges, weak chins, and sloping foreheads. They were highly carnivorous, and occasionally cannibalistic, so they were probably not above catching and eating the occasional EEMH.

However, despite their apelike image in popular culture, they're known to have made not only tailored animal-skin clothing and stone-tipped spears, but also tents and musical instruments, cave paintings and beaded necklaces. Given their long residence in Ice Age Europe, they were most likely pale-skinned, and as prone to sunburn as modern Norwegians. This didn't mean they were nocturnal, but they would probably have been at least somewhat photophobic if they knew what was good for them.

Researchers used to believe that ginger-colored hair passed into the *Homo sapiens* genome through contact with Neandertals, although this has since been disproven. However, the Neandertals did have a variety of genes related to hair and eye color, and very likely had as much variety in this area as modern Europeans. And for the same reason their skins were probably light, they likely had their own genes for blonde, brunette, and ginger, and perhaps light-colored eyes as well. And yes, even *H. sapiens* has the lipochrome pigment necessary to produce yellow irises, although they're rare. There's zero evidence that Neandertals had pointed ears; I totally made that up. However, there's also no evidence that they didn't, and it would certainly fit with a lot of our myths. Pointy ears occur sometimes in our own species as a random mutation, or as deliberate body modification, and they're relatively common in other primates as well, so it's actually not a very drastic speculation.

Based on reconstructions of their voiceboxes, Neandertals were anatomically capable of speech, but they probably really did have loud, shrill, nasal, gravelly voices that resembled, for example, the male actors from Monty Python badly presenting themselves as women. Interested readers can find an example at https://www.youtube.com/watch?v=o589CAu73UM, or by searching "Neanderthal high-pitched voice theory." Although they did possess the two key mutations in the FOXP2 language gene that set humans apart from other great apes and hominins, Neandertals had a slightly different version of the gene than we see today in anatomically modern humans. They also had differences in other genes that interact with FOXP2, and perhaps different levels of gene expression as well. Today, many researchers insist *Homo neanderthalensis* had the same power of speech as *Homo sapiens*, but there's no way to prove this, and as a technologist I tend to doubt it. Their progress was just too slow to indicate they were talking things over, or handing down oral traditions. My layman's guess is that, through a combination of cultural and biological factors, they had words but not complex grammar.

Even without pointed ears, all of this makes them a dead ringer for the trolls, ogres, goblins, and kobolds of European mythology, and this strikes me as a very unlikely coincidence indeed. Also, while Neandertals in movies and TV shows are inevitably portrayed as ugly brutes, their women and especially children would have been more gracile in appearance. An image search for "beautiful Neanderthal" will turn up facial reconstructions that, while not quite modern human, reveal a softer side to this species, and perhaps some hint as to why our two species might, at least occasionally, have wanted to mate with one another. Perhaps these are our elves and gnomes and pixies and dwarves?

None of this is intended to disparage the Neandertals, or to imply that they were in any way subhuman. In fact, they were among the cleverest members of the human genus, fully capable of interbreeding with us, and they would have had all the same thoughts and emotions we do. They buried their dead with flowers and trinkets, and for many thousands of years they were close competitors for the domination of Europe. We oughtn't be too smug about that; according to Dr. Jill Shapiro of Columbia University, over that kind of time frame a mere two percent difference in survival rates is enough for one population to crowd another off the map. However, we humans do love our differences, and have a sad tendency to dehumanize one another, and *that's* why Argur's people consider their neighbors to be "monsters." The opinions of a character in a book do not necessarily reflect those of the author.

The Humans: The Cro-Magnon or EEMH people were anatomically and genetically modern humans, though slightly larger (and larger-brained) than the people of today. As recent immigrants from East Africa, they were most likely brown-skinned and black-haired, and they brought with them a culture significantly more complex than that of the Neandertals. More specifically, Argur's people belong to the Gravettian culture, which was known to have rope, nets, cloth, pottery, fences, and a fondness for clay animals and voluptuous "Venus" figurines. And that's just the stuff that's survived for us to inspect; we only know about the rope and nets and textiles because we've found impressions of them in pottery fragments. Anything made of leather, wicker, wood, wool, or plant fiber has long since rotted away.

The valley of Nog La is loosely based on the Dolní Věstonice archaeological site in the Czech Republic. There is no evidence of wooden castles here, but fences made from bone suggest the idea would have been well within the bounds of Gravettian technology and imagination. The Knights of Ell are entirely made up, but Dolní Věstonice does appear to be the permanent home of an organized people who harvested wild grain and processed it into flour. That such a society might have a part-time warrior caste is hardly unlikely. Likewise there's no evidence for beer, but come on, seriously, they had grain and pottery, water and time. You do the math.

The "leverthrow" in this story is actually called an atlatl or spear thrower, whose appearance in Europe has only been conclusively dated to about 21,000 years ago (21 kya), and there's no direct evidence of these in Gravettian culture, either. However, the technology is suspected to have seen use in Europe as early as 30 kya (see *Science and Technology in World History: an Introduction*, by James Edward McClellan), before being gradually edged out by bows and arrows. If they were made of wood, we'd never find them, so it's a supportable speculation. Several threads of evidence suggest dogs were first domesticated around this time as well. All in all, the Gravettians appear to have more in common with later Neolithic farmers than they do with the "cave men" of popular imagination, implying that the roots of civilization go back a *lot* farther than we've thought.

One thing conspicuously absent from the archaeological record is evidence of large-scale conflict between Neandertals and EEMHs, who lived alongside one another in Europe for at least 5,400 years. Just for reference, 5,400 years ago the pyramids did not yet exist, Egypt was barely civilized, and the Sumerian cities of Ur, Uruk, and Eridu were the most advanced in the world. That's a long time, and if our two species coexisted for a similar span, they must have known each other very well indeed. Given the physical superiority of one group and the technological superiority of the other, one suspects there was a mutual reluctance to start anything more serious than the occasional skirmish, raid, rape, murder, or kidnapping.

Importantly, except in Spain the Neandertals are now thought to have become extinct in Europe no later than 39 kya, which would mean the humans overlapping with them were *not* Gravettians. The Gravettian culture didn't begin until around 33 kya, and the specific settlement at Dolní Věstonice, on which I've based this story, is dated at 26 kya. However, absence of evidence is not evidence of absence, and for purposes of this story I'm assuming that comparable Cro-Magnon settlements existed as early as approximately 30 kya, and also that the endangered species of "trolls" persisted until at least that time, and possibly longer, in isolated pockets whose remains we simply haven't uncovered. Improbable? Ask the dwarf mammoths of Wrangel Island, Russia, which survived until about 3,700 BP—eighty centuries after their extinction in the rest of Eurasia.

We should remember that modern Europeans are neither Cro-Magnon nor Neandertal, but a hybrid of the two species (or subspecies), with an additional 30–40 kiloyears of evolution into that environment, plus inward diffusion of genes from elsewhere in the world—notably India. The language of Nog La is based very loosely on Basque, which is non-Indo-European and could plausibly represent the last remnants of Cro-Magnon speech.

The Monsters: The Boolis (named for my wife's favorite cat, with a similar personality) is an Elasmothere or Siberian Unicorn—a burly, rhinoceroslike species that's thought to have gone extinct around 29 kya. The skulls of these creatures are dominated by a large horn socket between the eyes, although the horns themselves were made of keratin (basically, hair) and have not been preserved, so it's anyone's guess what they looked like. In speculative artwork the horn is usually portrayed as being very long and sharp, but the engineer in me finds this unlikely, as this would unbalance the head and require a lot of unnecessary energy to carry around. I suspect the horns were more like maces or war hammers: short, stout, and relatively blunt. This does not, however, rule out the possibility that younger boolises were thinner, lighter, and sharper-horned—more like the mythical Asian kirin or European unicorn—with the horn gradually growing wider (tree-ring style) as the animal grew. Some accounts suggest the elasmothere may have persisted into historical times in China, Mongolia, and Siberia as, again, a highly endangered species, although these reports sometimes describe the "unicorn" as deerlike rather than bovine in build. So who knows.

As for dragon bones... in her books *The First Fossil Hunters* and *Fossil Legends of the First Americans*, Adrienne Mayor makes clear that fossils were well known in the ancient world, and that "primitive" peoples were often capable of correctly deducing their origins and antiquity. In fact, later, more sophisticated societies tended to try to fit the bones to their own local mythologies (e.g., "hero's bones" to the Greeks), so their paleontology skills were actually worse. According to Mayor, mythical creatures such as the griffin are simply accurate descriptions of well-preserved fossils.

Notes on Part Three: The Garden

During the 2000s, when I was the science and technology correspondent for the SciFi channel (later renamed SyFy), I wrote three pop-science essays that were the genesis of this story: "Speaking in Tongues, Baby," "The Suburbs of Eden," and "Adam and Eve and Lara and Fox."

In the first of these, I reiterated the observations of others, that (a) the grammar of pidgin languages is the same all over the world, (b) babytalk is the same all over the world, and (c) this appears to reflect the "deep wiring" of the language centers of our brains. In other words, we may still carry the vestiges of an *innate* language.

Extinct ancient languages such as proto-Indo-European have been reconstructed by working backward from the words in their descendant languages, and even earlier languages have been reconstructed by examining the similarities between these proto-languages. Obviously this process gets less accurate the further you go back, but that hasn't stopped scientists from trying to reconstruct "Ursprache" or "Proto-Human," the hypothetical "original" human language. An interesting snapshot can be found in the 1997 NOVA episode "In Search of the First Language," and a more current summary at https://en.wikipedia.org/wiki/Proto-Human_language. If these controversial reconstructions have any validity, by the way, the name Tik-Tik means something like "fingers." Also, the word "puta," slang for vagina, occurs today in every language group throughout the world, and may in fact be an Ursprache noun that's been preserved in daily use for tens or even hundreds of thousands of years. Wow.

Still, my thought at the time was that this reconstruction

process, however fascinating and useful, skips over a rather obvious idea: that Ursprache likely combined a babytalk-esque vocabulary with a pidgin grammar. I also remember hearing, in a different documentary whose title I can no longer locate, that statistically speaking across all six thousand human languages and the backward reconstructions thereof, the words for mother contain an "M" sound too frequently to be a coincidence, while words for father tend to contain a "P" or "F." Hence, my use of "mama" and "pfo-pfo" as Ursprache words for mother and father.

In "Adam and Eve and Lara and Fox," I discussed the sudden arrival of the FOXP2 "language gene" mutation, which affects the development of certain key structures on the left side of the brain and enabled the rise of complex language. This was once thought to have occurred fairly recently—between 50,000 and 100,000 years ago—although the date has since been pushed back to at least 300 kya. However, FOXP2 doesn't exist in a vacuum, but interacts with a lot of other genes in complex ways. For example, mice with a genetically engineered human FOXP2 gene can sing like birds, but they can't repeat words the way a parrot can. And in the archaeological record, we see a sudden explosion in *Homo sapiens* technology and wanderlust at about 50 kya, plus or minus a few thousand, despite zero changes in anatomy or brain volume. I'm not alone in thinking that's a smoking gun for some kind of language revolution. A change in gene expression, maybe?

At the time the article was written, Y-Chromosome Adam was believed to have lived around 59 kya, plus or minus a few thousand. Another unlikely coincidence in our two-million-year history! Since then, older Y-chromosome haplogroups have been identified, pushing Adam's date back to 200–300 kya, but all this means is that *most* humans are descended from an Adam-like figure who lived right around the time complex new technologies started appearing. That's plenty good enough for our purposes here.

Anyway, the modern form of FOXP2 is strongly conserved in our genome, and revertant forms are strongly selected against. The mutation seems to have diffused rapidly through the African population, so it seemed to me there *must*, at some point in our ancient history, have been a small tribe of *really popular people* spreading it around. I'll admit I may have the date wrong, but even if we push it back to 300 kya and set it among the common ancestors of *H. sapiens* and *H. neanderthalensis*, a story much like this one probably did really occur.

In this book, the culture of the Talking People is loosely based on that of Africa's Khoi-san, who today are an endangered population, but were once prevalent across much of the continent, until crowded out by Bantu-speaking farmers. For a variety of linguistic and genetic reasons, the Khoi-san are believed to be the ancestors of all (or nearly all) non-African humans, so it's logical to place Adam among them, or whatever version of them existed back then. The Khoi-san language is tonal, like Mandarin, and includes various clicks and pops rarely found outside of Africa, which probably means Ursprache had these features as well.

In the final essay, "The Suburbs of Eden," I pointed out that social and sexual practices among the Khoi-san bore some striking parallels to modern suburbia, making them perhaps more relatable than other peoples with very different practices. Thus, my use of phrases like "housing development" and "commute to work."

For this book I've opted to follow the "deep wiring" language models, and assume that regardless of the actual words they used, the Talking People (who, mind you, *must actually have existed* in some form) would speak a tonal language full of African click noises, whose grammar would resemble pidgin and whose word construction would resemble babytalk. I'll happily buy a beer for anyone who can prove this hypothesis wrong.

Notes on Part Four: The Voyage

Species Identification: Is Ba a *Homo erectus*? Some archaeologists would classify him as *H. ergaster*, while others say *H. ergaster* and *H. erectus* are simply regional variants of the same species. For simplicity I've assumed the latter, although for purposes of this story it only matters because *H. erectus* is better known. Sexual practices within this species are not well known, but I have tried to place them about halfway between the habits of bonobos and the hunting/gathering societies of anatomically modern humans. The lack of violence and sexual jealousy when a strange male encounters a new tribe—in fact, the de-fusing of tension through sex—may seem strange to us, but really does occur with bonobos.

Art Among the Hominins? In England, a 500,000-year-old *H. erectus* hand axe has been found with a symmetrically placed fossil seashell in its handgrip area. Apparently, the fossil (pre-existing in the flint), had ornamental value, or some other value, and so the axe was made by carefully knapping away the stone around it. I've taken some artistic liberties by placing a similar axe in Morocco (and then Spain) at least 500,000 years earlier, but given the very slow pace of technological change at the time, this isn't much of a stretch. Other hand axes with less spectacular fossil inclusions have been found at other sites, as well as axes made from banded jasper, and some that appear to have hand-carved decorations as well. Thus, Ba's axe, while not typical, is well within the range of ornamented tools *H. erectus* are known to have made.

Ocean Travel: It's now widely accepted that the Indonesian island of Flores was colonized by *H. erectus* about 800,000 years ago, and that the only way to get there was by boat, with some sea crossings up to 100 kilometers along the way. (These people subsequently evolved into "hobbits," but that's another story entirely.) The evidence for sea travel in the Mediterranean around the same time is less ironclad, but in any case by 1.4 million years ago *H. erectus* groups were living in both Spain and Morocco (probably only about 10 kilometers apart at the time), and were anatomically just as smart as the Flores adventurers. So, yeah, that crossing would have been well within their ability. Modern swimmers can cross the modern beach-to-beach gap of 16 km in about four and a half hours, so for Ba to push a raft 60 percent of that distance in roughly 180 percent of the time seems not unreasonable.

Is it possible to cross the ocean without complex language? I don't see why not; a basic raft isn't a whole lot more complicated than a bird's nest. It does, however, imply that *H. erectus* knew how to how to chop logs into a uniform size and lash them securely together. Alternatively, a "coracle" is a type of one-man fishing boat found all around the world, that consists of a large, round basket covered in some combination of cloth, animal hides, resin, and pitch. I suspect large leaves could be used as well, especially if they're from a naturally gummy or sappy species of tree. This might be simpler to build than a raft, as it might not even require the invention of knots or twine. However, it would be a lot more treacherous for ocean crossings; since a coracle is somewhat tippy. It's also not naturally buoyant, so its ability to float is only as good as the maker's ability to keep it from leaking, and the pilot's ability to bail. A coracle would also not be capable of holding more than one or two people at a time—hardly enough to form a colony or a trading expedition.

To me, one of the most interesting moments in all of prehistory is the *first* time anyone decided to cross an ocean on a boat. It seems quite likely that this was an *H. erectus* fisherman staring across the Strait of Gibraltar. I suppose it could have been a fisher*woman*, but in all human cultures, dangerous stunts tend to be testosterone driven.

Notes on the Framing Story

The spread of Y-chromosome haplogroups is the subject of considerable study, and Harv's chromosome—from the D-M174 haplogroup—would certainly be anomalous in a white European. D-M174 dominates only in three small populations: the Tibetans, the brown-skinned Andamanese of the Indian Ocean, and the fair-skinned Ainu or Jomon people of Japan and Siberia (who, interestingly, have drowned Antediluvian sites of their own). However, D-M174 *is* present in India, and has been found at low frequency throughout central Asia, and in populations native to Eastern Europe. If there is an adventurer's chromosome that connects all the dots in this book, this is surely it.

The quantum computing jargon here is mostly accurate, although the idea of the Y chromosome as a quantum computer or quantum storage device is an unsupported literary invention. Sorry.

In all four of these "time travel" stories, what fascinates me is that these events, or something like them, must actually have happened. The plot and character details may be made up, but the evidence—genetic, linguistic, cultural and archaeological—point to these turning points as real moments in our collective history. Ice Age peoples really did build vast, megalithic settlements, and then the Ice Age really did end, flooding millions of square kilometers of inhabited territory. Cro-Magnon and Neandertal humans really did coexist and interbreed in Europe, and these interactions surely must, at times, have resembled our handed-down fairy tales. A spontaneous mutation of the FOXP2 neural development gene—the so-called "language gene"—really did occur and rapidly diffuse throughout the *Homo sapiens* population, turning clever hominins into a society of bards and teachers, historians and worrywarts.

Can meaningful stories be handed down, garbled but largely intact, for tens of thousands of years? The Rig Veda's descriptions of the extinct Saraswati River suggest that clear details can be retained for at least six thousand years, while some Aboriginal oral traditions accurately describe geological events and features from at least *ten* thousand years ago. The whole existence of complex language appears to cover a span only five to six times that long, and by definition there can be no oral traditions older than that. So is it really so crazy to imagine our oldest legends retain some authentic detail? If so, then we should lend a measure of actual scientific credence to everything from Scandinavian trolls to the Aboriginal Dreamtime to the Garden of Eden itself. Perhaps reconstructing the literal past is merely an exercise in matching ancient legends to provable scientific facts. The more I thought about these times and places and people, the more *inevitable* these stories felt to me, and it pleases me greatly to share them with you here.